First World War
and Army of Occupation
War Diary
France, Belgium and Germany

16 DIVISION
Divisional Troops
Royal Army Medical Corps
111 Field Ambulance
18 December 1915 - 30 April 1919

WO95/1967/1

The Naval & Military Press Ltd
www.nmarchive.com
Published in association with The National Archives

Published by

The Naval & Military Press Ltd

Unit 10 Ridgewood Industrial Park,

Uckfield, East Sussex,

TN22 5QE England

Tel: +44 (0) 1825 749494

www.naval-military-press.com

www.nmarchive.com

This diary has been reprinted in facsimile from the original. Any imperfections are inevitably reproduced and the quality may fall short of modern type and cartographic standards.

© Crown Copyright

Images reproduced by permission of The National Archives, London, England, 2015.

Contents

Document type	Place/Title	Date From	Date To
Heading	WO95/1967. 16 Division Divisional Troops Dec 1915-Apr 1919 111 Field Ambulance		
Heading	16th Division 111th Field Ambnce Dec 1915-1919 Apl		
Heading	16th Div. 111th F.A. December Dec 18		
Heading	War Diary Of The 111th Field Ambulance from Dec. 18th. 1915 to Dec. 31st 1915 Volume One (Part I.)		
War Diary	Haig Hutments Farnham	18/12/1915	18/12/1915
War Diary	Havre	19/12/1915	19/12/1915
War Diary	Labuissiere	20/12/1915	30/12/1915
War Diary	Amettes	30/12/1915	31/12/1915
Heading	111th F.A. Vol 2 Jan 1916		
Heading	War Diary of 111th Field Ambulance from Jan. 1st to Jan. 31st 1916 (Volume 2)		
War Diary	Amettes	01/01/1916	08/01/1916
War Diary	Ecquedecques	09/01/1916	17/01/1916
War Diary	Noeux-Les Mines	18/01/1916	31/01/1916
Heading	111th Field Ambulance Feb Mar 1916		
Heading	111th F.A. Vol 3		
Heading	War Diary of 111th Field Ambulance from February 1st, 1916 to February 29th, 1916 (Volume 3)		
War Diary	Noeux Les Mines	01/02/1916	12/02/1916
War Diary	Ecquedecques	13/02/1916	16/02/1916
War Diary	Les Tourbieres	16/02/1916	29/02/1916
Heading	War Diary of 111 Field Ambulance from 1st March 1916 to 31st March 1916 (Volume 4)		
War Diary	Bourecq	01/03/1916	08/03/1916
War Diary	Allouagne	08/03/1916	24/03/1916
War Diary	Noeux Les Mines	25/03/1916	31/03/1916
Heading	War Diary of 111 Field Ambulance from April 1st 1916 to April 30th, 1916 (Volume 5)		
War Diary	Noeux Les Mines	01/04/1916	30/04/1916
Heading	War Diary of 111 Field Ambulance from 1st May 1916 to 31st May 1916 (Volume 6)		
War Diary	Noeux Les Mines	01/05/1916	31/05/1916
Heading	War Diary of 111 Field Ambulance from 1st June 1916 to 30th June 1916 (Volume 7)		
War Diary	Noeux Les Mines	01/06/1916	30/06/1916
Heading	16th Division 111th Field Ambulance. July 1916		
Heading	War Diary 111th Field Amb. R A M C 1st. July to 31st. July 1916. Volume No. 8		
War Diary	Noeux Les Mines	01/07/1916	31/07/1916
Heading	War Diary. 111th Field Ambulance Month Of August. 1916. Volume. 9		
War Diary	Noeux Les Mines	01/08/1916	11/08/1916
War Diary	Loos	12/08/1916	13/08/1916
War Diary	Noeux Les Mines	14/08/1916	18/08/1916
War Diary	Loos	19/08/1916	20/08/1916
War Diary	Noeux Les Mines	21/08/1916	25/08/1916
War Diary	Hurionville	26/08/1916	30/08/1916
War Diary	Longueau	30/08/1916	30/08/1916

Type	Location/Description	Start	End
War Diary	Daours	31/08/1916	31/08/1916
Heading	War Diary 111th Field Ambulance RAMC For Month of September, 1916. Volume 10		
War Diary	Dive Copse	31/08/1916	06/09/1916
War Diary	Carnoy	07/09/1916	10/09/1916
War Diary	Bronfay Farm (1)	11/09/1916	22/09/1916
War Diary	Corbie	23/09/1916	23/09/1916
War Diary	Bailleul	24/09/1916	24/09/1916
War Diary	Scherpenberg	25/09/1916	30/09/1916
Heading	War Diary Month of October, 1916. Volume 11 111th Field Ambulance R.A.M.C.		
War Diary	Scherpenberg	01/10/1916	06/10/1916
War Diary	Meteren	07/10/1916	31/10/1916
Heading	War Diary. For Month of November, 1916 Volume 12 111th Field Ambulance R.A.M.C.		
War Diary	Meteren	01/11/1916	30/11/1916
Heading	War Diary For Month Of December, 1916. Volume 13 111th Field Ambulance R.A.M.C.		
War Diary	Meteren	01/12/1916	31/12/1916
Heading	War Diary for month of January, 1917. Volume 14 RAMC. 111th Field Ambulance		
War Diary	Meteren	01/01/1917	31/01/1917
Heading	War Diary For Month of February, 1917. Volume 15 Unit 111th Field Ambulance R.A.M.C.		
War Diary	Meteren	01/02/1917	28/02/1917
Heading	War Diary For Month of March, 1917 Volume 16 Unit 111th Field Ambulance R.A.M.C.		
War Diary	Meteren	01/03/1917	31/03/1917
Heading	War Diary For Month of April, 1917. Volume 17 Unit 111th Field Ambulance R.A.M.C.		
War Diary	Meteren	01/04/1917	30/04/1917
Heading	War Diary Volume 18 For Month of May, 1917 Unit RAMC 111th Fd Ambce		
War Diary	Meteren	01/05/1917	31/05/1917
Heading	War Diary For Month of June, 1917. Volume No 19 Unit R.A.M.C. 111th Field Ambulance		
Miscellaneous	B.E.F. 16th Div. Summary of Medical War Diaries Of 111th F.A./8th Corps. 5th Army.	22/06/1917	22/06/1917
Miscellaneous	B.E.F. 16th Div. Summary Of Medical War Diaries Of 111th F.A. 8th Corps. 5th Army	22/06/1917	22/06/1917
Miscellaneous	B.E.F. 16th Div. 111th F.A/8th Corps. 5th Army.	00/06/1917	00/06/1917
War Diary	Meteren	01/06/1917	02/06/1917
War Diary	Meteren (X.15.d Sheet 27)	03/06/1917	19/06/1917
War Diary	Godewaers Velde Q.18.B.1.2 Sh. 27	20/06/1917	21/06/1917
War Diary	Peenhof Farm. B.16.C.5.5 Sh. 27	22/06/1917	30/06/1917
Miscellaneous	Appendix 1. Extracts From Medical Arrangements by A.D.M.S., 16th Division, d/31.5.17 Distribution of Personnel	31/05/1917	31/05/1917
Miscellaneous	Appendix 2 A.D.M.S 16th Division No 192/101 d/18.6.17	18/06/1917	18/06/1917
Miscellaneous	Appendix 3 A.D.M.S. 16th Division No. S192/103	19/06/1917	19/06/1917
Miscellaneous	Appendix 3 47th Inf. Bde Administrative Order No 4	19/06/1917	19/06/1917
Miscellaneous	Appendix 4 Extracts from O.O. No 20 issued by A.D.M.S., 16th Division	22/06/1917	22/06/1917
Heading	War Diary For Month Of July, 1917. Volume 20 Unit 111th Field Ambulance RAMC		

Miscellaneous	B.E.F. 16th Div. Summary Of Medical War Diaries Of 111th F.A./8th Corps. 5th Army.	23/07/1917	23/07/1917
Miscellaneous	B.E.F. 16th Div. 111th F.A./8th Corps. 5th Army.	08/07/1917	08/07/1917
War Diary	B.E.F. 111th F.A. 19th Corps. 5th Army.	22/08/1917	22/08/1917
Miscellaneous	B.E.F. 16th Div. 111th F.A./8th Corps. 5th Army.	23/07/1917	23/07/1917
Miscellaneous	B.E.F. 111th F.A. 19th Corps. 5th Army.	22/08/1917	22/08/1917
War Diary	Peenhof Farm B.16.C.5.5 Sh.27	01/07/1917	23/07/1917
War Diary	Winnezeele J.15.b.5.6 Sh 27	24/07/1917	25/07/1917
War Diary	Hilhoek (Sh 27. L.20.b.7.7)	26/07/1917	31/07/1917
Heading	War Diary. For Month Of August, 1917. Volume 21 Unit 111th Field Ambulance R A M C		
Heading	War Diary of 111 Field Ambulance for period from 1st August 1917 to 31st August 1917 Volume XXI		
Miscellaneous	B.E.F. 16th Div. Summary of Medical War Diaries Of 111th F.A./8th Corps.	22/08/1917	22/08/1917
Miscellaneous			
War Diary	Hilhoek Sheet 27 L.20.b.7.7	01/08/1917	05/08/1917
War Diary	Moated Farm S.28.H.2. d.7.2	06/08/1917	20/08/1917
War Diary	Eecke	21/08/1917	22/08/1917
War Diary	Gomiecourt (57 C. A 23.D.1.1)	23/08/1917	27/08/1917
War Diary	Hamelincourt (51B 329.d.9.6)	28/08/1917	31/08/1917
War Diary		30/08/1917	31/08/1917
Heading	War Diary. For Month Of September, 1917. Volume 22 Unit R.A.M.C. 111th Field Ambulance		
Heading	War Diary of 111 Field Ambulance for period from 1st September 1917 to 30th September 1917 Volume XXII		
War Diary	Hamelincourt 51B S 29.d.9.6	01/09/1917	30/09/1917
Heading	War Diary For Month Of October, 1917. Unit 111th Fd. Ambce RAMC Volume Number 23		
Heading	War Diary of 111 Field Ambulance for period from 1st October 1917 to 31st October 1917 Volume XXIII		
War Diary	Hamelincourt S.29.d.9.6 (Sh 51B)	01/10/1917	02/10/1917
War Diary	Hamelincourt S.29.d.9.6.	03/10/1917	23/10/1917
War Diary	Hamelin-Court S.29 D.9.6. Sh 51B.	24/10/1917	27/10/1917
War Diary	Hamelincourt S.29.d.9.6	27/10/1917	31/10/1917
Heading	War Diary For Month Of November, 1917. Volume 24 Unit 111th Field Ambulance RAMC		
Heading	War Diary of 111th. Field Ambulance for Period from 1st. November, 1917 to 30th. November, 1917. Volume XXIV.		
War Diary	Hamelin Court. S.29.d.9.6	01/11/1917	19/11/1917
War Diary	St Leger (T.27.b)	20/11/1917	22/11/1917
War Diary	Hamelin Court (S.29.d.9.6)	23/11/1917	27/11/1917
War Diary	Hamelin Court	28/11/1917	30/11/1917
Miscellaneous	Officer Commanding, 111th. Field Ambulance. Appendix I	13/10/1917	13/10/1917
Miscellaneous	Officer Commanding 111th. Field Ambulance. Appendix II	28/10/1917	28/10/1917
Heading	War Diary For Month Of December, 1917. Volume 25 Unit 111th Field Ambulance R.A.M.C.		
Heading	War Diary. of 111th. Field Ambulance. for Period December 1 to 31, 1917. Volume XXV.		
War Diary	Hamelin Court Sh 57. B. S. 29.d.9.6.	01/12/1917	01/12/1917
War Diary	Gomie-Court	02/12/1917	02/12/1917
War Diary	Beaulen-Court	03/12/1917	04/12/1917
War Diary	Beaulen-Court Sh 57C N.24.d.8.4	04/12/1917	07/12/1917

Type	Description	From	To
War Diary	Tincourt (Sh 62c J.18.d.8.3)	07/12/1917	09/12/1917
War Diary	Peronne Sh 62C 1.27.b	10/12/1917	23/12/1917
War Diary	Civil Hospital Peronne Sh.62.C 1.27.b.	24/12/1917	31/12/1917
Heading	War Diary of 111 Field Ambulance. Vol. XXV. Appendix 1.	26/11/1917	26/11/1917
Heading	War Diary For Month of January, 1918. Volume 26 Unit 111th Fd Ambce R.A.M.C.		
War Diary	Peronne (Civil Hospital) I.27.B.	01/01/1918	01/01/1918
War Diary	Civil Hospital Peronne (1.27.b)	01/01/1918	31/01/1918
Heading	War Diary. For Month of February, 1918. Volume 27 Unit 111th Field Ambulance R.A.M.C.		
Heading	War Diary Vol. XXVII February 1918. 111 Field Ambulance.		
War Diary	Civil Hospital Peronne (I.27.B) Sh 62 C	01/02/1918	02/02/1918
War Diary	Civil Hospital Peronne I.27.b	03/02/1918	24/02/1918
War Diary	Civil Hospital Peronne I.27.D.	25/02/1918	28/02/1918
Miscellaneous	No. 111 F.A. Mar. 1918.		
Heading	War Diary Vol XXVIII 111th Field Ambulance		
War Diary	Civil Hospital Peronne I.27.B.	01/03/1918	23/03/1918
War Diary	Herbecourt (Amiens Sh 17) (Sh 62C.H.32.A.9.8)	23/03/1918	23/03/1918
War Diary	Sh. 62.C. G.27.C.4.8	24/03/1918	24/03/1918
War Diary	Sh. 62 D L. 23.d.4.3	24/03/1918	24/03/1918
War Diary	Querrieu (Sh. 62 D H.17.)	25/03/1918	25/03/1918
War Diary	Sh 62 D P. 20.A.5.4.	25/03/1918	27/03/1918
War Diary	(Sh 62 D. N. 28.C)	28/03/1918	31/03/1918
Miscellaneous	No. 111 F.A. Apr. 1918.		
Heading	111th Field Ambulance War Diary Volume XXIX For April. 1918 Original Copy		
War Diary	Amiens-St Qventin Road. Sh 62 D N. 28. C.	01/04/1918	01/04/1918
War Diary	N. 26. D. 5.6.	01/04/1918	02/04/1918
War Diary	Sh. 62. D. N.26.D.5.6.	03/04/1918	03/04/1918
War Diary	Saleux (Amiens. 17)	03/04/1918	05/04/1918
War Diary	Morival Sh. Dieppe. 16	05/04/1918	08/04/1918
War Diary	Ault Sh. Abbeville 14.	09/04/1918	10/04/1918
War Diary	Bandrighem. (Sh. Hazebrouck. 5.A.)	10/04/1918	11/04/1918
War Diary	Ouve-Wirquin Sh. Hazebrouck 5 A	12/04/1918	15/04/1918
War Diary	La Lacque (W Aire) Sh Hazebrouck 5A.	16/04/1918	16/04/1918
War Diary	La Lacques Sh 5A	16/04/1918	16/04/1918
War Diary	Isbergue	16/04/1918	25/04/1918
War Diary	Sh 36A H.30.C.2.3.	26/04/1918	30/04/1918
Miscellaneous	Training Programme Appendix. 1	01/05/1917	01/05/1917
War Diary	Training Programme 111th Field Ambulance	30/04/1918	30/04/1918
Heading	War Diary 111th Field Ambulance Vol XXX May 1918.		
War Diary	Sh 36A. H.30.C.4.3	01/05/1918	17/05/1918
War Diary	Upen D'Aval (Sh Hazebrouck 5A) Square C.5	17/05/1918	18/05/1918
War Diary	(Sh. Calais 13)	18/05/1918	18/05/1918
War Diary	(Calais. Sh 13) Wierre Au Bois	19/05/1918	31/05/1918
Heading	Original War Diary 111th Field Ambulance Volume XXXI June 1918.		
War Diary	Wierre Au Bois Sh. Calais 13	01/06/1918	03/06/1918
War Diary	Square D.5.	04/06/1918	06/06/1918
War Diary	Wierre Au Bois Calais Sh 13.	06/06/1918	30/06/1918
Heading	111th F.A. July 1918.		
War Diary	Wierre Au Bois Sh. Calais 13	01/07/1918	05/07/1918
War Diary	Beauval Sheet Lens II	06/07/1918	31/07/1918

Heading	War Diary Volume XXXIII August 1918 111th Field Ambulance Original Copy.		
War Diary	Beauval Sh. Lens 11	01/08/1918	24/08/1918
War Diary	Mont Renault Farm (Sh. Lens II)	25/08/1918	28/08/1918
War Diary	Doullens (Sh Lens 11)	29/08/1918	29/08/1918
War Diary	Barlin Sh. 44B K.33.A.8.8.	30/08/1918	31/08/1918
Heading	111th Field Ambulance War Diary Vol. XXXIV. "Original" Copy.		
Heading	140/3259. Sept. 1918		
War Diary	Barlin Sh 44B K.33.a.8.3	01/09/1918	02/09/1918
War Diary	Barlin K.33.A.8.3	03/09/1918	11/09/1918
War Diary	K.33.A.8.3	11/09/1918	29/09/1918
War Diary	J.24.b.3.8	30/09/1918	30/09/1918
Heading	111th F.A. Oct. 1918		
War Diary	Haillicourt J.24.b.3.8	01/10/1918	07/10/1918
War Diary	La Bourse L.2.A.7.6	08/10/1918	19/10/1918
War Diary	Berclau B.18.D.2.8. (Sheet 44 N) D.21 C 2.1	20/10/1918	20/10/1918
War Diary	Camphin D. 21. & 2.1.	21/10/1918	21/10/1918
War Diary	Pont A. Marcq E 18. D. 9.1.	22/10/1918	31/10/1918
Heading	111th F.A. Nov 1918		
War Diary	Pont. A. Marcq E. 18. D.9.1	01/11/1918	05/11/1918
War Diary	Pont A Marcq	06/11/1918	09/11/1918
War Diary	Rumes (Sheet 5 Tournai)	10/11/1918	16/11/1918
War Diary	La Tanarderie Sh 44A K.21.A	17/11/1918	31/11/1918
Miscellaneous	Time Table of 111th Field Ambulance Classes for November 1918 Appen I		
Miscellaneous	Present Arrangements of 111th Field Ambulance Classes	25/11/1918	25/11/1918
Miscellaneous	No. 111 Field Ambulance Dec 1918		
War Diary	La. Tanarderie Sheet 44a K.21.A.	03/12/1918	31/12/1918
Heading	16 Div Box 1674 111th Field Ambulance War Diary XXXVII Jan. 1919		
War Diary	La Tanarderie Sh 44A K.21.A	01/01/1919	31/01/1919
Miscellaneous	111th Field Ambulance. List of Classes For January 1919.	07/01/1919	07/01/1919
Miscellaneous	111th Field Ambulance Education		
Miscellaneous	Parchment Certificates Appendix III		
Miscellaneous	No. 111 Field Ambulance Feb. 1919.		
War Diary	La Tanarderie Sh 44A K.21.A.	01/02/1919	28/02/1919
Heading	War Diary (111 Field Ambulance) March 1919 Vol 40		
War Diary	Sheet 44 A K.21.A.	01/03/1919	28/03/1919
War Diary	Sheet 44 A F 17 C 2.4. Templeuve	29/03/1919	31/03/1919
Heading	111th F.A. Apr. 1919		
War Diary	Templeuve	01/04/1919	30/04/1919

① WO 95/1964

16 Division

Headquarters Branches of Services
Divisional Troops.

Dec ~~Jan~~ 1915 — Apr 1919.

111 FIELD AMBULANCE

16TH DIVISION

111TH FIELD AMBNCE
DEC 1915 — 1918
1919 APL

111 F.A.

December 1917

Dec '16

16 mps
F/147

111 F.A.
tot I

D
7935

Confidential

WAR DIARY

of the

111th FIELD AMBULANCE

from Dec. 18th 1915 to Dec. 31st 1915

Volume One. (Part I.)

WAR DIARY or INTELLIGENCE SUMMARY

Army Form C. 2118

Place	Date	Hour	Summary of Events and Information	Remarks and references to Appendices
HAIG HUTMENTS FARNHAM	18th Dec 1915	2.30 AM / 4 AM	The Unit left Camp in two parties composed of B + 1/2 C sections and A + other 1/2 C sects, and marched to FARNBOROUGH STATION, left this station at 6.10 AM + 7.30 AM and arrived at SOUTHAMPTON Docks at 7.35 AM + 8.35 AM. Sailed from SOUTHAMPTON at 5 P.M.	Autographs Maj. RAKE
HAVRE	19th Dec 1915	8 AM	Disembarked at 8 AM and remained at Docks all day, left Docks at 5.30 P.M. and marched to the GARE MARITIME. Entrained and left GARE MARITIME at 9.30 P.M. Halted at ABBEVILLE at 8.45 AM and left at 9.37 AM. 20.XII.15. Proceeded via ST OMER to FOUQUEREUIL. Arrived 6.20 PM Disentrained and marched to LABUISSIÈRE.	Autographs
LABUISSIÈRE	20th Dec 1915	1.20 AM	Arrived here at the hour and been into billets (barns).	Autographs
do	21st Dec 1915		In billets resting and fitting things in order for lot.	Autographs
do	22nd Dec 1915		In billets the same as yesterday	Autographs
do	23rd Dec 1915		Record Office opened. Major Awdell proceeded to Hospital for treatment of local sick.	Autographs Major PM17

Army Form C. 2118

WAR DIARY
or
INTELLIGENCE SUMMARY
(Erase heading not required.)

Instructions regarding War Diaries and Intelligence Summaries are contained in F.S. Regs., Part II. and the Staff Manual respectively. Title Pages will be prepared in manuscript.

Place	Date	Hour	Summary of Events and Information	Remarks and references to Appendices
LA BUSSIERE	24th Dec 1915		Unit Received here in billets. No accommodation for a hospital.	Arothers Maj. RAMC
"	25 Dec.		Same place. Nothing beyond ordinary routine work	Civrs
"	26 Dec.		Same place. Four Motor Ambulances + two Horse Ayles arrived Reg Personnel	Civrs
"	27 Dec.		Routine work.	Civrs
"	28 Dec.		Routine work. Sgt SHUTTS B (The Unit shd 15) Unit St. Mds.	Civrs
"	29 Dec.		Received orders to move to new military area.	Civrs
"	30 Dec.		Clen up the town at 8 AM and marched via ARCHES + TERFAY to AMETTES.	Civrs
AMETTES	30th Dec.		Arrived at the Place at 1.30 PM. Settled in billets (Horses). B section found hospital in a school, not accommodation for 30 Cases.	Civrs
"	31st Dec.		Road men work. 3 Cases in Hospital this morning.	Arothers Maj. RAMC

111th F.A.
Vol: 2

16th Div
F/148/2

Jan 1916

Confidential.

War Diary

of

111th Field Ambulance

from Jan. 1st to Jan. 31st 1916.

(Volume 2.)

Army Form C. 2118

WAR DIARY
or
INTELLIGENCE SUMMARY
(Erase heading not required.)

Instructions regarding War Diaries and Intelligence Summaries are contained in F.S. Regs., Part II. and the Staff Manual respectively. Title Pages will be prepared in manuscript.

Place	Date	Hour	Summary of Events and Information	Remarks and references to Appendices
AMETTES	1st Jan 1916	.....	Routine work. Weather wet & windy. No. of Cases in Hospital NCOs & Men 4 & Officers. Transferred to Hospital 6 & the Hospitals 1. Transferred to duty. 1	Maj. RAMC
"	2nd Jan 1916	.....	Routine work. No. of cases in Hospital – NCOs & men. 6 Transfd to other Hospitals 1. Transferred to duty. 1	Officers
"	3rd Jan 1916	.....	Routine work. No. of cases in Hospital. NCOs & men 4. Disch to duty 2.	Officers
"	4th Jan 1916	.....	Routine work. No. of cases in Hospital NCOs & men 7. Transferred to CCS 1. Discharged to duty 2.	Officers
"	5th Jan 1916	.....	Routine work. No. of cases in Hospital NCOs & men 6. Transferred to CCS 3. Discharged to duty. N.L. Stroud billeted for the unit.	Officers
"	6th Jan 1916	.....	Routine work. No. of cases in Hospital NCOs & men 7. T.B.C.C.2. To duty 1. One case Q.S.N. left most (Procantral) admitted.	Officers
"	7th Jan 1916	.....	Routine work. No. of cases in Hosp. NCOs & men 7. Transferred to CCS 4. Discharged to duty 1. Recvd message from DAA & QMG 16th Div. that 3rd Amb. must move to new billet at ECQUEDECQUES	Airothren Maj. RAMC

Army Form C. 2118

WAR DIARY
or
INTELLIGENCE SUMMARY
(Erase heading not required.)

Instructions regarding War Diaries and Intelligence Summaries are contained in F.S. Regs., Part II. and the Staff Manual respectively. Title Pages will be prepared in manuscript.

Place	Date	Hour	Summary of Events and Information	Remarks and references to Appendices
AMETTES	7th Jan 1916		Cont:- Sent C. Sect. to ECQUEDECQUES this afternoon (3 pm) to open New Hospital and act as advance billeting party and to be ready to receive the sick at present with B. Sect. first thing tomorrow morning. Sgt. SHUTTS & the Unit returned from No. 141 Ft Amb.	Another truly RAMC
"	8th Jan 1916		The remaining sections of the F.A. left this place and arrived in new billets at about midday today. The billets on farms, good, but accommodation for a hospital is not so good. No. 6 NCOs & men to Stop 8. Gone to C.C.S.2. Io duty. Nil.	Pivots
ECQUEDECQUES	9th Jan 1916		No. 6 NCOs & men in Stop 8. Gone to C.C.S. Nil. Io duty 3.	Pivots
"	10th Jan 1916		No. 6 NCOs & men in C.deck Stop 7. Gone to C.C.S. Nil. Io duty Nil.	Pivots
"	11th Jan 1916		A section opens Hospital here in private house. No. of NCOs & men in Hospital 8. Gone Nil. Io duty 1.	Pivots
"	12th Jan 1916		Routine work. No. 8 Evac. in Hospital 12. Evac. 2. Io duty 1.	Pivots
"	13th Jan 1916		Nothing unusual. in Hospital 10. Evac. 3. Io duty 4.	Pivots

WAR DIARY or INTELLIGENCE SUMMARY

Army Form C. 2118

Place	Date	Hour	Summary of Events and Information	Remarks and references to Appendices
ECQUEDECQUES	13th Jan 1916		Routine work. No. 1 over in Hospital 10. Stone 2 on duty 1. Weather fine but wet. No previous in Area.	Chapman Maj RAMC Q505
"	14th Jan 1916		Routine work. No previous in Hospital 16. Some men to duty 1.	Q505
"	15th Jan 1916		Routine work. Orders Received from ADMS 16th Div to proceed to hospital. 1 Ewn to No 6 C.C.S. Qew 10 112th 30 Mn6 6 to Sub 2	Q505
"	16th Jan 1916		Hospital packed ready to move.	Q505
"	17th Jan 1916		Field Ambulance moved at 7 am this morning to new area at NOEUX-LES-MINES. The ambulance arrived and 105th Dec the State school in NOEUX-LES-MINES from the 5th LONDON F.A. at 12.30 heads day	Q505
NOEUX-LES MINES	18th Jan 1916		A section + C section opened up as a hospital and during the day took in 11 Cases and evacuated one. Some wounded at hutted battery.	Q505

Army Form C. 2118

WAR DIARY
or
INTELLIGENCE SUMMARY
(Erase heading not required.)

Place	Date	Hour	Summary of Events and Information	Remarks and references to Appendices
NOEUX-LES-MINES	19th Jan 1916		Routine work. No. of Cases in Hospital NCOs & Men 7 sick & 2 wounded.	
"	20th Jan 1916		No. of Crew wounded 7. to duty 0. Officers admitted I.S. Evacuated 1.	Brothels Reg/Adm Cloth
"	21st Jan 1916		No. of Cases in Hospital NCOs & men 1 wounded 4 sick. Evacuated to C.C.S. 3	
"			No. of Cases in Hospital NCOs & Men 3 W. 4 S. Evac. to C.C.S. 2. Lt. G.E. LLOYD and party of 2 NCOs & 4 men proceeded to Adv. Dressing Station of No. 47 F Amb. at PHILOSOPHE & LOOS for instruction	Brothels
"	22nd Jan 1916		No. of Cases in Hospital NCOs & men sick 4 wounded 0 Evac Nil Officers sick 1. Evac. 1. Lt. T.H. OLIVER and party of NCOs & men proceeded to 146th F.A. Adv. Dressing Station at Le RUTOIRE for instruction	Brothels
"	23rd Jan 1916		No. of Cases admitted to Hospital NCOs & men 4 wounded. 12 sick. Evac. 1 sick 7 4 wounded	Brothels Hol[?]

Army Form C. 2118

WAR DIARY
or
INTELLIGENCE SUMMARY
(Erase heading not required.)

Place	Date	Hour	Summary of Events and Information	Remarks and references to Appendices
NOEUX-LES-MINES	24th July 1916		No. 9 Areas admitted 2 Officers sick. NCOs & men sick 1 wounded 0. NCOs & men sick 9 wounded 6. 11 Dick. Gone to C.C.S. 2 Officers 6 other ranks. To Rest Station 5 other ranks. 1 Lt T.H. OLIVER & party returned from Adv. Dressing Station of 46th F.A. as it had 15 to Warn Ord.	[signature]
"	25th July 1916		Lt. G.E. STEPHENSON and party NCOs & men proceeded to 47th F.A. at LOOS & PHILOSOPHE for instruction at their Adv. Dressing Station. Lt G.E. LLOYD & party returned from Adv. Dressing Station 47th F.A. No 9 Areas in Hospital Officers sick 1 wounded 0. NCOs & men sick 9 wounded 2. From C.C.S. 6 or 3 Officers 1. To duty 5.	[signature]
"	26th July 1916		No. 9 Areas in Hospital Officers sick 1. NCOs & men wounded 5 sick 16. To duty 5. From C.C.S. 1 Officer 8 other Ranks.	[signature]

WAR DIARY or INTELLIGENCE SUMMARY

Army Form C. 2118

Place	Date	Hour	Summary of Events and Information	Remarks and references to Appendices
NOEUX LES MINES	27th Jan 1916		No Offrs in Hospital. Offrs Nil. OR 6 wounded 11 sick. Evac. to C.C.S. q.o.R. So duty 23. To Rest Station 1.	Airman run over
"	28th Jan 1916		No Offrs in Hospital. Offrs nil. OR 14 sick 10 Evac Sick.	AD5/8
"	29th Jan 1916		No 1 Casu in Hospital Offrs nil. OR 7 wounded 7 sick. Evac. to C.C.S. 3. To duty one. Lt G.E. STEPHENSON and party returned from ADV. Dressing Station $\frac{1}{9}$/47th JA. Lt A.H. LITTLE & party proceeded to ADV. Dressing Station $\frac{1}{9}$46th JA at HAZINGARBE. Received orders to hand over the schools to 47th JA. and to take over the Mains Schools from them and to open Hospital there. Met Lt Du Sheton. A Section opened a hospital. aux B & C sections met	AD5/8

WAR DIARY
or
INTELLIGENCE SUMMARY

Army Form C. 2118

Place	Date	Hour	Summary of Events and Information	Remarks and references to Appendices
NOEUX-LES-MINES	29th Jan 1916		Conti- travel into hituto at ECQUEDECQUES. They had a stop at the JA at 10.30 AM and went into Indane Mulep Ons. The unit has bryon.	Crofton Maj RAMC
"	30th Jan 1916		No Officers in Hospital Officers S.I. W.noe N.C.Os & men S.3 W14. Give losses Officers S.I., OR 34. So duty!. Lt. J.W. RUTHERFURD at the 16th Div Grenade School. Lt. T.H. OLIVER relieved. Two men of the unit evac ICCS suffering from shell shock.	Cook
"	31st Jan 1916		Lt. A.H. LITTLE & party returned from 46th JA. Party of N.C.Os when proceeded to Adv dressing station of 47th JA this morning to Instruction. Admitted to Hospital 9R W.B. sick 9 Evac 16CCS. Wounded 9. So duty!.	Crofton Maj RAMC

111th Field Ambulance

Feb } 1916
Mar }

111th 7.a.
vol: 3

Confidential.

War Diary
of
111th Field Ambulance

from February 1st, 1916 to February 29th, 1916.

(Volume 3).

Army Form C. 2118

WAR DIARY
or
INTELLIGENCE SUMMARY
(Erase heading not required.)

Place	Date	Hour	Summary of Events and Information	Remarks and references to Appendices
NOEUX LES MINES	1st Feb 1916		Routine work in the Mining Schools. Admitted N.C.Os nil. O.R. seen 7. wounded 5. Evac. 10 C.C.S. O.R. 12. To duty 4.	CaptBrown Maj R.A.M.C.
"	2nd Feb 1916		No. of Beds ad mitted N.C.Os nil. O.R. seen 7. wounded 7. Evac. to C.C.S. 7. To duty 2. Lt. W. J. MacDonald and party N.C.Os & men proceed to Advanced Dressing Station of 46th Div for instruction	CaptBrown
"	3rd Feb 1916		Ab.lt DTR for instruction. No. of Beds ad mitted Offr nil. O.R 2 wounded. 6 sick Evac. to C.C.S. 10. To duty 2. Lt Rutherford and party returned from Adv Dressing Station 47th Div.	CaptOR
"	4th Feb 1916		No. of Beds ad mitted Offrs wounded 1. O.R. 9 wounded 6 sick. Evac. to C.C.S 14 O.R. 1 Officer. To duty 2 (OR)	CaptOR

WAR DIARY
or
INTELLIGENCE SUMMARY
(Erase heading not required.)

Army Form C. 2118

Place	Date	Hour	Summary of Events and Information	Remarks and references to Appendices
Noeux Les Mines	5th Aug 1916		No. of cases admitted Officers Nil OR Sick 9. To CCS 2. Evacuated sick to Base today.	App. Min. May RAMC
"	6th Aug 1916		No. of cases admitted Officers Nil OR Sick 7. To CCS 5. Sgt. Maj. PITT. 15 kinds admitted sick to Base today. To CCS 5 on duty.	App. B
"	7th Aug 1916		Lt F.A. ANDERSON and party proceed to Adv. Dressing Station B/46th FA for instruction. Capt. TR. TRIST arrives from ECQUEDECQUES and out a party of NCO's and men proceed to Adv. Dressing Station B/47th FA for instruction. No. of cases admitted Officers seen 1 OR. 2 Sick 11. To CCS Officers 1 OR 10.	App. B. App. B
"	8th Aug 1916		No. of cases admitted Officers seen 1 OR wounded 7 sick 10 To CCS Officers 1. OR 7 wounded. To duty 1. NCO's & men proceed to 46th F.A. Adv. Dressing Station	App. B

Place	Date	Hour	Summary of Events and Information	Remarks and references to Appendices
NEUVE LES MINES	9th Feb 1916		No. of Cas. Wounded OR wounded 6. Men 6. Evac. to CCS. 5. On duty 1. NCO's & men proceeded to 47th S.A. Adv. Dressing Station for instruction.	Another from ADMS
"	10 Feb 1916		Officers Wounded Nil. OR Wounded 1. Sick 7. Evac. to CCS. OR 9. On duty 6.	Evac. to CCS
"	11th Feb 1916		Officers Wounded 1 wounded OR 5 wounded, 7 sick. Evac to CCS 25 OR. 1 Officer. On duty 14. Capt J.R. TRIST and party returned from Adv. Dressing Station at 47th S.A. NCO's & men returned from Adv. Dr. Station drawn for 46th S.A.	Evac to CCS
"	12th Feb 1916		The S.A. received the Manin schools & handed over to the HQ. S.A. at 10:30 am this morning.	Evac.

Army Form C. 2118

WAR DIARY
or
INTELLIGENCE SUMMARY
(Erase heading not required.)

Instructions regarding War Diaries and Intelligence Summaries are contained in F.S. Regs., Part II. and the Staff Manual respectively. Title Pages will be prepared in manuscript.

Place	Date	Hour	Summary of Events and Information	Remarks and references to Appendices
NOEUX LES MINES	12th Jan 1916		The Unit:— The HQrs & B section of the S.A. marched to ECQUEDECQUES and formed up with A & C sections arrived today at 4.15 P.M.	Cunningham Lieut/R.A.M.C
ECQUEDECQUES	13.2.16		In truck in this place where he was before. No hospital being found here trying to locate B.C.M.S. suitable buildup for A. hospital. Hunt if the men of the F.A. is good.	
"	14.2.16		Nothing doing here waiting to know. Received orders if probable move tomorrow to BLESSY.	Cunjob.
"	15.2.16		And moved at 8.30 A.M. ans took up hens quarters at LES TOURBIERS. C section opened hospital in Shower stores.	Rivers
"	16.2.16		Pte Willoughby Cpn had very cramped Hospital ready to take in sick	Rivers Cunjob

1875 Wt. W593/826 1,000,000 4/15 J.B.C. & A. A.D.S.S./Forms/C. 2118.

Army Form C. 2118

WAR DIARY
or
INTELLIGENCE SUMMARY

(Erase heading not required.)

Instructions regarding War Diaries and Intelligence Summaries are contained in F.S. Regs., Part II. and the Staff Manual respectively. Title Pages will be prepared in manuscript.

Place	Date	Hour	Summary of Events and Information	Remarks and references to Appendices
LES TOURBIERES	16/2/16		Took over temporary command of F. Amb. from Major C.W. O'Brien, R.A.M.C., proceeding to England on leave	RRF 1st Cpl. same
	17/2/16		Lieut. G.E. STEPHENSON, R.A.M.C., left 1st F. Amb. for duty as m.o. i/c 9th Royal Dublin Fusiliers. t/Lieut. J.T. MURPHY, R.A.M.C. from 9th Royal Dublin Fusiliers joined this unit. Officers admitted NIL. O.R. wounded NIL. Sick 4. Evac. F.C.C.S. nil. To duty nil.	RRF
	18/2/16		Officers admitted NIL. O.R. wounded nil. Sick nil. Evac. F.C.C.S. 1. To duty nil Hospital and Officer Men views by D.D.M.S. 1st Corps.	pent
	19/2/16		Officers admitted NIL. O.R. wounded nil. Sick 6. Evac. F.C.C.S. 2. To duty nil	RRF
	20/2/16		Officers admitted Sick 2 (Measles, Mumps 1), wounded nil. O.R. Wounded nil. Sick 10. Evac. F.C.C.S. Officers 2. O.R. nil. Dischgd to duty nil.	RRF
	21/2/16		Officers admitted Wounded nil. Sick 1 (Scabies). O.R. wounded nil. Sick 12. Evac. F.C.C.S. Officers 1. O.R. 5. Discharged to duty 1.	RRF
	22/2/16		t/Lr. A.L. McCREERY, R.A.M.C. joined the F. Amb. Officers admitted NIL. O.R. Wounded nil. Sick 19. Evac. F.C.C.S. 5. Discharged to duty 6.	RRF

WAR DIARY or INTELLIGENCE SUMMARY

Army Form C. 2118

Place	Date	Hour	Summary of Events and Information	Remarks and references to Appendices
LES TOURBIERES	23/2/16		1/Lt. T.H. OLIVER, R.A.M.C., posted to 16th. DIV. GRENADE SCHOOL as m.o. i/c is struck off the strength of 1 F. Amb. Officers admitted Wounded Nil Sick 3. O.R. Wounded nil Sick 14. Evac. to C.C.S. Officers 3 (Number 2: Gonorrhoea 1). O.R. 3. Disch'd to duty O.R. 10.	R.R.S. sick Ct. Rank
"	24/2/16		Officers admitted Nil. O.R. Wounded nil. Sick 23. Evac. to C.C.S. Officers Nil. O.R. 14. (Scabies 11: M.Y.D. 2. Haemorrhoids 1) Disch'd to duty O.R. 4.	R.R.S.
"	25/2/16		Officers admitted Nil. O.R. Wounded nil. Sick 13. Evac to C.C.S. Officers nil. O.R. 5 Disch'd to duty 4 (O.R.)	past
"	26/2/16		Officers admitted Wounded nil. Sick Nil. O.R. Wounded nil. Sick 13. Evac. to C.C.S. O.R. 4 Disch'd to duty 7. (O.R.)	past
"	27/2/16		Officers admitted, Wounded nil Sick 1 (German measles) O.R. Wounded nil. Sick 10. Disch'd to duty. Evacuated Officers 1 (German measles) O.R. 4. Disch'd to duty 6.	past
"	28/2/16		Officers Ad mitted nil O.R sick 4. Evacuated O.R. 18. To Convalescent Dépôt 9. To duty 4. MAJOR C.W. O'BRIEN. R.A.M.C. returned from leave Australia from CAPT J.R. R.T.R.S.T.	R.A.D.C (SC)

WAR DIARY
INTELLIGENCE SUMMARY

Place	Date	Hour	Summary of Events and Information	Remarks and references to Appendices
LES TOURBIERES	20/2/16		Officers admitted Nil. OR 4 sick One to CCS one been Bombay men. This place & area the Brigade form Hospital at BOURECQ. The tropher is places in bomber huts built by the RE + another mas used before we took over by No 100 T.A.	

111 F.Amb
Vol 4

No Dio

Confidential

War Diary
of
111 Field Ambulance

from 1st March 1916 to 31st March 1916.

(Volume 4).

WAR DIARY
or
INTELLIGENCE SUMMARY

(Erase heading not required.)

Army Form C. 2118

Instructions regarding War Diaries and Intelligence Summaries are contained in F. S. Regs., Part II. and the Staff Manual respectively. Title Pages will be prepared in manuscript.

Place	Date	Hour	Summary of Events and Information	Remarks and references to Appendices
BOURECQ	1/3/16		Billets good. Hospital in two wooden huts: accommodation good; approaches bad: road-making begun. Officers admitted Wounded NIL Sick NIL O.R. adm. Wounded nil. Sick 20. Evac. to C.C.S. Officers nil O.R. 4. Disch. to duty O.R. 2	RRT nil Capt. RAMC (S.R.)
	2/3/16		Officers admitted wounded nil sick nil. O.R. wounded nil Sick 16. Evac. to C.C.S. Off nil. O.R. 10. Disch. to duty 4.	RRT nil
	3/3/16		Officers adm. NIL. O.R. Sick 22. Evac. to C.C.S. O.R. 17. Disch. to duty 3.	RRT nil
	4/3/16		Officers adm. NIL. O.R. Sick 17. Evac. to C.C.S. O.R. 8. Disch. to duty 12.	RRT nil
	5/3/16		Officers 2 adm. Sick 1. O.R. Sick 16. Evac. to C.C.S. Officers 1. O.R. 9. Disch. to duty. O.R. 8. Prev. dis. (3 and nev of daily admissions) Sore Throat, having been sick in quarters since 4/3/16.	RRT nil
	6/3/16		MAJOR C.W. O'BRIEN, R.A.M.C., (Serial no. 21) and was shewn 'admitted' in F. Ambs. A&D. book (officers)(3 + over) daily adm.) Bronchitis. transferred to No. 6 C.C.S. President dis. Temporary command taken over by CAPT. J.R.R. TRIST, R.A.M.C. (S.R.) Officers adm. Sick 2. O.R. 15. Evac. to C.C.S. Officer 1. O.R. 9. Disch to duty O.R. 5.	RRT nil Capt. RAMC (S.R.)
	7/3/16		P/Lt. G.E. LLOYD, A.H. LITTLE, A.L. Mc CREERY sick in Quarters. Officers adm. nil. O.R. Sick 15. Evac. to C.C.S. O.R. 7. Disch. to duty O.R. 2 Prevalent Disease (3 and over of daily admission) Bronchitis.	RRT

1875 Wt. W593/826 1,000,000 4/15 T.R.C. & A. A.D.S.S./Forms/C. 2118.

Army Form C. 2118

WAR DIARY
or
INTELLIGENCE SUMMARY
(Erase heading not required.)

Place	Date	Hour	Summary of Events and Information	Remarks and references to Appendices
BOURECQ	8/3/16		F. Amb. moved to new billets taking over hospital from 6 H. London F. Amb (T)(47th.Div) at ALLOUAGNE. Thirty two sick men were taken along to the new hospital.	1pt 5 iny Capt. R.Amc. (S.R)
ALLOUAGNE	8/3/16		Billets good. Hospital good. Hospital in Theatre buildings. 2/Lieuts G. E. LLOYD, A. L. Mc CREERY of this unit eleven admitted to 'Distangres' in A+D from 8/6. Lt. LLOYD to No 6 C.C.S. diagnosis P.O.U.O. Lt. Mc. CREERY to No. 7 General Hosp. diagnosis German Measles. Lt. Little of this unit sick taken along in amb. Officers adm. 3 Sick; O.R. Sick 15. Evac. t.c.c.s. Officers 3. O.R. nil. Died. nil. Prevalent disease (Influenza). 1/Lt. LITTLE returns to duty from t.c.c.s. r/Lt. MURPHY sick in quarters (Influenza). Sick in Quarters.	1pt F.
ALLOUAGNE	9/3/16		Officers adm. nil; O.R. Sick 16. Evac. t.c.c.s. Officers nil. O.R. 2. To Duty O.R. 3. Prevalent Disease (to 3 ams new f.sick admissions) Influenza.	

WAR DIARY or INTELLIGENCE SUMMARY

Army Form C. 2118

Place	Date	Hour	Summary of Events and Information	Remarks and references to Appendices
ALLOUAGNE	10/3/16		T/Lt. J.T. MURPHY of this unit still sick in quarters (sleeps in 'Admin') took and on Daily State as 'Awaiting transfer to Rest Station.' Sick and their ailments from 47th INF. BDE, 48th INF. BDE, 180th Bde. RFA, 182nd Bde RFA, 177th Bde. RFA, 77th Bde. (How.) RFA, 164 Div. Amm Column and admits to this unit hospital. Sick and being seen for 153rd F. Co. R.E. (M.O. R.E. at a distance) and 6th Royal Irish Regt. (M.O. sick in quarters with QUINSY). Officers adm. Sick 3. O.R. adm. b.t.c.c. Officers trans 2. O.R. Cm 3. Died. W/N of Officer ad. O.R.S. Duaiv. & Rens Station. O.R. 4 Rect (Temp) w.J. RUTHERFORD. R.A.M.C. posted to 6/ ROYAL IRISH REGt.	R/O.F/W/V Capt. P/W/R. (S.R.)
	11/3/16		Joined 111th F. Amb. to take over temporary command. Field Ambulance Transport inspected this afternoon by Brig. Gen. Pereira, 47th Brigade. He expressed himself as very pleased both with the condition of the horses and the appearance of the horses + vehicles.	Major. Pell Capt. Ramel

Army Form C. 2118

WAR DIARY
or
INTELLIGENCE SUMMARY
(Erase heading not required.)

Place	Date	Hour	Summary of Events and Information	Remarks and references to Appendices
ALLOUAGNE	12/3/16		Off. Admitted:- Officers nil, other ranks, Sick 10.	2/Lt Bell Capt. Rams
			Evacuated to C.C.S:- Officers: nil; other ranks, 11.	
			Transferred to Convalescent Dep't;- Officers 1, other ranks, nil.	
			Discharged to duty;- other ranks, 8.	
	13/3/16		Admitted. Officers: Sick, 1. other ranks, sick, 14.	S.
			Evacuated to C.C.S. Officers, 1. other ranks, 5.	
			Transferred to Corps Rest Station. Officers, 1, other ranks, 6.	
			Discharged to duty." other ranks, 10.	
			The D.D.M.S. 1st Corps visited the Unit in the evening	

Army Form C. 2118

WAR DIARY
or
INTELLIGENCE SUMMARY
(Erase heading not required.)

Instructions regarding War Diaries and Intelligence Summaries are contained in F.S. Regs., Part II. and the Staff Manual respectively. Title Pages will be prepared in manuscript.

Place	Date	Hour	Summary of Events and Information	Remarks and references to Appendices
ALLOUAGNE	14/3/16		Admitted, other ranks, 16. (sick)	(W) = Rev. Capt. Rowe
			Evacuated to C.C.S. other ranks, 3. (sick)	
			Discharged to duty. other ranks, 8. (sick)	
			D.A.D.M.S. 16th Div'n visited the Field Ambulance.	
			Temp'y Lieut't C.J. Brady Rowe joined unit for duty to-day.	
	15/3/16		Admitted. Other ranks, sick 14	
			Evacuated to C.C.S. other ranks, sick 18	
			Discharged to duty. other ranks. 11	
			A.D.M.S. 16th Div'n inspected the Dressing Station etc of the Field Ambulance	R

1875 Wt. W593/826 1,000,000 4/15 T R.C. & A. A.D.S.S./Forms/C.2118.

Army Form C. 2118

WAR DIARY
or
INTELLIGENCE SUMMARY
(Erase heading not required.)

Place	Date	Hour	Summary of Events and Information	Remarks and references to Appendices
ACUVAQ NO 16	3/16		Admitted. Other ranks, sick 10	W/O Pell Capt Maud
			Evacuated to C.C.S. Other ranks 10	
			Transferred to Rest Station. Other ranks 5	
			Discharged to duty. Other ranks 11.	
	3/16		Admitted. Officers nil; other ranks 13.	B
			Evacuated to C.C.S. other ranks 3.	
			Discharged to duty. 10.	

Army Form C. 2118

WAR DIARY
or
INTELLIGENCE SUMMARY
(Erase heading not required.)

Instructions regarding War Diaries and Intelligence Summaries are contained in F. S. Regs., Part II. and the Staff Manual respectively. Title Pages will be prepared in manuscript.

Place	Date	Hour	Summary of Events and Information	Remarks and references to Appendices
ALLOUAGNE	18/3/16		Admitted. Other ranks 14	Nom. Roll Cpl Rams
			Evacuated to C.C.S. Other ranks 7	
			Discharged to duty. 2	
			Visited the 46th Field Ambulance at NOEUX LES MINES and VAUDRICOURT.	
	19/3/16		Admitted. Other Ranks 13. Officers 2. Other ranks 12	B
			Evacuated to C.C.S. Other ranks 2. Officers 2. Other ranks 6.	
			Rest Station not 1.	
			Duty "	
	20/3/16		Admitted. Officer 1. Other ranks 15	B
			Evacuated Officer 1. " " 13	
			Corps Rest Station Officer 1. and 8	
			Duty	

Army Form C. 2118

WAR DIARY
or
INTELLIGENCE SUMMARY
(Erase heading not required.)

Instructions regarding War Diaries and Intelligence Summaries are contained in F. S. Regs., Part II. and the Staff Manual respectively. Title Pages will be prepared in manuscript.

Place	Date	Hour	Summary of Events and Information	Remarks and references to Appendices
ALLOUAGNE	20/3/16 (contin)		Saw A.D.M.S. 16th Div in Divn. Office.	10 pm (Bn) Capt. Rapol
	21/3/16		Admitted Officers Sick 1, Other ranks Sick 25. Evacuated to C.C.S. Officers 1, other ranks 11. To duty Other ranks 7.	B
	22/3/16		Admitted. Officers nil; other ranks, Sick 12. Evacuated. Other ranks 15. To duty. Other ranks 9. Corps rest station. Other ranks 4.	B
	23/3/16		Admitted. Other ranks, Sick 24. Evacuated. Other ranks 32. Rest Station nil Duty 13.	B

WAR DIARY
or
INTELLIGENCE SUMMARY

Army Form C. 2118

Place	Date	Hour	Summary of Events and Information	Remarks and references to Appendices
ALLOUAGNE	24/3/16		Admitted: Officers Sick 2, Other Ranks Sick 22. Evacuated: Officers 2, Other Ranks 30. Rest Station: nil. Duty: Other Ranks 8. Capt. H.E.M. Wall Ramli (temp) joined the unit from the 8/R. Munst. Fus., Lieut J.T. Murphy RAMC (temp) (attached to 8/Royal Munst. Fus.) These Officers and 22 Other Ranks proceeded to take over the advanced dressing stations and Head Quarters of the 46th Field Ambulance at MAZINGARBE, VAUDRICOURT and NOEUX LES MINES respectively.	AF. B.213 Capt. Wall Ramli
NOEUX LES MINES	25/3/16		The unit moved to NOEUX LES MINES taking over the Dressing Stations and billets of No 46 Field Ambulance and Divisional baths at NOEUX LES MINES and MAZINGARBE.	L.23.b.3.9 K.14.a.4.5 K.18.b.9.4 K.18.b.9.11 K.18.b.9.11 L.23.b.2.9

Army Form C. 2118

WAR DIARY
or
INTELLIGENCE SUMMARY
(Erase heading not required.)

Instructions regarding War Diaries and Intelligence Summaries are contained in F. S. Regs., Part II. and the Staff Manual respectively. Title Pages will be prepared in manuscript.

Place	Date	Hour	Summary of Events and Information	Remarks and references to Appendices
NOEUX LES MINES	25/3/16		Also the Advanced Dressing Station at MAZINGARBE + VAUDRICOURT. Admitted: Officers, nil., other ranks, nil. 13. Evacuated: officers 1., other ranks 4.	Major Bell Capt Moore L.23.1.39. R.4.a. 4.5
	26/3/16		Admitted. other ranks, nil. 18 Evacuated. other ranks 2.	B
	27/3/16		Admitted. officers, nil., other ranks nil 15. Evacuated. other ranks 2. Duty. other ranks. 4. Lieut (temp) A.H. LITTLE R.A.M.C. posted to 9/ ROYAL MUNST! FUS!	B

Army Form C. 2118

WAR DIARY
or
INTELLIGENCE SUMMARY
(Erase heading not required.)

Instructions regarding War Diaries and Intelligence Summaries are contained in F. S. Regs., Part II. and the Staff Manual respectively. Title Pages will be prepared in manuscript.

Place	Date	Hour	Summary of Events and Information	Remarks and references to Appendices
NOEUX LES MINES.	28/3/16		Admitted. Other ranks: wounded, 2; sick, 18.	Lt. Bell Capt. Read
			To C.C.S. Other ranks, 14.	
			To Corp Rest Station. Nil.	
			To Duty. Nil.	
	29/3/16		Admitted. Officers, pick 2; Other ranks sick. 8.	B
			C.C.St? Officers sick 2, other ranks, 10.	
			Corp Rest St? Other ranks 1.	
			Duty. Other ranks 6.	
	30/3/16		Admitted. Other ranks: wounded 2; sick 11.	B
			C.C. St? Other ranks, 6.	
			Corp Rest St? Other ranks 3.	
			Duty. " 10.	

WAR DIARY
or
INTELLIGENCE SUMMARY

(Erase heading not required.)

Army Form C. 2118

Place	Date	Hour	Summary of Events and Information	Remarks and references to Appendices
NOEUX LES MINES	31/3/16		Admitted. Officers, nil 3. Other ranks; sick 23. Cas: Ct. S. Other ranks 10. Officers, 8. Cops Rest Sc. Nil Duty 8. W/a. Bell Capt Manne	W/a. Bell Capt Manne

111 F Amb
Vol 5

Confidential

War Diary

of

111 Field Ambulance

from April 1st 1916 to April 30th, 1916

(Volume 5.)

April 1916

COMMITTEE FOR THE
MEDICAL HISTORY OF THE WAR
Date   9 - JUN. 1915

Army Form C. 2118

(VOLUME 5)

WAR DIARY
or
INTELLIGENCE SUMMARY
(Erase heading not required.)

Instructions regarding War Diaries and Intelligence Summaries are contained in F.S. Regs., Part II. and the Staff Manual respectively. Title Pages will be prepared in manuscript.

Place	Date	Hour	Summary of Events and Information	Remarks and references to Appendices
NOEUX LES MINES	1/4/16		LIEUT: F.A. ANDERSON transferred to 8/ R. MUNSTER FUS.	by M.Bell Capt Major
			Admitted. Officers. sick. 1. Other ranks. sick 14.	
			Cas. Cl. St? " " " " " " 5	
			to Duty. " " " " " " 4	
			Corps Rest St?. NIL.	
	2/4/16		Admitted. Officers NIL. Other ranks. wounded 2, sick 12.	B
			Cas. Cl. St?. " " " " " 2 " 7	
			to Duty. " " " " NIL " 3	
			Corps Rest St?. " " " " " " 4	
	3/4/16		Admitted. Officers. wounded NIL; sick 1. Other ranks. wounded NIL. sick 27	B
			" " " " " " " 1; " NIL; " " 9	
			to Duty. " " " " " NIL; " " 9	
			Corps Rest St?. " " " " " " " 2	

Army Form C. 2118

WAR DIARY
or
INTELLIGENCE SUMMARY
(Erase heading not required.)

Place	Date	Hour	Summary of Events and Information	Remarks and references to Appendices
NOEUX LES MINES	4/4/16		Admitted. Officers NIL. Other ranks, Sick wounded, 2; Sick 18. Cas. Cl. St⁵ " " " " 2; " 9 to duty. " " " " " " 3 Corps Rest St⁵. " " " " NIL; " NIL.	15/r. Bell Capt. Name
	5/4/16		CAPT. E.C. BLACK. R.A.M.C. and CAPT. J.R. McGILVRAY posted to 111ᵀᴴ FIELD AMB: this day. Authority A.D.M.S. 16ᵀᴴ DIV: 2/143 of 5/4/16 CAPT: E.C. BLACK. R.A.M.C. temporarily detached for duty with 112ᵀᴴ FIELD AMB: authority ibid. Admitted. Officers NIL; Other ranks, wounded NIL, Sick 29 Cas. Cl. St⁵ " " " " " " 25 to duty " " " " " " 6 Corps Rest St⁵ " " " " " " 4.	

WAR DIARY
or
INTELLIGENCE SUMMARY

(Erase heading not required.)

Army Form C. 2118

Instructions regarding War Diaries and Intelligence Summaries are contained in F.S. Regs., Part II. and the Staff Manual respectively. Title Pages will be prepared in manuscript.

Place	Date	Hour	Summary of Events and Information	Remarks and references to Appendices
NOEUX LES MINES	6/4/16		Admitted. Officers wounded 1, Sick, Nil; other ranks, wounded 1, sick 36.	injured Capt Rampet
			to Can. C.S. " " " " Nil " " 20	
			to Isolation " " " " Nil " 1 "	
			at VAUDRICOURT " " " " " " 9	
			Dis. to duty " " " 1 Nil " 4	
			to Corps Rest St. " " " Nil Nil " 3	
			Lieut E.G. INGE R.A.M.C. proceeded on leave.	
	7/4/16		Admitted. Officers wounded Nil, Sick Nil; other ranks, wounded Nil, sick 20	B
			to Can. C.S. " " " " " " 9	
			Dis. to duty " " " " " 1	
			to Corps Rest St. " " " " " 6	

Army Form C. 2118

WAR DIARY
or
INTELLIGENCE SUMMARY
(Erase heading not required.)

Instructions regarding War Diaries and Intelligence Summaries are contained in F.S. Regs., Part II. and the Staff Manual respectively. Title Pages will be prepared in manuscript.

Place	Date	Hour	Summary of Events and Information	Remarks and references to Appendices
NOEUX LES MINES	8/4/16		Admitted. Officers, wounded NIL, sick NIL; Other Ranks. wounded 10, sick 14	Major C. Bell Capt. Rennie
			to Cor. C.S. " " " " " " 8	
			Ron to duty. " " " " " " 5	
			to Corps Rest St. " " " " " " 2	
	9/4/16		Admitted. Officers NIL; O.R. wounded 1, sick 13	3
			to C.C.S. " " " " " " 5	
			Day to duty. " " NIL " " 3	
			to C.R.S. " " " " " " 4	
	10/4/16		Admitted. Officers NIL; O.R. wounded NIL, sick 15	3
			to C.C.S. " " " " " " 5	
			Dis: to duty " " " " " " 3	
			to C.R.S. " " " " " " 2	

Army Form C. 2118

WAR DIARY
or
INTELLIGENCE SUMMARY
(Erase heading not required.)

Instructions regarding War Diaries and Intelligence Summaries are contained in F. S. Regs., Part II. and the Staff Manual respectively. Title Pages will be prepared in manuscript.

Place	Date	Hour	Summary of Events and Information	Remarks and references to Appendices
NOEUX LES MINES	11/4/16		Admitted. Officers, wounded NIL, sick 1; O.R. wounded 1, sick 18	(Sgd) Bell Capt R.A.M.C
			to C.C.S. " " 1; " " 13	
			Dis. to duty " " " 1; " " 6	
			to C.D.R.S. " " NIL; " " 3.	
	12/4/16		Admitted. Officers wounded NIL, sick 1; O.R. wounded NIL, sick 19	B
			to C.C.S. " " 1; " " 14	
			Dis. to duty " " NIL; " " 4	
			to C.D.R.S. " " " " " 6	
			Lieut J.T. MURPHY R.A.M.C. Reported the unit for duty.	
	13/4/16		Admitted. Officers wounded 1, sick NIL; O.R. wounded NIL, sick 11	B
			to C.C.S. " " 1; " " 7	
			Dis. to duty " " NIL " " 9	
			to C.D.R.S. NIL.	

WAR DIARY or **INTELLIGENCE SUMMARY**

Army Form C. 2118

Place	Date	Hour	Summary of Events and Information	Remarks and references to Appendices
NOEUX LES MINES	14/4/16		Admitted. Officers Nil; O.R. wounded 4, sick 23 to C.C.S. „ „ 4 „ 12 Rej. to duty „ „ Nil „ 10 to C.R.S. „ „ „ Nil Lieut C.F. BRADY R.A.M.C. transferred to 7/ R.I. RIFLES as M.O.	14 - R.H. Capt Rance
	15/4/16		Admitted. Officers wounded Nil, sick 3; O.R. wounded Nil, sick 16 to C.C.S. „ „ „ 3 „ „ „ 16 Rej. to duty „ „ „ „ „ „ 4 to C.R.S. „ „ „ „ „ „ 1	B
	16/4/16		Admitted. Officers Nil; O.R. wounded Nil, sick 24 to C.C.S. „ „ „ „ 13 Rej. to duty „ „ „ „ 6 to C.R.S. „ „ „ „ 5	B

WAR DIARY
or
INTELLIGENCE SUMMARY

Army Form C. 2118

Place	Date	Hour	Summary of Events and Information	Remarks and references to Appendices
NOEUX LES MINES	17/4/16		Admitted. Officers. Nil., O.R. wounded 5, sick 15	by-in-chief Capt Ramsay
			to C.C.S. Officers " " " 5 " 7	
			Gro. to duty " " " " " 4	
			to C.R.S. " " " " " 4	
			Capt E.C. BLACK R.A.M.C reported for duty with this unit	B
	18/4/16		Admitted. Officers Nil. O.R. wounded 5, sick 20	
			to C.C.S. " " " 3 " 10	
			Gro. to duty. " " " " " 1	
			to C.R.S. " " " 1 " 1	
			CAPT. J.R.R. TRIST. R.A.M.C. left the unit and proceed to join the 2/YORKS and LANCS as Medical Officer.	B

Army Form C. 2118

WAR DIARY
or
INTELLIGENCE SUMMARY
(Erase heading not required.)

Instructions regarding War Diaries and Intelligence Summaries are contained in F. S. Regs., Part II. and the Staff Manual respectively. Title Pages will be prepared in manuscript.

Place	Date	Hour	Summary of Events and Information	Remarks and references to Appendices
NOEUX LES MINES	19/4/16		Admitted Officers wounded NIL, Sick 1; O.R. wounded 2, Sick 48	19th Rpt rept Recd
			to C.C.S. " " 1, " 25	
			dis. to duty " " " 8	
			to C.R.S. " NIL, " 3	
	20/4/16		Admitted Officers wounded NIL, Sick 1; O.R. wounded 1, Sick 18	R
			to C.C.S. " 2, " 1, " 1, o.R. " 17	
			dis. to duty " " NIL, " 15	
			to C.R.S. " " " 3	
	21/4/16		Admitted Officers wounded NIL, Sick 1; O.R. wounded 1, Sick 19	R
			to C.C.S. " " 1, " 2, " 21	
			dis. to duty " " " 1, " 7	
			to C.R.S. " NIL, " 2	
			LIEUT. F.A. ANDERSON R.A.M.C. rejoined the unit from duty with 8/ R. MUNSTER FUS.	

Army Form C. 2118

WAR DIARY
or
INTELLIGENCE SUMMARY

(Erase heading not required.)

Instructions regarding War Diaries and Intelligence Summaries are contained in F. S. Regs., Part II. and the Staff Manual respectively. Title Pages will be prepared in manuscript.

Place	Date	Hour	Summary of Events and Information	Remarks and references to Appendices
NOEUX LES MINES	21/9/16 (cont)		LIEUT. J.T. MURPHY R.A.M.C. taking his place	
	22/9/16		Admitted Officer NIL; O.R. wounded 1, Sick 24	B
			to C.C.S. " " 14	
			dis to duty " NIL " NIL	
			to C.R.S " 1 " 3	
			" NIL	
	23/9/16		Admitted Officer NIL; O.R. wounded 2, Sick 15	B
			to C.C.S. " 2 " 10	
			dis to duty " 1 " 4	
			to C.R.S. " NIL	

Army Form C. 2118

WAR DIARY
or
INTELLIGENCE SUMMARY
(Erase heading not required.)

Instructions regarding War Diaries and Intelligence Summaries are contained in F. S. Regs., Part II. and the Staff Manual respectively. Title Pages will be prepared in manuscript.

Place	Date	Hour	Summary of Events and Information	Remarks and references to Appendices
NOEUX LES MINES	24/4/16		Admitted Officers NIL ; O.R. Wounded 1 ; Sick 19	W/a Rev. Capt. Dean
			to C.C.S. " " " 10	
			do. to duty " NIL " 4	
			to C.R.S. " " " NIL	
	25/4/16		Admitted Officers Wounded NIL, Sick 1 ; O.R. Wounded 1 ; Sick 21	B
			to C.C.S. " " " 1 ; " " 2 " 14	
			do. to duty " " " " " " NIL " 6	
			to O.R.S. " " " NIL " " " " 3	
			to Cpl Seaton Dressing Station ; O.R. 1	
	26/4/16		Admitted Officers Wounded NIL, Sick 1 ; O.R. Wounded 3 ; Sick 34	B
			to C.C.S. " " " 1 " " " " 13	
			do. to duty " " " " " NIL " 5	
			to O.R.S. " " " NIL " " " " 3	

WAR DIARY
or
INTELLIGENCE SUMMARY
(Erase heading not required.)

Army Form C. 2118

Instructions regarding War Diaries and Intelligence Summaries are contained in F. S. Regs., Part II. and the Staff Manual respectively. Title Pages will be prepared in manuscript.

Place	Date	Hour	Summary of Events and Information	Remarks and references to Appendices
	27/4/16		Admitted. Officers wounded Nil, Sick 3, O.R. wounded 37, Sick 32.	Kshall Copy Retrc
			To C.C.S. " Nil " 3, OR " 26, " 47	
			To Duty " " " Nil OR " 1, " 19	
			To CRS " Nil " Nil OR " Nil " 1	
	28/4/16		Admitted. Officers wounded Nil, Sick 3, OR wounded 10, Sick 26.	
			To C.C.S. " Nil " 3, OR " 27, " 23	
			To Duty " " " Nil OR " 1, " 2	
			To CRS " Nil " Nil " Nil " Nil	
	29/4/16		Admitted " " " Nil " 26, " 19	
			To CCS " " " Nil " 25, " 20	
			To Duty " " " Nil " 1, " 1 HSN	

Army Form C. 2118

WAR DIARY
or
INTELLIGENCE SUMMARY
(Erase heading not required.)

Instructions regarding War Diaries and Intelligence Summaries are contained in F. S. Regs., Part II. and the Staff Manual respectively. Title Pages will be prepared in manuscript.

Place	Date	Hour	Summary of Events and Information	Remarks and references to Appendices
	30/4/16		Admitted. Officers wounded Nil, Sick 1. O.R wounded 6. Sick 15.	ASW
			To C.C.S. " " " 1. " " 6 " 11.	
			To Duty " Nil " Nil " Nil	
			To C.R.S " " " " "	

Confidential.   16th Div.   111 F. Amb.
                                    Vol 6

War Diary

of

111 Field Ambulance

from 1st May 1916 to 31st May 1916.

(Volume 6).

COMMITTEE FOR THE
MEDICAL HISTORY OF THE WAR
Date   26 JUN. 1915

Army Form C. 2118

WAR DIARY
or
INTELLIGENCE SUMMARY
(Erase heading not required.)

Instructions regarding War Diaries and Intelligence Summaries are contained in F.S. Regs., Part II. and the Staff Manual respectively. Title Pages will be prepared in manuscript.

Volume 6.

Place	Date	Hour	Summary of Events and Information	Remarks and references to Appendices
NOEUX LES MINES.	May 1/1916		Admitted. Officer wounded 1; Sick NIL, O.R. wounded 1, Sick 9	Major Bell Major Plesser
			to C.C.S. " " 1 " " 7	
			to duty " " " " " " 1	
			to C.Q.S. " " NIL " " 1	
			MAJOR W.J.E BELL R.A.M.C. proceeded to England on leave.	
			LIEUT H.E ALLANSON R.A.M.C. (T.C.) joined the unit for duty.	
	May 2/1916		Admitted. Officer wounded NIL, Sick 1; O.R. wounded 3, Sick 14	B
			to C.C.S. " " " " 1 " " 3 NIL " " 7	
			to duty " " " " NIL " " 1 3	
			to C.Q.S. " " " " NIL " " NIL NIL	
	May 3/1916		Admitted. Officer wounded NIL, Sick 1; O.R. wounded 3, Sick 13	B
			to C.C.S. " " " " 1 " " 3 6	
			to duty " " " " NIL " " NIL NIL	
			to C.Q.S. " " " " " " " " 1	

Army Form C. 2118

WAR DIARY
or
INTELLIGENCE SUMMARY
(Erase heading not required.)

Instructions regarding War Diaries and Intelligence Summaries are contained in F. S. Regs., Part II. and the Staff Manual respectively. Title Pages will be prepared in manuscript.

Place	Date	Hour	Summary of Events and Information	Remarks and references to Appendices
NOEUX LES MINES	May 4 1916		Admitted Officers wounded NIL, Sick 1; O.R. wounded 1, Sick 18.	M a Bell Major Royal
			to C.C.S. " " " " " 1, " 20	
			to duty " " " NIL " " 2	
			to C.Q.M.S. " " " " " NIL " NIL	
			LIEUT: A.L. M°CREERY R.A.M.C. (T.C.) proceeded to the 9th ROYAL	
			IRISH RIFLES for temporary duty	
	May 5 1916.		Admitted Officers wounded 1, Sick NIL, O.R. wounded 1, Sick 23	B
			to C.C.S. " " " 1, " " 1, " 11	
			to duty " " NIL " " " " 3	
			to C.Q.M.S. " " " " " NIL " 1	
			LIEUT. W.J. MAC DONALD R.A.M.C. (T.C.) proceed to the 8th Royal	
			Dublin Fusiliers for temporary duty as M.O. in charge.	

WAR DIARY or INTELLIGENCE SUMMARY

Army Form C. 2118

(Erase heading not required.)

Instructions regarding War Diaries and Intelligence Summaries are contained in F.S. Regs., Part II. and the Staff Manual respectively. Title Pages will be prepared in manuscript.

Place	Date	Hour	Summary of Events and Information	Remarks and references to Appendices
NOEUX LES MINES	May 6 1916		Admitted. Officers wounded Nil, sick 2; O.R. wounded 1, sick 12	Major Bell Major Reed
			to C.C.S. " " " 2, " " " Nil " " 13	
			to duty " " " Nil " " " 4 " " 3	
			to C.R.S. " " " " " " Nil " " 2	
	May 7 1916		Admitted. Officers wounded Nil, sick Nil; O.R. wounded 4, sick 11	B
			to C.C.S. " " " " " " 1 " " 8	
			to duty " " " " " " 1 " " 1	
			to C.R.S. " " " " " " 1 " " 9	
	May 8 1916		Adm. Off. wounded Nil. " sick Nil. O.R. wounded 1, sick 13.	B
			C.C.S. " " " " " " 2 " " 11	
			duty " " " " " " Nil " " Nil	
			C.R.S. " " " " " " " " " "	

Army Form C. 2118

WAR DIARY
or
INTELLIGENCE SUMMARY
(Erase heading not required.)

Instructions regarding War Diaries and Intelligence Summaries are contained in F.S. Regs., Part II. and the Staff Manual respectively. Title Pages will be prepared in manuscript.

Place	Date	Hour	Summary of Events and Information	Remarks and references to Appendices
NOEUX LES MINES.	May 9/16.		Adm. Off. wounded NIL, Sick 1, O.R. wounded NIL, Sick 28.	W/o Bell Major Read
			C.C.S. " 1 " " 1	
			duty " NIL " " 3	
			C.R.S. " " " " 2	
			CAPT E.C. BLACK R.A.M.C. (T.C.) transferred for temp duty as M.O.	
			t/c 9th Royal Dublin Fusiliers.	
	May 10/16.		Adm. Off. wounded 2, Sick NIL, O.R. wounded 4, Sick 13.	B
			C.C.S. " " 2 " " " " 6	
			duty " NIL " " " " NIL	
			C.R.S. " " " " " 1	
	May 11/16.		Adm. Officer wounded NIL, Sick 1, O.R. wounded 6, Sick 27	B
			C.C.S. " " 1 " " 5 " 16	
			duty " " " " " 1 " 6	
			C.R.S. " " NIL " " NIL " NIL	

Army Form C. 2118

WAR DIARY
or
INTELLIGENCE SUMMARY
(Erase heading not required.)

Place	Date	Hour	Summary of Events and Information	Remarks and references to Appendices
NOEUX LES MINES	May 12/16		Adm. Off. wounded 1, Sick Nil. O.R. wounded 3, Sick 1) C.C.S. " " 1 " " " 16 duty " " Nil " " 2 " Nil C.R.S. " " " " " " " 1	Capt. Bell Major Reid
	May 13/16		Adm. Off. wounded Nil. Sick 1. O.R. wounded 4, Sick 8 C.C.S. " " " 1 " " " 4 " 11 duty " " " Nil " " Nil " 6 C.R.S. " " " " " " " 2	
	May 14/16		Adm. Off. wounded Nil, Sick Nil. O.R. wounded Nil, Sick 12 C.C.S. " " " " " " " 3 duty " " " " " " " 4 C.R.S. " " " " " " " 1	

WAR DIARY or INTELLIGENCE SUMMARY

Army Form C. 2118

Place	Date	Hour	Summary of Events and Information	Remarks and references to Appendices
NOEUX LES MINES	May 15/16		Adm. Off. wounded Nil, Sick 13. O.R. wounded 1. Sick 13. C.C.S. " " " " " " 6 duty " " " " " " 1 C.Q.M.S. " " Nil " " " 9	Lyon Bell Major Reserve
	May 16/16		Adm. Off. wounded Nil. Sick Nil. O.R. wounded Nil. Sick 26. C.C.S. " " " 2 " " " 20 duty " " Nil " " " 4 C.Q.M.S. " " " " " " Nil	
	May 17/16		Capt. H.E.M. WALL R.A.M.C. (T.C.) proceeded on leave. Adm. Off. wounded Nil. Sick 1. O.R. wounded 1. Sick 15 C.C.S. " " " 1 " " " 16 duty " " Nil " " " 2 C.Q.M.S. " " " " Nil " " 4	

WAR DIARY
INTELLIGENCE SUMMARY

Army Form C. 2118

Place	Date	Hour	Summary of Events and Information	Remarks and references to Appendices
NOEUX LES MINES	May 17/16 (cont)		Lieut W.J. MACDONALD. R.A.M.C. (T.C.) returned to unit from the 8th Royal Scottish Fusiliers.	Mr. Bell Major Ross
	May 18/16		Adm. Off. wounded NIL. Sick 1. O.R. wounded NIL. Sick 35	
			C.C.S. " " " 1 " " " 16	
			duty " " " NIL " " " 1	
			C.D.S. " " " " " " NIL	
	May 19/16		Adm. Off. wounded NIL. Sick NIL. O.R. wounded NIL. Sick 22	
			C.C.S " " " " " " 26	
			duty " " " " " " 2	
			C.D.S. " " " " " " 5	
			Lieut A.J. HICKEY R.A.M.C. (T.C.) posted to this unit.	

Army Form C. 2118

WAR DIARY
or
INTELLIGENCE SUMMARY

(Erase heading not required.)

Instructions regarding War Diaries and Intelligence Summaries are contained in F. S. Regs., Part II. and the Staff Manual respectively. Title Pages will be prepared in manuscript.

Place	Date	Hour	Summary of Events and Information	Remarks and references to Appendices
NOEUX LES MINES	May 20th / 1916		Adm. Off. wounded NIL, sick NIL. O.R. wounded 2, sick 22	10/a Roll Map's Read
			C.C.S. " " " 2 " 22	
			duty " " " " " 11	
			C.R.S. " " " NIL " 11	
	May 21st / 1916		Adm. Off. wounded NIL, sick 1. O.R. wounded 8, sick 31	
			C.C.S. " " " 1 " 10	
			duty " " " NIL " 1	
			C.R.S. " " " NIL " NIL	
			CAPT. BLACK R.A.M.C. (T.C) returned to this unit for duty from the 9th Royal Dublin Fusiliers. Enemy shelled this end of the town near the evening station.	K.18.b.9.1

Army Form C. 2118

WAR DIARY
or
INTELLIGENCE SUMMARY
(Erase heading not required.)

Instructions regarding War Diaries and Intelligence Summaries are contained in F. S. Regs., Part II. and the Staff Manual respectively. Title Pages will be prepared in manuscript.

Place	Date	Hour	Summary of Events and Information	Remarks and references to Appendices
NOEUX LES MINES	May 22 1916		Adm. Officers wounded NIL, Oth. R., O.R. wounded 3, Sick 36,	10th Batt Major Reed
			C.C.S. " " " 2, " " 1, " 11	
			duty " " " NIL, " " 2, " NIL	
			C.R.S. " " " " , " " NIL, " 4	
	May 23rd 1916		Lieut F.A. ANDERSON. R.A.M.C. (T.C.) proceeded to England on leave.	
			Adm. Officers wounded NIL, Oth. pick NIL, O.R. wounded 1, Sick 67	
			C.C.S " " " , " " NIL, " " 1, " 15	
			Section C.D.S " " " , " " " , " " 1, " 1	
			duty " " " , " " " , " " 2, " 2	
			C.R.S " " " , " " " , " " NIL, " NIL	
	May 24th 1916		Adm. Officers NIL " " O.R. wounded 1, Sick 15	
			C.C.S " " " , " " " , " " 11, " 11	
			Section C.D.S. " " " , " " " , " NIL, " 2	
			duty " " " , " " " , " " 2, " 17	
			C.R.S " " " , " " " , " NIL, " NIL	

WAR DIARY or INTELLIGENCE SUMMARY

Army Form C. 2118

Place	Date	Hour	Summary of Events and Information	Remarks and references to Appendices
NOEUX LES MINES	May 25th 1916		Adm. Officer wounded NIL, Sick 1, O.R. wounded NIL, Sick 25	Roy. J. Bell Major R.A.M.C
			C.C.S. " " " " " " " 26	
			duty " " 1 " " " NIL " 8	
			C.R.S. " " NIL " " " " 6	
			Enemy shelled the town near the Dressing Station.	
	May 26th 1916		Adm. Officer wounded NIL, Sick NIL, O.R. wounded 1, Sick 15.	R.15 6-7-91
			C.C.S. " " " " " " 3 " 7	
			duty " " " " " NIL " 4	
			C.R.S. " " " " " " " 4	
	May 27th 1916		Adm. Officer NIL, O.R. wounded 2, Sick 18	
			C.C.S. " " " " " 2 " 8	
			Scabies C.D.S. " " " 2	
			duty " " " NIL " 9	
			C.R.S. " " " " NIL	
			Lieut H.E. ALLANSON R.A.M.E.(T.C.) proceeded to 6th Royal Irish Regt for temp: duty as M.O.	

Army Form C. 2118

WAR DIARY
or
INTELLIGENCE SUMMARY
(Erase heading not required.)

Instructions regarding War Diaries and Intelligence Summaries are contained in F. S. Regs., Part II. and the Staff Manual respectively. Title Pages will be prepared in manuscript.

Place	Date	Hour	Summary of Events and Information	Remarks and references to Appendices
NOEUX LES MINES	May 28th 1916		Adm: Officers wounded NIL, O.R. 1, O.R. wounded 2, Sick 10.	19th Bgy Maps Recd
			C.C.S. " " " " 1, " " " " " 8	
			duty " " " NIL " " " " NIL " " 9	
			C.R.S. " " " " " " " NIL	
			CAPT: E.C. BLACK R.A.M.C. (T.C.) transferred for 6 days training to 1st Army School of Rescue.	
			HON'Y LIEUT: E.G. INGE R.A.M.C. (T.C.) admitted to Hospital No. 9 C.C.S. suffering from Pleurisy.	B
	May 29th 1916		Adm: Officers NIL. O.R. wounded NIL, Sick 14	
			C.C.S. " " " " " " " 9	
			duty " " " " " " " NIL	
			C.R.S. " " " " " " " 3	

WAR DIARY or INTELLIGENCE SUMMARY

Army Form C. 2118

Place	Date	Hour	Summary of Events and Information	Remarks and references to Appendices
NOEUX LES MINES	May 30/1916		Adm. Officers wounded NIL, Sick 1. O.R. wounded 1, sick 28 C.C.S. " " " 1 " 2 " " 9 Scabies D.S. " " " " " " 2 " " 1 duty " " " NIL " " " " NIL C.R.S. " " " " " " " " NIL	Men Roll Maps Plans
	May 31/1916.		Adm. Officers wounded NIL, sick 1. O.R. wounded 3, sick 12 C.C.S. " " " 1 " " 3 " " 11 Scabies D.S. " " " " NIL " " NIL " " 1 duty " " " " " " " " 8 C.R.S. " " " " " " " " 4 Capt H.E M. WALL R.A.M.C (T.C.) returned from leave to-night. LIEUT F.A. ANDERSON R.A.M.C (T.C) also returned from leave.	B

111 F Amb
Vol 7
Jun

Confidential

WAR DIARY

of

111 Field Ambulance

from 1st June 1916 to 30th June 1916

(Volume 7.)

Army Form C. 2118

WAR DIARY
or
INTELLIGENCE SUMMARY
(Erase heading not required.)

Volume 7.

Place	Date	Hour	Summary of Events and Information	Remarks and references to Appendices
NOEUX LES MINES	June 1 1916		One man of unit wounded (shell)	Mitchell Major Rowe
			Adm. Officers sick NIL, wounded NIL, O.R. sick 24, wounded 2	
			C.C.S. " " " " " 15 " 2	
			duty " " " " " 4 " NIL	
			C.R.S. " " " " " NIL " NIL	
			Capt H.F.M. WALL. R.A.M.C. (T.C.) proceeded for duty to 12th Division.	
	June 2 1916		Adm. Officers wounded 1, sick 3. O.R. wounded NIL, sick 31	B
			C.C.S. " " " 1 " 3 " " " 33	
			duty " " " " " 3 " " " 3	
			C.R.S. " " " NIL " NIL " " " NIL	
	June 3 1916		Adm. Officers wounded NIL, sick NIL. O.R. wounded 2, sick 7	B
			C.C.S. " " " " " " " " " 12	
			duty " " " " " NIL " " " 1	
			C.R.S. " " " " " " " " " NIL

Army Form C. 2118

WAR DIARY
or
INTELLIGENCE SUMMARY
(Erase heading not required.)

Instructions regarding War Diaries and Intelligence Summaries are contained in F. S. Regs., Part II. and the Staff Manual respectively. Title Pages will be prepared in manuscript.

Place	Date	Hour	Summary of Events and Information	Remarks and references to Appendices
NOEUX LES MINES	June 4 1916		Adm. Officers wounded NIL, Sick 2. O.R. wounded NIL, sick 10	B
			C.C.S. " " " " " 2 " " 9	
			duty " " " " " 1 " " 5	
			C.R.S. " " " NIL " " " NIL	
			Number in hospital, 31.	
	June 5 1916		Steady state.	B
			Number in hospital, 25	
	June 6 1916		Number in hospital, 32.	
			Capt J.E. RUTHERFORD and Capt C.M. ROW, both Rand (T.C.) reported for duty with this unit.	B
	June 7 1916		Number in hospital, 34.	B

Army Form C. 2118

WAR DIARY
or
INTELLIGENCE SUMMARY
(Erase heading not required.)

Instructions regarding War Diaries and Intelligence Summaries are contained in F. S. Regs., Part II. and the Staff Manual respectively. Title Pages will be prepared in manuscript.

Place	Date	Hour	Summary of Events and Information	Remarks and references to Appendices
NOEUX LES MINES.	June 8th 1916		Remaining in Hospital. 37	
	June 9th 1916		Remaining in Hospital. 40	
	June 10th 1916		One driver A.S.C. (H.T) joined unit	
	June 11th 1916		Remaining in Hospital. 42.	
	June 12th 1916		" " " 44	
	June 13th 1916		" " " 36.	
			" " " 27	

Army Form C. 2118

WAR DIARY
or
INTELLIGENCE SUMMARY
(Erase heading not required.)

Instructions regarding War Diaries and Intelligence Summaries are contained in F.S. Regs., Part II. and the Staff Manual respectively. Title Pages will be prepared in manuscript.

Place	Date	Hour	Summary of Events and Information	Remarks and references to Appendices
NOEUX LES MINES	April 14/1916		Remaining in Hospital. 27.	
	April 15/1916		" " 28.	
	April 16/1916		New draft of 6 men joined the unit.	
			Remaining in Hospital. 19.	
			1 man struck off the strength of unit to proceed to the Clyde Shipbuilding etc Lim. Glasgow. *	Appen. 1
			* Authority W.O. Letter 19/Releases/440. A.G.5.	
	April 17/1916		Remaining in Hospital. 30	
	April 18/1916		Remaining in Hospital. 41	

Army Form C. 2118

WAR DIARY
or
INTELLIGENCE SUMMARY
(Erase heading not required.)

Instructions regarding War Diaries and Intelligence Summaries are contained in F. S. Regs., Part II. and the Staff Manual respectively. Title Pages will be prepared in manuscript.

Place	Date	Hour	Summary of Events and Information	Remarks and references to Appendices
NOEUX LES MINES	June 19/1916		Remaining in Hospital. 21	
	June 20/1916		" " " 26.	
			Began the construction of a small Officer's Hospital to consist of two cubicles and a central dining and sitting room.	
	June 21/1916		Remaining in Hospital. 26.	
	June 22/1916		" " " 30	

Army Form C. 2118

WAR DIARY
or
INTELLIGENCE SUMMARY
(*Erase heading not required.*)

Instructions regarding War Diaries and Intelligence Summaries are contained in F. S. Regs., Part II. and the Staff Manual respectively. Title Pages will be prepared in manuscript.

Place	Date	Hour	Summary of Events and Information	Remarks and references to Appendices
NOEUX LES MINES	June 23 1916		Remaining in Hospital, 35	
	June 24 1916		Capt C.H. DENHAM (T.C.) and 22 Other ranks proceeded to AUCHEL to-day to take over the Corps Scabies Dressing Station.	
	June 25 1916		Remaining in Dressing Station 26.	
	June 26 1916		" 29	
			" 30	

Army Form C. 2118

WAR DIARY
or
INTELLIGENCE SUMMARY

(Erase heading not required.)

Place	Date	Hour	Summary of Events and Information	Remarks and references to Appendices
NOEUX LES MINES	Aug 27 1916		Remaining in Dressing Station. 39. One Officer admitted to the "Officer's hospital".	B
	Aug 28 1916		Remaining in Dressing Station 44. Visited the Corps Scabies Dressing Station at AUCHEL.	B
	Aug 29 1916		Remaining. 47	
	Aug 30 1916		Remaining 45. Nine (9) wounded admitted owing to Shelling at MAZINGARBE.	L.23. Sheet 36B

W.J.C. Bell
Major R.A.M.C.
O.C. 11th F. Amb.

16th Division

111th Field Ambulance

July 1916

WAR DIARY

111th Field Amb. RAMC

1st. July to 31st. July 1916.

VOLUME No. 8

Army Form C. 2118

WAR DIARY
or
INTELLIGENCE SUMMARY
(Erase heading not required.)

Volume 8.

Instructions regarding War Diaries and Intelligence Summaries are contained in F.S. Regs., Part II. and the Staff Manual respectively. Title Pages will be prepared in manuscript.

Place	Date	Hour	Summary of Events and Information	Remarks and references to Appendices
NO BOX LES MINES	July 1/1916		Patients remaining 37	B
	July 2/1916		" 27	B
	July 3/1916		Officers wounds are now in line for slight cases which will not require more than four days treatment. Remaining 27. One private of this unit admitted slightly wounded due to shelling at MAZINGARBE.	RS L.23 (Sheet 36B)
	July 4/1916		Remaining 42. Still shelling MAZINGARBE. One private of this unit admitted wounded.	R
	July 5/1916		Remaining 47	B

Army Form C. 2118

WAR DIARY
or
INTELLIGENCE SUMMARY
(Erase heading not required.)

Instructions regarding War Diaries and Intelligence Summaries are contained in F. S. Regs., Part II. and the Staff Manual respectively. Title Pages will be prepared in manuscript.

Place	Date	Hour	Summary of Events and Information	Remarks and references to Appendices
NOEUX LES MINES	July 5 1916 (cont)		Ordered by A.D.M.S. 16th Division to discontinue preparation for bathing at the station, MAZINGARBE, on account of the frequent shelling of that place.	K. 18 Sheet 36B
			Patients remaining: 43	L. 23 Sheet B
	July 6 1916		" 33	B
	July 7 1916		Lieut. & A. ANDERSEN struck off the strength	B
	July 8 1916		Patients remaining 47. Included are sick and one wounded Officer. Hostile shelling of MAZINGARBE in Bearing Station area occurred between 10 & 11 p.m. and was very severe. Capt. J. a. Rutherford transferred to 6th Bn. L. Regt. in medical charge vice Lieut. H.E. Adamson who rejoined the unit.	B

Army Form C. 2118

WAR DIARY
or
INTELLIGENCE SUMMARY
(Erase heading not required.)

Instructions regarding War Diaries and Intelligence Summaries are contained in F. S. Regs., Part II. and the Staff Manual respectively. Title Pages will be prepared in manuscript.

Place	Date	Hour	Summary of Events and Information	Remarks and references to Appendices
NOEUX LES MINES	July 9/1916		Remaining 37 no officers	C.2.5 d 6.5
	July 10/1916		Lt W. E. Allerson transferred for duty to Corps Scabies Bathing Station AUCHIEL.	B
	July 11/1916		Patients remaining 37	B
	July 12/1916		" Sick 41, wounded 1	B
	July 13/1916		Patients remaining Sick 43, wounded 2.	B
			" 52 (2 officers) wounded 5	B

1875 Wt. W593/826 1,000,000 4/15 J.B.C. & A. A.D.S.S./Forms/C. 2118.

Army Form C. 2118

WAR DIARY
or
INTELLIGENCE SUMMARY
(Erase heading not required.)

Instructions regarding War Diaries and Intelligence Summaries are contained in F. S. Regs., Part II. and the Staff Manual respectively. Title Pages will be prepared in manuscript.

Place	Date	Hour	Summary of Events and Information	Remarks and references to Appendices
NOEUX LES MINES	July 14 1916		Patients remaining Sick 49 (2 officers) Wounded 2.	B
"	July 15 1916		Patients remaining Sick 49 (2 officers) Wounded 2.	B
"	July 16 1916		" 44 (2 officers) " 1	B
"	July 17 1916		" 38 (2 officers) " Nil	B
"	July 18 1916		" 41 " Wounded 1	B

WAR DIARY
or
INTELLIGENCE SUMMARY

Army Form C. 2118

Place	Date	Hour	Summary of Events and Information	Remarks and references to Appendices
NOEUX LES MINES	July 19/16		21 wounded moved through Dressing Station.	B
	July 20/16		MAZINGARBE heavily shelled. Remainot - Sick 42. Wounded 2.	B
	July 21/16		Remaining Sick 33. (1 Officer) wounded 2. Lieut J.S.P. KNIGHT R.A.M.C. proceeded to 9th O Inish Fusiliers for temporary duty	B
	July 22/16		Remaining Sick 36 (1 Officer) wounded 3.	B
			Remaining Sick 46 (Officers 3) wounded 3	B

Army Form C. 2118

WAR DIARY
or
INTELLIGENCE SUMMARY
(Erase heading not required.)

Instructions regarding War Diaries and Intelligence Summaries are contained in F. S. Regs., Part II. and the Staff Manual respectively. Title Pages will be prepared in manuscript.

Place	Date	Hour	Summary of Events and Information	Remarks and references to Appendices
NOEUX LES MINES	July 23 1916		Remaining Sick 40 (2 Officers) Wounded 3. Capt C. H. DENHAM & Lieut ALLANSON. E. H. returned from the Corps Scabies Station and Auchel after handing over the Scabies Station to 96th Fd. Amb. 32nd Division	K 18/7-9/1. (36.R) 4B C.17/7-8.5 (Sheet 36c)
	July 24 1916		Remaining Sick 43 (2 Officers)	B
	July 25 1916		" 41 (2 Officers)	B
	July 26 1916		" 41 (2 Officers)	B

Army Form C. 2118

WAR DIARY
or
INTELLIGENCE SUMMARY
(Erase heading not required.)

Instructions regarding War Diaries and Intelligence Summaries are contained in F. S. Regs., Part II. and the Staff Manual respectively. Title Pages will be prepared in manuscript.

Place	Date	Hour	Summary of Events and Information	Remarks and references to Appendices
NOEUX LES MINES	July 27/1916		Remaining - Sick 37 (2 Officers) Wounded 3 men joined - nil till to-day	B
	July 28/1916		" 43 (1 Officer)	B
	July 29/1916		" 43	B
	July 30/1916		" 39 Lieut & Qr Mr E.G. INGE R.A.M.C. 14th Fd Amb. admitted to Dressing Station with Hernia. Rt. Inguinal.	B

1875. Wt. W593/826 1,000,000 4/15 J.B.C. & A. A.D.S.S./Forms/C. 2118.

Army Form C. 2118

WAR DIARY
or
INTELLIGENCE SUMMARY
(Erase heading not required.)

Instructions regarding War Diaries and Intelligence Summaries are contained in F.S. Regs., Part II. and the Staff Manual respectively. Title Pages will be prepared in manuscript.

Place	Date	Hour	Summary of Events and Information	Remarks and references to Appendices
NOEUX LES MINES	July 31 1916		Remaining Sch 29.	B
			1st G. Bell Major General O.C. 11th Fd Amb	

August 1916

WAR DIARY.

111th Field Ambulance.

MONTH OF AUGUST, 1916.

VOLUME :— 9

COMMITTEE FOR THE
MEDICAL HISTORY OF THE WAR
Date 30 OCT. 1916

Army Form C. 2118

WAR DIARY
or
INTELLIGENCE SUMMARY
(Erase heading not required.)

———— VOLUME 9 ————

Place	Date	Hour	Summary of Events and Information	Remarks and references to Appendices
NŒUX LES MINES	Aug 1 1916		Remaining Sick 46. Bomb dropped from hostile aeroplane near 113 Field Ambulance about 9.30 P.M.	K.18.b.9.1 ®
	Aug 2 46		Remaining Sick 47, wounded 1. In company with Capt Row & Capt HICKEY RAMC visited Brewery PHILOSOPHE and ST PATRICK and FORT GLATZ in LOOS, all three being Dressing Stations held by a field Ambulance of the 40th Division. No 36194 Corporal Berry. C.F awarded a Parchment Certificate by the Divisional Commander for devotion to duty and gallant conduct in the field on April 29th 1916.	Quartier R ~~G Snigget~~ R G.20.a.3.0 G.35.d.3.7 G.35.b.3.8 ®
	Aug 3 46		Remaining Sick 46 (1 Officer)	

WAR DIARY
or
INTELLIGENCE SUMMARY

(Erase heading not required.)

Army Form C. 2118

Instructions regarding War Diaries and Intelligence Summaries are contained in F. S. Regs, Part II. and the Staff Manual respectively. Title Pages will be prepared in manuscript.

Place	Date	Hour	Summary of Events and Information	Remarks and references to Appendices
NŒUX LES MINES	Aug 4/16		Remaining. Sick 42.	B
	Aug 5/16		Remaining. Sick 40. The town near Station was shelled to-day. A bomb was also dropped from an aeroplane about the same place.	B
	Aug 6/16		Remaining. Sick 36. A few Baths on Station.	B
	Aug 7/16		Remaining. 83. A few shells in vicinity of station	B

WAR DIARY
or
INTELLIGENCE SUMMARY
(Erase heading not required.)

Army Form C. 2118

Place	Date	Hour	Summary of Events and Information	Remarks and references to Appendices
NOEUX LES MINES	Aug 7 1916 (cont)		Advanced party of 2 Officers and 10 men sent to advanced dressing stations held by the 137th Field Ambulance, 46th Division at the Brewery, PHILOSOPHE and St Patrick and Fort Glatz at LOOS. Capt C.H. DENHAM, R.A.M.C. (T.C.) struck off strength (contract ended)	B G.20.a.20 G.35.d.3.9 G.25.b.3.8
	Aug 8 1916		Took over Advanced dressing stations at Brewery, PHILOSOPHE and St Patrick & Fort Glatz in LOOS from 137th Field Ambulance, 46th Division. Handed over Advanced Dressing Station MAZINGARBE and Divisional Baths at MAZINGARBE	B L.22.b.2.9

WAR DIARY
or
INTELLIGENCE SUMMARY
(Erase heading not required.)

Army Form C. 2118

Place	Date	Hour	Summary of Events and Information	Remarks and references to Appendices
NOEUX LES MINES	Aug 8/1916 (cont)		and the Divisional Baths NOEUX LES MINES to 113th Field Ambulance, 16th Division	B
	Aug 9/1916		Collecting wounded from Loos section and from 14 bis section up to RAILWAY ALLEY.	B
	Aug 10/1916		Remaining. Sick 31, wounded 12. " 25 (1 officer) wounded 12. " 19 (1 officer) " 8	B
	Aug 11/1916		Went to Advanced Dressing Station (St Patricks) in LOOS.	B

WAR DIARY
or
INTELLIGENCE SUMMARY
(Erase heading not required.)

Army Form C. 2118

Place	Date	Hour	Summary of Events and Information	Remarks and references to Appendices
LOOS	Aug 12/1916		Visited the Regimental Aid Posts in LOOS and made myself acquainted with the methods of evacuation.	G.35.ot.3.4
			At H.Q. of unit NOEUX LES MINES	
			Remaining Sick 21 (1 Officer) Wounded 14.	
	Aug 13/1916		Visited Regimental Aid Posts in LOOS with the O.B.S. A.D.M.S. 16th Division	Q.323.8
			Visited TOSH KEEP with the same Officer with a view to establishing a Regimental Aid Post for the Battalion in 14 bis section.	G.36.9.79
			At H.Q. of unit. NOEUX LES MINES	
			Remaining Sick 24 (2 officers) Wounded 7	

Army Form C. 2118

WAR DIARY
or
INTELLIGENCE SUMMARY
(Erase heading not required.)

Place	Date	Hour	Summary of Events and Information	Remarks and references to Appendices
NOEUX LES MINES	Aug 14 1916		Returned to H.Q. of unit early this morning. Remaining Sick 20 (2 officers) wounded 11.	AB K.18.b.9.1.
	Aug 15 1916		Capt. D.M. JOHNSTON R.A.M.C. (T.F.) joined the unit for duty and is taken on the strength accordingly. Remaining Sick 23 (officers 2) wounded 14. Two men joined unit from the base.	
	Aug 16 1916		Remaining. Sick 22 (2 officers) wounded 11.	

Army Form C. 2118

WAR DIARY
or
INTELLIGENCE SUMMARY
(Erase heading not required.)

Instructions regarding War Diaries and Intelligence Summaries are contained in F. S. Regs., Part II. and the Staff Manual respectively. Title Pages will be prepared in manuscript.

Place	Date	Hour	Summary of Events and Information	Remarks and references to Appendices
NOEUX LES MINES	Aug 18/1916		Remaining Sick 19 (2 Officers) Wounded 16. Inspected London Road Dug-out with the D.A.D.M.S. 16th Division. This Dug-out is to be used as a rest station where tea + soup can be given to walking wounded cases coming down London Road Trench.	G.25.a.1.2. BETHUNE (trench sheet) 1:40,000.
	Aug 18/1916		Remaining Sick 24, (1 Officer) Wounded 24 (2 Officers) Lieut D.M. Hunt transferred to 7th Inniskilling Regt. on temp. duty. Went to Adv. Dressing Station (ST PATRICK'S) in LOOS. Remaining Sick in Dressing St. NOEUX LES MINES.	G.35.d.3.7
LOOS	Aug 19/1916		Sick 19 (1 Officer) Wounded 22.	

Place	Date	Hour	Summary of Events and Information	Remarks and references to Appendices
LOOS	Aug 20 1916		Raid by 6th Royal Irish Regt. preceded by Heavy & a minie Casualties few and slight. About 25 pierced through Advanced Searing Stations Nearly all flight wounds by rifle bullet and machine gun fire The regiment lost 3 Officers. 2 killed and one missing. Remaining at Searing Station NOEUX LES MINES Sick 18. Wounded 15.	B
NOEUX LES MINES	Aug 21 1916		Returned to H.Q. at NOEUX LES MINES. Remaining Sick 21. Wounded 9 (1 Officer)	R K.13.b.9.1

Army Form C. 2118

WAR DIARY
or
INTELLIGENCE SUMMARY
(Erase heading not required.)

Instructions regarding War Diaries and Intelligence Summaries are contained in F.S. Regs., Part II. and the Staff Manual respectively. Title Pages will be prepared in manuscript.

Place	Date	Hour	Summary of Events and Information	Remarks and references to Appendices
NOEUX LES MINES	Aug 22/1916		Remaining. Sick 4 (1 officer) wounded. 15 (1 officer). Hostile shelling of town to-day. Ruined about Station.	B
	Aug 23/1916		Remaining. Sick 29 (2 officers) wounded 9.	B
	Aug 24/1916		Remaining. Sick 23 (1 officer) wounded 5.	B
	Aug 25/1916		The unit closed down preparatory to moving. Remaining: nil.	B

1875 Wt. W593/826 1,000,000 4/15 T.R.C. & A. A.D.S.S./Forms/C. 2118.

WAR DIARY or INTELLIGENCE SUMMARY

Army Form C. 2118

Place	Date	Hour	Summary of Events and Information	Remarks and references to Appendices
HURIONVILLE	Aug 26/1916		The unit moved into billets in HURIONVILLE in accordance with 16th Division R.A.M.C. Operation order No 8 dated 24th Aug. 1916. It is responsible for the pick of the 49th Brigade and 16th Divisional Artillery. Cases requiring admission to Hospital to be evacuated to No 112 Field Ambulance at ALLOUAGNE by Motor Ambulance Car.	U.20.d.8.3 (sheet 36ᴬ)
	Aug 27/1916		One aid admitted & transferred to 112th Field Ambulance.	C.12.b.9.6 (sheet 36ᴮ)

Army Form C. 2118

WAR DIARY
or
INTELLIGENCE SUMMARY
(Erase heading not required.)

Instructions regarding War Diaries and Intelligence Summaries are contained in F.S. Regs., Part II. and the Staff Manual respectively. Title Pages will be prepared in manuscript.

Place	Date	Hour	Summary of Events and Information	Remarks and references to Appendices
HURIONVILLE	Aug 25/16		Admitted 13 sick and transferred all to 112th Fd Amb.	112th Fd Amb.
	Aug 29/16		Admitted 8 sick. Transferred to 112th Fd Amb.	
	Aug 30/16	2.0 AM	In accordance with 16th Division movement order No 7371 dated 25th, 27th and 28th August the unit marched to CHOCQUES and entrained.	
		7.12 AM	Train started.	

Army Form C. 2118

WAR DIARY
or
INTELLIGENCE SUMMARY
(Erase heading not required.)

Instructions regarding War Diaries and Intelligence Summaries are contained in F. S. Regs., Part II. and the Staff Manual respectively. Title Pages will be prepared in manuscript.

Place	Date	Hour	Summary of Events and Information	Remarks and references to Appendices
LONGUEAU	Aug 30/16	2.30 P.M.	Train arrived and the unit detrained and marched to DAOURS where it moved into billets (16th Division Order No 737 dated 29th August 1916)	
DAOURS	Aug 31/16		In accordance with 16th Division R.A.M.C Operation Order No 9 dated 30th August 916 The Bearer Division moved to CITADEL joining 49th Infantry Brigade Group on arrival. The Tent Division marched to the Corps Main Dressing Station DIVE COPSE and reported to Officer Commanding for duty.	E. 18. d (sheet) S 24 c (sheet 62D NE)

10/a Rall
Major [?]
O.C. 10th F. Amb.

Sept. 1916

WAR DIARY

111th Field Ambulance. R.A.M.C.   16th Div

FOR MONTH OF SEPTEMBER, 1916.

VOLUME 10

COMMITTEE FOR THE
MEDICAL HISTORY OF THE WAR
Date -9 DEC. 1916

140/13/9

Army Form C. 2118

WAR DIARY
or
INTELLIGENCE SUMMARY
(Erase heading not required.)

Volume 10 —

Instructions regarding War Diaries and Intelligence Summaries are contained in F. S. Regs., Part II. and Staff Manual respectively. Title Pages will be prepared in manuscript.

Place	Date	Hour	Summary of Events and Information	Remarks and references to Appendices
DIVE COPSE	Aug 31 1916 (continued)		Prepared to open.	J.24.c. (Sheet 62 D) N.E.
	Sept 1 1916		Opened Dressing Station	"S"
	Sept 2 1916		Capt. C. M. Rew Rand ordered to report to Eastern Command Head Quarters 50 Pall Mall, London for the purpose of giving evidence at a Court Martial (Adm.S. 16th Div. 43/7 dated 2 Sep. 1916) Bearer Division ordered to proceed to BRONFAY FARM and report to O.C. Bearer Div. 20th Div. (ADn.S 16th Div. 192/18 dated 2 Sep. 1916)	Q Q R F. Eq. 6.7.11 Albert (continued Sheet)

1875 Wt. W 593/826 1,000,000 4/15 T.B.C. & A. A.D.S.S./Forms/C. 2118.

Army Form C. 2118

WAR DIARY
or
INTELLIGENCE SUMMARY
(Erase heading not required.)

Instructions regarding War Diaries and Intelligence Summaries are contained in F.S. Regs., Part II. and the Staff Manual respectively. Title Pages will be prepared in manuscript.

Place	Date	Hour	Summary of Events and Information	Remarks and references to Appendices
DIVE COPSE (1)	Sept 3/1916		Treating a large number of wounded from the attack made by the 16th Division on (2) GUILLEMONT. Bearer Division opened Advanced Dressing Station at BERNAFAY WOOD (3) and BRIQUETERIE (4)	(1) S.18.d ALBERT (continued sheet) B (2) T.19.c B (3) S.22.d.9.1 (4) A.4.b B
	Sept 4/1916		Treated a large number of wounded	
	Sept 5/1916		Routine. Lieut A.E. Allanson Reed proceeded to 1st Mounted Fusiliers in temporary medical charge.	AB
	Sept 6/1916		I received an order to take over charge of the Advanced Dressing Station CARNOY (5) from Capt. Van den Bijuen Reed and proceeded forthwith.	(5) A.13.6. B

Army Form C. 2118

WAR DIARY
or
INTELLIGENCE SUMMARY
(Erase heading not required.)

Instructions regarding War Diaries and Intelligence Summaries are contained in F.S. Regs., Part II. and the Staff Manual respectively. Title Pages will be prepared in manuscript.

Place	Date	Hour	Summary of Events and Information	Remarks and references to Appendices
CARNOY (1)	Sept 7 1916		Treated a large number of wounded. Lieut R.M. Hunt evacuated sick to No 5 C.C.S.	(1) A.B.6. Regd 43 ALBERT (Ordnance Fleet)
	Sept 8 1916		Routine	(2) J.18.d
	Sept 9 1916		Tent Division proceeded from DIVE COPSE (3) to BRONFAY FARM (3) and prepared to open.	(3) 43 F.24.b.7.1
	Sept 10 1916		Rejoined Tent Division at BRONFAY FARM heading over command of Advanced Dressing Station CARNOY (4) to a representative of the Guards Division. Beaver Division moved to Camp at HAPPY VALLEY. Lieut Allanson Rawd wounded in shoulder and evacuated.	(4) A.B.6. 65

Army Form C. 2118

WAR DIARY
or
INTELLIGENCE SUMMARY
(Erase heading not required.)

Instructions regarding War Diaries and Intelligence Summaries are contained in F. S. Regs., Part II. and the Staff Manual respectively. Title Pages will be prepared in manuscript.

Place	Date	Hour	Summary of Events and Information	Remarks and references to Appendices
BRONFAY FARM (1)	Sept 11 1916		Beaver Division moved to Camp at VAUX SUR SOMME (2)	(1) F.29.6.7.1 (2) J.26.c
	Sept 12 1916		Routine	(3)
	Sept 13 1916		Capt. A. Baldie and Lieut W.W. Jones Royal T.C. posted to this unit. (AD3/18 16th Div. 143/23 dated 13 Sep 1916)	(4)
	Sept 14 1916		Routine	(5)
	Sept 15 1916		Routine	(6)

Army Form C. 2118

WAR DIARY
or
INTELLIGENCE SUMMARY
(Erase heading not required.)

Instructions regarding War Diaries and Intelligence Summaries are contained in F. S. Regs., Part II. and Staff Manual respectively. Title Pages will be prepared in manuscript.

Place	Date	Hour	Summary of Events and Information	Remarks and references to Appendices
BRONFAY FARM (1)	Sept 16 1916		Fewer wounded coming in. Routine.	F.29.6.9.1
	Sept 17 1916		Routine. Very few wounded coming in.	
	Sept 18 1916		Beaver division moved to HUPPY by motor omnibus. One officer of this unit and six men were wounded in the recent operations.	
	Sept 19 1916		Routine. Handed over Dressing station to 1/2nd London Field Ambulance.	

Army Form C. 2118

WAR DIARY
or
INTELLIGENCE SUMMARY
(Erase heading not required.)

Place	Date	Hour	Summary of Events and Information	Remarks and references to Appendices
BRONFAY FARM.	Sept 20/1916		Reserve Division moved to METEREN entraining at BAILLEUL at 8.30 a.m. on	X 15 d. (Sheet 27)
	Sept 21/1916		Reserve Division entraining at ABBEVILLE at 1.30 a.m. and detraining at Pontru	
	Sept 22/1916		Tent Division marched to CORBIE and moved into billets in company with the Tent Division of No 112 Fd Ambulance and various details from No 113 Fd Ambulance.	

Army Form C. 2118

WAR DIARY
or
INTELLIGENCE SUMMARY
(Erase heading not required.)

Instructions regarding War Diaries and Intelligence Summaries are contained in F. S. Regs., Part II. and the Staff Manual respectively. Title Pages will be prepared in manuscript.

Place	Date	Hour	Summary of Events and Information	Remarks and references to Appendices
CASSIE	Sept 23 1916		Entrained at 8.15 P.M. with advance detachments from No 112 and No 113 Fd Ambulance.	
BAILLEUL	Sept 24 1916		Detrained at 8.20 a.m. and leaving the junior from No 112 & 113 Fd Ambulance with their respective units we marched to SCHERPENBERG where we reported to the Bearer Division who had marched from METEREN arriving about an hour before us.	M. T.B. 513 attached
SCHERPEN-BERG	Sept 25 1916		The unit is now in camp. The men are provided with wooden huts and tents. The officers with the exception of myself are in tents.	

WAR DIARY
or
INTELLIGENCE SUMMARY

Army Form C. 2118

Place	Date	Hour	Summary of Events and Information	Remarks and references to Appendices
SCHERPEN-BERG	Sept 26/1916		The unit is classed as far as taking in O.R. wounded and select duty from the following units and transport to the 112 a 113 to Ambulance Battalion in camp at M.G.L. 11th Brents of DE 20H CAMP Militia 136th Army Troop Coy M.17. G.B.9 250th Tunnelling Coy LA CLYTTE N.T.& T.S. We detain a few cases for 24 hours if we judge that they will be fit for duty at the end of that period	

Army Form C. 2118

WAR DIARY
or
INTELLIGENCE SUMMARY
(Erase heading not required.)

Place	Date	Hour	Summary of Events and Information	Remarks and references to Appendices
SCHERPEN-BERG	Sept 27/16		Routine work consists in improving the drainage of the camp sites, levelling the ground, construction of paths, steps etc. construction of latrines, incinerators, adjustment in benches, dodge pits, grease traps & so on. We have taken over a standing hopping & on horse which requires roofing and flooring. There is enough work to carry us on for several months.	B
	Sept 28/16		Routine	B
	Sept 29/16		Routine	B

WAR DIARY
or
INTELLIGENCE SUMMARY

Army Form C. 2118

Place	Date	Hour	Summary of Events and Information	Remarks and references to Appendices
SCHERPEN-BERG	Sept 29 1916 (cont.)		A.D.M.S. 16th Division visited Camp and made a short inspection of the site	
	Sept 30 1916		Routine. Addendum. On Sept 25th the D.D.M.S. XIV Corps made a short inspection of the Camp in company with the A.D.M.S. 16th Division. F/C Bell Major Reuvers O.C. 111th Fd. Amb.	

WAR DIARY

MONTH OF OCTOBER, 1916.

VOLUME

111th Field Ambulance
R.A.M.C.

Army Form C. 2118

WAR DIARY
or
INTELLIGENCE SUMMARY
(Erase heading not required.)

Volume II.

Instructions regarding War Diaries and Intelligence Summaries are contained in F.S. Regs., Part II. and the Staff Manual respectively. Title Pages will be prepared in manuscript.

Place	Date	Hour	Summary of Events and Information	Remarks and references to Appendices
SCHERPEN-BERG	Oct 1/1916		Lieut W.J. MacDonald found proceeded to the 11/Hants Regt. for temporary duty. Capt A.P. Bisley. Rouen temporary duty. Capt McGilvray Raynal temporary duty.	M.V. 53 Sheets
	Oct 2/1916		Routine	1/R. Irish Rifles for tem— 8/R. Innyskilling Fusiliers for
	Oct 3/1916		Lieut W.W. Jones Rouen attached to see proto of 1st attending Coy. and supervise the sanitary arrangements of that unit.	

Army Form C. 2118

WAR DIARY
or
INTELLIGENCE SUMMARY
(Erase heading not required.)

Instructions regarding War Diaries and Intelligence Summaries are contained in F.S. Regs., Part II. and the Staff Manual respectively. Title Pages will be prepared in manuscript.

Place	Date	Hour	Summary of Events and Information	Remarks and references to Appendices
SCHERPENBERG	Oct 3/1916 (cont)		About 50 O.R. of unit sent out to police vacant horse & wagon lines left by Canadian Divisional Artillery until the 16th Divisional Artillery arrive	Mappin 53 Place
	Oct 4/1916		Routine	
	Oct 5/1916		Capt. A. Baldie R.A.M.C. and 1 unit advanced party from B Section proceeded to Divisional Rest Station METEREN X.15.d to take on from the 59th Field Ambulance. 19th Division Platoon. A Section Transport & material proceeded to the same place later in the day. 1 N.C.O. and 1 man took over the Divisional Rest Station at CAESTRE.	X.15.d METEREN 19th Division Platoon W.S.a Slater R

WAR DIARY or INTELLIGENCE SUMMARY

Army Form C. 2118

Place	Date	Hour	Summary of Events and Information	Remarks and references to Appendices
SCHERPEN BERG	Oct 6/1916		A Section lent transport proceeded to METEREN taking over the Divisional Rest Station at that place & at CAESTRE from the 58th Field Ambulance. 19th Division Patients taken over 62., at METEREN. D.R.S. at CAESTRE is at present closed, no patients being taken in.	
METEREN	Oct 7/1916		D.R.S. Admitted O. Remained 47. 1 to Amb. " " 3 Cases all evacuated to C.C.S. or transferred to the IX Corps Rest Station at MONT DES CATS.	Appx A.15.of 24.4.9.
	Oct 8/1916		D.R.S. Admitted O. Remaining 32. Fd Amb. " " Officer 1 O.R. 12. Remaining O.R. 9	R.19.a H.4.9.

Army Form C. 2118

WAR DIARY
or
INTELLIGENCE SUMMARY
(Erase heading not required.)

Place	Date	Hour	Summary of Events and Information	Remarks and references to Appendices
MÉTÉREN	Oct 9/1916		D.R.S. Admitted O. Remaining 25. 1st Aust. Admitted 0.412. Remaining O.R. 18.	X 15 d 86.27
	Oct 10/1916		D.R.S. Admitted O. Remaining 24 1st Aust. " " 2 " 18 Men detached for police duty at Artillery Horse & horse lines rejoined unit (visited by acting ADMS and SA&MS 16th Division)	
	Oct 11/1916		D.R.S. Admitted 9. Remaining 29 1st Aust. " 1 " 17. The Unit is at present installed in a State School.	B

Army Form C. 2118

WAR DIARY
or
INTELLIGENCE SUMMARY
(Erase heading not required.)

Instructions regarding War Diaries and Intelligence Summaries are contained in F.S. Regs., Part II. and the Staff Manual respectively. Title Pages will be prepared in manuscript.

Place	Date	Hour	Summary of Events and Information	Remarks and references to Appendices
METEREN	Oct 11/16		There is one large ward holding 45 cases, two smaller ones holding about 15 each and a left building about 25 cases during the accommodation up to 150. There is also unlimited space for pitching tents	X.15.of Sh.27
	Oct 12/16		Admitted 28. Remained 59. Visited Rest Station at CAESTRE which we are at present holding with a small detachment. At 10.15 pm. relieved of duty with 1st Entrenching Coy.	W.8.a Sh.27.
	Oct 13/16		Admitted 12. Remaining 62.	

1875. Wt. W593/826 1,000,000 4/15 J.B.C. & A. A.D.S.S./Forms/C. 2118.

Army Form C. 2118

WAR DIARY
or
INTELLIGENCE SUMMARY
(Erase heading not required.)

Place	Date	Hour	Summary of Events and Information	Remarks and references to Appendices
METEREN	Oct 14/16		Admitted 12. Remaining 66. 1 N.C.O and 10 men reported to O.C. 156th Fd Coy R.E at BEAVER FARM for work in the trenches	N.15.c.0.7 Sh 28
	Oct 15/16		Admitted 7. Remaining 64 " 22 " 67	
	Oct 16/16		Visited by D.D.M.S. IX Corps. Day room opened to-day. Furnished with arm chairs, Linoleum etc obtained from British Red Cross.	R

WAR DIARY
or
INTELLIGENCE SUMMARY

(Erase heading not required.)

Army Form C. 2118

Place	Date	Hour	Summary of Events and Information	Remarks and references to Appendices
METEREN	Oct 17/16		Admitted 12., Remaining 71. Reinforcements arrived. 1 Cpl and 15 men. Capt Baldie found detailed to see sick at Rest Station CAESTRE daily.	
	Oct 18/16		Admitted 10., Remaining 71. Capt A.J. Hickey Rayne reported for duty.	
	Oct 19/16		Admitted 12., Remaining 63. Capt (a.). Macdonald proceeded on leave without rejoining from the 11th Hants Regt to which he was temporarily Reg attached.	☒

Army Form C. 2118

WAR DIARY
or
INTELLIGENCE SUMMARY
(Erase heading not required.)

Instructions regarding War Diaries and Intelligence Summaries are contained in F. S. Regs., Part II. and the Staff Manual respectively. Title Pages will be prepared in manuscript.

Place	Date	Hour	Summary of Events and Information	Remarks and references to Appendices
METEREN	Oct 20/16		Admitted 18. Remaining 67. Award of Military Medal to 36/94 Corpl Beavy, C.A. of this unit appeared in IXth Corps Orders.	
	Oct 21/1916		Admitted 22. Remaining. 85.	
	Oct 22/16		Admitted 17. Remaining 82. Capt D.M. Johnston Reval (T.F.) left unit. He reports to D.A.D.M.S. Ambulance Trains.	
	Oct 23/16		Admitted 19. Remaining 91. Lieut W.W. Jones Reval reported to Chemical Adviser, 2nd Army for "Gas Course". Capt C.M. Rox Reval rejoined unit.	B

Army Form C. 2118

WAR DIARY
or
INTELLIGENCE SUMMARY
(Erase heading not required.)

Instructions regarding War Diaries and Intelligence Summaries are contained in F.S. Regs., Part II. and the Staff Manual respectively. Title Pages will be prepared in manuscript.

Place	Date	Hour	Summary of Events and Information	Remarks and references to Appendices
METEREN	Oct 24/16		Admitted 13. Remaining 94. Capt A. Hopwell Paul reported for duty.	
	Oct 25/16		Admitted 15. Remaining 95	
	Oct 26/16		Admitted 21. Remaining 72 Lt Jones Round returned from "Gas Course".	
	Oct 27/16		Admitted 22. Remaining 95 Capt A. Baldie David detailed for duty with 180th Bde Q.A.A. at RAMPARTS, YPRES.	1.14.6.14.5 Sheet 28 B

Army Form C. 2118

WAR DIARY
or
INTELLIGENCE SUMMARY
(Erase heading not required.)

Instructions regarding War Diaries and Intelligence Summaries are contained in F.S. Regs., Part II. and the Staff Manual respectively. Title Pages will be prepared in manuscript.

Place	Date	Hour	Summary of Events and Information	Remarks and references to Appendices
METEREN	Oct 28/16		Admitted 8. Remained 71	
	Oct 29/16		Admitted 7. Remaining #61 Capt. J.B. McGilvray rejoined unit for duty	
	Oct 30/16		Admitted Nil. Remaining 49 Lieut W.W. Jones detailed for duty with 16th D.A.C.	
	Oct 31/16		Admitted 18. Remaining 54	

W.a. Bell
Major R.a.m.c.
O.C. 111th F. Amb.

WAR DIARY.

FOR

MONTH OF NOVEMBER, 1916.

VOLUME 12

111th Field Ambulance R.A.M.C.

Army Form C. 2118

WAR DIARY
or
INTELLIGENCE SUMMARY
(Erase heading not required.)

Volume 12.

Instructions regarding War Diaries and Intelligence Summaries are contained in F.S. Regs., Part II. and the Staff Manual respectively. Title Pages will be prepared in manuscript.

Place	Date	Hour	Summary of Events and Information	Remarks and references to Appendices
METEREN	Mar 1/1916		Admitted 11. Remaining 48	X.15.d
	Mar 2/1916	7:00	Admitted 28. Remaining 60. Capt Hopwell. A. Plane detailed for temporary duty with 8/R. Dublin Fus. Lieut. Jones b/o. Rennie returned to unit. Capt. Macdonald 109 Renal rejoined unit from leave.	
	Mar 3/1916		Admitted 26. Remained 76. Dressing Station inspected by D.A. and Q.M.G. of IX Corps.	

Army Form C. 2118

WAR DIARY
or
INTELLIGENCE SUMMARY

(Erase heading not required.)

Instructions regarding War Diaries and Intelligence Summaries are contained in F.S. Regs., Part II. and the Staff Manual respectively. Title Pages will be prepared in manuscript.

Place	Date	Hour	Summary of Events and Information	Remarks and references to Appendices
METEREN	Nov 4/1916		Admitted 26. Renamed 94. 1 Pte. A.S.C. joined unit as farrier.	X.15.d.
	Nov 5/1916		Admitted 12. Renamed 94. Unit vacated billets to 25th Divisional Schools by order of D.A. & Q.M.G. IX Corps. Visited A.D.M.S. 16th Division.	
	Nov 6/1916		Admitted 5. Renamed 92. Capt. A. Baldie Lane posted to 186 Bde R.F.A. is struck off the strength of the unit to-day.	

WAR DIARY
INTELLIGENCE SUMMARY

Army Form C. 2118

Place	Date	Hour	Summary of Events and Information	Remarks and references to Appendices
METEREN	Nov 7/1916		Admitted 19. Remaining 109.	X.15.d Sheet 27
	Nov 8/1916		Admitted 17. Remaining 114. A.D. & D.M.S. 16th Division inspected Rest Station accompanied by the D.A.D.M.S.	
	Nov 9/1916		Admitted 25. Remaining 130. The above "Remaining" figure shows cases who are at the Army Rest Station MENT DES CATS remain in the books of this unit until disposal of	R.19.b Sheet 27

Army Form C. 2118

WAR DIARY
or
INTELLIGENCE SUMMARY
(Erase heading not required.)

Instructions regarding War Diaries and Intelligence Summaries are contained in F.S. Regs., Part II. and the Staff Manual respectively. Title Pages will be prepared in manuscript.

Place	Date	Hour	Summary of Events and Information	Remarks and references to Appendices
METEREN	Nov 10 1916		Rest station inspected by the D.D.M.S. IX Corps.	X.15.d
	Nov 11 1916		Routine	
	Nov 12 1916		Lieut Is. W. Jones dental invalided for temporary duty to 8/ Royal Munster Fusiliers	
	Nov 13 1916		Routine	

Army Form C. 2118

WAR DIARY
or
INTELLIGENCE SUMMARY
(Erase heading not required.)

Instructions regarding War Diaries and Intelligence Summaries are contained in F. S. Regs., Part II. and the Staff Manual respectively. Title Pages will be prepared in manuscript.

Place	Date	Hour	Summary of Events and Information	Remarks and references to Appendices
METEREN	Nov 15/1916		Routine	X.15.d
	Nov 16/1916		Capt. Hipwell rejoined unit from temporary duty with 181 Royal Dublin Fusiliers	
	Nov 17/1916		Routine	
	Nov 18/1916		Thoch's Disinfector taken on charge at CAESTRE. Orders have been received for the unit to prepare to open a FK Corps Scabies Station at the above place	W.3.9 sector

WAR DIARY
or
INTELLIGENCE SUMMARY
(Erase heading not required.)

Army Form C. 2118

Place	Date	Hour	Summary of Events and Information	Remarks and references to Appendices
HETEREN	Nov 19 1916		Visit by D.D.M.S. IX Corps. Recommended an extension of accommodation by erection of three Nissen Bow huts	X.15.d.
	Nov 20 1916		Telephone installed in office by 25th Division Signalling School. Capt. J.R. McGilvray proceeded for 3 days duty at Northumbrian C.C.S. in order to learn the procedure of a Scabies Cleansing Station. "C" Section Ammunition Transport Personnel stationed between Quarters and SCHERPENBERG Camp has been handed over to the Divisional Artillery	M.18.a.

Army Form C. 2118

WAR DIARY
or
INTELLIGENCE SUMMARY
(Erase heading not required.)

Place	Date	Hour	Summary of Events and Information	Remarks and references to Appendices
METEREN	Nov 21/1916		Routine	
	Nov 22/1916		Visit to CAESTRE with A.D.M.S.	
	Nov 23/1916		Lt. W. W. Jones returns to duty. 8th Battalion R. Munster Fus absorbed by 1st Batt R. Munster Fus. Capt. J.R. McGelvany returns to duty.	
	Nov 24/1916		Routine	
	Nov 25/1916		Capt. McGelvany R.A.M.C. & Sergt. & 2 Cpls. & 24 men proceeded to open Corps Scabies Station at CAESTRE (see appx No 3a (Scabies))	No 3a Scabies appx 27
	Nov 26/1916		Routine	

WAR DIARY or INTELLIGENCE SUMMARY

Army Form C. 2118

Place	Date	Hour	Summary of Events and Information	Remarks and references to Appendices
METEREN	Nov 27/1916		Visit to CAESTRE with A.D.M.S. Visit to Rest Station by D.D.M.S.	
	Nov 27/1916	10.10 am	proceeded for duty as M.O. to 11 Hants (auth'y ADMS 3/45 Nov 27/1916)	
			addl personnel for CAESTRE, 2 SOS from 76.3. Amb. 1 Officer, 26 men. (25-Div) from 108 F. Amb. (36 Div) 5 men	
	Nov 28/1916		Routine	
	29/1916		1 Officer from 108 F.A. additional personnel for CAESTRE Corps Series D.S.	
	30/1916		Corps Scabies D.S. opened. Return for duty Personnel Non U(T.C) RAMC E.S. Ince	

Dec 1916

WAR DIARY FOR MONTH OF DECEMBER, 1916.

VOLUME 12

111th Field Ambulance RAMC

16th Div.

Vol III
141/902

COMMITTEE FOR THE MEDICAL HISTORY OF THE WAR
Date 31 JAN 1917

Army Form C. 2118

WAR DIARY
or
INTELLIGENCE SUMMARY
(Erase heading not required.)

Volume XIII

Instructions regarding War Diaries and Intelligence Summaries are contained in F.S. Regs., Part II. and the Staff Manual respectively. Title Pages will be prepared in manuscript.

Place	Date	Hour	Summary of Events and Information	Remarks and references to Appendices
METEREN	Dec 1/1916		Capt MacDonald RAMC att. for temp duty with 2nd Royal Irish Rif.	
	Dec 2/1916		Routine	
	Dec 3/1916		Routine	
	Dec 4/1916		Routine	
	Dec 5/1916		Visit by DDMS to CAESTRE	
	Dec 6/1916		Routine	
	Dec 7/1916		Routine	
	Dec 8/1916		Evacuation of sick from Div. Rest commenced.	
	Dec 9/1916		Lt. Groves has ret'd to duty from 11th Hants. Capt. Fox. temp. duty with 2nd R. Orleans	

Army Form C. 2118

WAR DIARY
or
INTELLIGENCE SUMMARY
(Erase heading not required.)

Place	Date	Hour	Summary of Events and Information	Remarks and references to Appendices
METEREN	Dec 10 1916		Capt. MacDonald returned from leave	X.15.d.
	Dec 11 1916		C.O. returns from leave. Erection of NISSEN-BOW huts completed	
	Dec 12 1916		Visit by G.O.C. IX Corps. Visit by A.D.M.S. 16th Division. IX Corps Scabies Treatment Station at CAESTRE also visited.	W.S.a.
	Dec 13 1916		Visit by D.D.M.S. IX Corps. Routine.	
	Dec 14 1916		Capt. T.R. Grant R.A.M.C. (T.C.) joined the unit	

Army Form C. 2118

WAR DIARY
or
INTELLIGENCE SUMMARY
(Erase heading not required.)

Instructions regarding War Diaries and Intelligence Summaries are contained in F. S. Regs., Part II. and the Staff Manual respectively. Title Pages will be prepared in manuscript.

Place	Date	Hour	Summary of Events and Information	Remarks and references to Appendices
METEREN	Dec 15/1916		Capt. A. J. Hickey proceeded on leave. (Period of leave. 16/12/16 to 26/12/16)	
	Dec 16/1916		Routine	
	Dec 17/1916		Capt. A. Whitwell detached for medical duty with 1st R. Munster Fusiliers	
	Dec 18/1916		Routine	
	Dec 19/1916		Capt. W. J. Macdonald detached for duty with the 7th R. Inniskilling Fusiliers	

Army Form C. 2118

WAR DIARY
or
INTELLIGENCE SUMMARY
(Erase heading not required.)

Instructions regarding War Diaries and Intelligence Summaries are contained in F.S. Regs., Part II. and the Staff Manual respectively. Title Pages will be prepared in manuscript.

Place	Date	Hour	Summary of Events and Information	Remarks and references to Appendices
METEREN	Dec 20 1916		Routine	
	Dec 21 1916		Routine	
	Dec 22 1916		Routine	
	Dec 23 1916		Routine	
	Dec 24 1916		Capt. Q. Hopwell returned to duty. Visit paid by A.D.M.S. 16th Division (informal)	

Army Form C. 2118

WAR DIARY
or
INTELLIGENCE SUMMARY
(Erase heading not required.)

Instructions regarding War Diaries and Intelligence Summaries are contained in F.S. Regs., Part II. and the Staff Manual respectively. Title Pages will be prepared in manuscript.

Place	Date	Hour	Summary of Events and Information	Remarks and references to Appendices
METEREN	Dec 25 1916		Christmas dinner to patients followed by concert given by 25th Divisional School.	
	Dec 26 1916		Christmas dinner for personnel of unit followed by a ping pong. Lieut W.W. Jones R.A.M.C. posted as M.O. i/c 2nd R. Dublin Fusiliers	
	Dec 27 1916		Capt C.S. Ettoes Crichton Rankin (T.C) posted for duty Capt R.T. Grant (T.C) detailed for temporary duty as M.O. i/c 250th Tunnelling Coy R.E.	

WAR DIARY
or
INTELLIGENCE SUMMARY

Army Form C. 2118

Place	Date	Hour	Summary of Events and Information	Remarks and references to Appendices
METEREN.	Dec 28/16		Promoted to rank of Acting Lieut. Colonel under Section VII of C.R.S. 384a. D.R.O. 1864. (16th Div A 1/14 and A 1/115.	
	Dec 29/16		Routine	
	Dec 30/16		Routine	
	Dec 31/16		Visited Advanced Dressing Stations in Divisional area with A.D.M.S.	19.a Bell Lt. Col. Reid

WAR DIARY for month of JANUARY, 1917.

VOLUME 14

R.A.M.C. 111th Field Ambulance

Date 13 MAR. 1917
COMMITTEE FOR THE
MEDICAL HISTORY OF THE WAR

Army Form C. 2118

WAR DIARY
or
INTELLIGENCE SUMMARY
(Erase heading not required.)

Instructions regarding War Diaries and Intelligence Summaries are contained in F. S. Regs., Part II. and the Staff Manual respectively. Title Pages will be prepared in manuscript.

Place	Date	Hour	Summary of Events and Information	Remarks and references to Appendices
METEREN	Jan 1 1917		Capt. W.J. Macdonald returned to unit for duty from the 7th Inniskilling Fus.	X.15.d. Sheet 27
			Capt. A. Hickey returned to unit from leave.	
			Capt. A. Hipwell proceeded on leave. Duration 2/1/17 to 12/1/17	
	Jan 2/3/4 1/1/17		Routine	
	Jan 5 1917		Visit by A.D.M.S. and A.A. & Q.M.G. 16th Division. Opening of an extension of the Divisional Laundry at METEREN discussed.	

Army Form C. 2118

WAR DIARY
or
INTELLIGENCE SUMMARY
(Erase heading not required.)

Instructions regarding War Diaries and Intelligence Summaries are contained in F.S. Regs., Part II. and the Staff Manual respectively. Title Pages will be prepared in manuscript.

Place	Date	Hour	Summary of Events and Information	Remarks and references to Appendices
METEREN	Jan 6/1917		Routine	X.15.d. Sheet 27
	Jan 7/1917		Capt A.J. Hickey detailed for temporary medical duty with 7th Kenston (Ref. ADMS 433/4 : 4/1/17) Lecture by Mr. Ashton on "Boy Scouts and Sports" Illustrated by magic lantern in B Block.	
	Jan 8/1917		Routine	
	Jan 9/1917		A German balloon picked up at X.15.d.4.4. field (admist) dressing Station. Small electric lamp and battery attached. Deflated, packed and sent to 1X Corps "g" Balloon made of paper and about 4½ feet in length.	

Army Form C. 2118

WAR DIARY
or
INTELLIGENCE SUMMARY
(Erase heading not required.)

Place	Date	Hour	Summary of Events and Information	Remarks and references to Appendices
METEREN	Jan 10/1917		Routine	X.15 d. Sheet 27
	Jan 11/1917		Capt R.T. Grant returned detached for duty from the 250th Tunnelling Company.	
	Jan 12/1917		Routine	
	Jan 13/1917		Captain A.J Hickey rejoined unit. (See under 7th inst)	
	Jan 14/1917		Capt. R.T. Grant R.a.m.c proceeded on leave. Duration 15th – 28th Jan.	

WAR DIARY
or
INTELLIGENCE SUMMARY
(Erase heading not required.)

Army Form C. 2118

Place	Date	Hour	Summary of Events and Information	Remarks and references to Appendices
METEREN	Jan 14 1917 (cont)		One Staff Sergeant joined unit as a reinforcement. Capt. C.S. Crichton R.A.M.C. detailed for duty with 9th R. Dublin Fusiliers on relief of Captain J.M. Wrigley detailed for a course of sanitation.	X 15 d Sheet 27
	Jan 15 1917		Capt Lieut. Macdonald Reuval proceeded for duty with the 177th Bde R.F.A. in relief of Capt A.D. Moffat Reuval 177th Bde R.F.A. in relief of Capt A.D. Moffat Reuval proceeding on leave.	
	Jan 16 1917		Routine.	
	Jan 17 1917		Visit by A.D.M.S. 16th Division to Divisional Rest Station and to IX Corps Scabies Draining Station at CAESTRE	W.R.a Sheet 27

Army Form C. 2118

WAR DIARY
or
INTELLIGENCE SUMMARY
(Erase heading not required.)

Instructions regarding War Diaries and Intelligence Summaries are contained in F.S. Regs., Part II. and the Staff Manual respectively. Title Pages will be prepared in manuscript.

Place	Date	Hour	Summary of Events and Information	Remarks and references to Appendices
METEREN	Jan 18/1917		Capt C.S. Crichton. Leave granted 30 days leave by War Office	X.15. of 8th/17
			(AuthY. W.O. Letter 24/0/219 A.M.D.1. dated 10/1/17	
			D.G.M.S. B/480/31 dated 12/1/17)	
			Capt. O. Hipwell R.A.M.C. detailed for duty with 9th Bn.	
			Dublin Fusiliers in relief of Capt C.S. Crichton.	
			Reinforcements. 2 Pts.	
	Jan 19/1917		Routine	
	Jan 20/1917		Capt. A.J. Hipwell rejoined unit	

Army Form C. 2118

WAR DIARY
or
INTELLIGENCE SUMMARY

(Erase heading not required.)

Instructions regarding War Diaries and Intelligence Summaries are contained in F.S. Regs., Part II. and the Staff Manual respectively. Title Pages will be prepared in manuscript.

Place	Date	Hour	Summary of Events and Information	Remarks and references to Appendices
METEREN	Jan 21/1917		Capt. A.J. Haley detailed for medical duty with 8th Bn Royal Innskilling Fusiliers.	X.15.d Sheet 27
	Jan 22/1917		Routine	
	Jan 23/1917		Capt. C.M. Row posted for duty with 2nd Bn Royal Welsh Fus: Lieut. W.W. Jones reported for duty	
	Jan 24/1917		Routine	
	Jan 25/1917		Lieut. W.W. Jones Reame departed for England on termination of Contract.	

1875 Wt. W593/826 1,000,000 4/15 J.B.C. & A. A.D.S.S./Forms/C. 2118.

Army Form C. 2118

WAR DIARY
or
INTELLIGENCE SUMMARY
(Erase heading not required.)

Place	Date	Hour	Summary of Events and Information	Remarks and references to Appendices
METEREN	Jan 26 1917		Routine	X.15 of Photry
	Jan 27 1917		Hon: Lieut. & W. Ms. E. Jones Asgn Dep't of Medical Stores R.A.M.C. posted as O.C. No 32 Advanced Depot of Medical Stores	
	Jan 28 1917		Capt. A.J. Throlog returned to unit from 2th R. Irwin Aux. Divisional Rest Station and IX Corps Scabies Station visited by A/Adsmus and D.A.D.M.S. 16th Div.	
	Jan 29 1917		Capt. R.T. Grant rejoined unit from leave. 34th Division has come into area and a considerable number of their sick are being received here.	

Army Form C. 2118

WAR DIARY
or
INTELLIGENCE SUMMARY

(Erase heading not required.)

Instructions regarding War Diaries and Intelligence Summaries are contained in F. S. Regs., Part II. and the Staff Manual respectively. Title Pages will be prepared in manuscript.

Place	Date	Hour	Summary of Events and Information	Remarks and references to Appendices
J.B.	Jan 30 1917		Visit by D.D.M.S. to Corps.	X.15.d. Sheet 27
METEREN	Jan 31 1917		Routine	

W.J.a. Bell
Lieut, Act: Revue
O.C. 111th Field Ambulance

WAR DIARY.

FOR MONTH OF FEBRUARY, 1917.

VOLUME 15

UNIT:- 111th Field Ambulance.
R.A.M.C.

WAR DIARY
or
INTELLIGENCE SUMMARY

(Erase heading not required.)

Army Form C. 2118

Instructions regarding War Diaries and Intelligence Summaries are contained in F.S. Regs., Part II. and the Staff Manual respectively. Title Pages will be prepared in manuscript.

Place	Date	Hour	Summary of Events and Information	Remarks and references to Appendices
METEREN	Feb 1 1917		Capt. T.O.J. Macdonald returned from 177 Bde R.F.A. to unit	X.15.d
	Feb 2 1917		Route	
	Feb 3 1917		Capt. R.T. Grant detailed for duty with 16th Divisional Train (temporary)	
	Feb 4 1917		Hon. Lt. & Qr. Master G.J. Landa Reeve (T.C.) joined unit for duty and taken on strength accordingly.	
	Feb 5 1917		Capt. Leig. Liddesdale Reeve (T.C.) posted to and taken on the strength of this unit	
	Feb 6 1917		Capt. A. Hopwell Reeve (T.C.) detailed for temporary duty with 7 K. Royal Rifles.	

Army Form C. 2118

WAR DIARY
or
INTELLIGENCE SUMMARY

(Erase heading not required.)

Place	Date	Hour	Summary of Events and Information	Remarks and references to Appendices
METEREN	Feb 7/17		Reinforcements. — 1 Private Q.S.C.M.T. (car driver)	X.15.d
	Feb 8/17		As METEREN Laundry (south) is at present taken over by the 34th Division arrangements have been made for washing of hospital clothing by inhabitants of village.	
	Feb 9/17		Routine	
	Feb 10/17		Capt. R.T. Grant returned from duty with 16th Divisional Train.	
	Feb 11/17		Capt to/Lt. Macdonald Raoul detailed for temporary duty with 177th Brigade, R.F.A.	

Army Form C. 2118

WAR DIARY
or
INTELLIGENCE SUMMARY
(Erase heading not required.)

Instructions regarding War Diaries and Intelligence Summaries are contained in F.S. Regs., Part II. and the Staff Manual respectively. Title Pages will be prepared in manuscript.

Place	Date	Hour	Summary of Events and Information	Remarks and references to Appendices
METEREN	Feb 12 1917		Return of Capt. J.R. McGilvray from leave.	X.13.d.
	Feb 13 1917		Routine	
	Feb 14 1917		Entertainment in "B" Block by one of Third Army Ashwell's Concert Parties.	
	Feb 15 1917		Routine	
	Feb 16 1917		Routine	

Army Form C. 2118

WAR DIARY
or
INTELLIGENCE SUMMARY
(Erase heading not required.)

Instructions regarding War Diaries and Intelligence Summaries are contained in F. S. Regs., Part II. and the Staff Manual respectively. Title Pages will be prepared in manuscript.

Place	Date	Hour	Summary of Events and Information	Remarks and references to Appendices
METEREN	Feb 17 1917		Capt. W.J. Macdonald returned from duty with the 117th Bde R.F.A.	X.19.d. Sheet 27.
	Feb 18 1917		Capt. W.G. Liddesdale Pearse detailed for duty with the 11th Hants (Pioneers)	
	Feb 19 1917		Entertainment in "B" Block by party from 76th Fd. Amb. 1 N.C.O and 5 men detailed for a course of instruction in Sanitation at Tx Corps H.Q. BAILLEUL (No 4 San Sect)	
	Feb 20 1917		Visited Tx Corps Scabies Dressing Station. A.D.M.S. and D.A.D.M.S. 16th Division visited 16th Div. Rest Station and Tx Corps Scabies Dressing Station.	

ns regarding War Diaries and Intelligence Summaries are contained in F.S. Regs., Part II. and the Staff Manual respectively. Title Pages will be prepared in manuscript.

WAR DIARY
or
INTELLIGENCE SUMMARY

(Erase heading not required.)

Army Form C. 2118

Place	Date	Hour	Summary of Events and Information	Remarks and references to Appendices
METEREN	Feb 20/1917 (Contd)		Entertainment in "B" Block by a Troupe from 15th Royal Irish Rifles (25th Division)	X. 115. d. Sheet 27.
	Feb 21/1917		Capt. R.S. Crichton returned from leave. Entertainment in "B" Block by the officers of the 15th Royal Irish Rifles.	
	Feb 22/1917		Routine	
	Feb 23/1917			
	Feb 24/1917		Staff Sgt. Brotlu W.C. struck of strength. To proceed to transportation depot Boulogne. Capt. Liddesdale 10.g. R. Gme. rejoined unit from 11th Hants Regt. (R)	

Army Form C. 2118

WAR DIARY
or
INTELLIGENCE SUMMARY
(Erase heading not required.)

Place	Date	Hour	Summary of Events and Information	Remarks and references to Appendices
METEREN.	Feb 25 1917		Capt. A. Hipwell Rame returned from duty with the 7th Royal Irish Rifles.	X.15.d. Sheet 27
	Feb 26 1917		Capt. W.G. Liddesdale detailed for a course of Sanitation at II Army School of Sanitation. Hagebrouck. (HAZEBROUCK)	
	Feb 27 28 1917		Routine	

W.J.E. Bell
Lieut. Col. Rame
O.C. 111th Field Ambulance.

Mar 1917

WAR DIARY
FOR MONTH OF MARCH, 1917.

VOLUME 16

UNIT:- 111th Field Ambulance R.A.M.C.

16@/w

14/2/042.

Vol. 16

COMMITTEE FOR THE
MEDICAL HISTORY OF THE WAR
Date 11 MAY 1917

Army Form C. 2118

WAR DIARY
or
INTELLIGENCE SUMMARY
(Erase heading not required.)

Instructions regarding War Diaries and Intelligence Summaries are contained in F.S. Regs., Part II. and the Staff Manual respectively. Title Pages will be prepared in manuscript.

Place	Date	Hour	Summary of Events and Information	Remarks and references to Appendices
METEREN	March 1 1917		Routine	X.15.d. Sheet 27
	March 2 1917		One man detached from unit to join Advanced H.T. Depôt at ABBEVILLE for duty with New Roads Construction Unit.	
	March 3 1917		Attended meeting of 2nd Army Medical Society at REMY SIDINGS. Capt. A. Wipwell took over medical charge of 8th Royal Dublin Fusiliers and is struck off the strength of this unit. Capt. A. Macey joins the unit and taken on the strength.	L.17.d. Sheet 27
	March 4 1917		One G.S. Wagon with Driver and two horses H.D. attached temporarily to 171 Tunnelling Company. PONT DE NIEPPE.	B.23.a. 0.10 Sheet 36

Army Form C. 2118

WAR DIARY
or
INTELLIGENCE SUMMARY
(Erase heading not required.)

Instructions regarding War Diaries and Intelligence Summaries are contained in F.S. Regs., Part II. and the Staff Manual respectively. Title Pages will be prepared in manuscript.

Place	Date	Hour	Summary of Events and Information	Remarks and references to Appendices
METEREN	March 5 1917		Capt G.S. Crichton detailed to attend a course of Sanitation at 2nd Army School of Sanitation. HAZEBROUCK.	
	March 6 1917		Capt R.T. Grant detailed for temporary duty as M.O. i/c 8th Royal Inniskilling Fusiliers	
	March 7 1917		Capt A. Mossey and six men sent to the IX Corps Scabies Treating Station to replace one Officer and six men of the 76th Field Ambulance who have rejoined their unit	
	March 8 1917		Routine.	
	March 9 1917		Routine	

Army Form C. 2118

WAR DIARY
or
INTELLIGENCE SUMMARY
(Erase heading not required.)

Instructions regarding War Diaries and Intelligence Summaries are contained in F.S. Regs., Part II. and the Staff Manual respectively. Title Pages will be prepared in manuscript.

Place	Date	Hour	Summary of Events and Information	Remarks and references to Appendices
METEREN	March 10 1917		Visited Head Quarters of British Red Cross Society at ST OMER. Capt. C.S. Crichton returned from course of Instruction at Second Army School of Sanitation. One Driver A.S.C. joined as reinforcement.	
	March 11 12 1917		Routine	
	March 13 1917		Capt. C.S. Crichton took medical over charge of 16th Divisional School. Retained on strength of unit.	
	March 14 1917		Two horsed-ambulance-wagons detailed to collect sick daily of 47th Infantry Brigade at THIEUSHOVEK and surrounding area.	9.35. &c. Sheet 27

WAR DIARY
or
INTELLIGENCE SUMMARY

Army Form C. 2118

Place	Date	Hour	Summary of Events and Information	Remarks and references to Appendices
METEREN	March 14 1917 (cont)		One "other rank" 7th Leinster Regt admitted with "Measles".	
	March 15 1917		One Officer 1st Royal Munster Fusiliers admitted with "Measles".	
	March 16 17 18 1917		Routine.	
	March 19 1917		Capt. J.R. McGilvray detailed to temporary medical charge of the 77th Army Field Artillery Brigade R.F.A.	

Army Form C. 2118

WAR DIARY
or
INTELLIGENCE SUMMARY
(Erase heading not required.)

Instructions regarding War Diaries and Intelligence Summaries are contained in F. S. Regs., Part II. and the Staff Manual respectively. Title Pages will be prepared in manuscript.

Place	Date	Hour	Summary of Events and Information	Remarks and references to Appendices
METEREN	March 20 1917		Reinforcements. 5 men.	
			1 case admitted 34th Division. 10th Lincolns. A.9.E. ? Diphtheria.	
	March 21 1917		Routine.	
	March 22 1917		Routine.	
	March 23 1917		1 man 2nd Royal Irish Regt. admi: on 15th inst with P.U.O and later sent to No 2 C.C.S. now diagnosed Cerebro Spinal Meningitis. Occupants of Hut C.1 isolated pending visit of Bacteriologist.	
	March 24 1917		Capt R.T. Grant returned from duty with 8th Royal Inniskilling Fusiliers	

1875 Wt. W593/826 1,000,000 4/15 I.R.C. & A. A.D.S.S./Forms/C. 2118.

Army Form C. 2118

WAR DIARY
or
INTELLIGENCE SUMMARY
(Erase heading not required.)

Place	Date	Hour	Summary of Events and Information	Remarks and references to Appendices
METEREN	March 24 1917 (cont)		1 Officer admitted with Measles. 1 O.R. " " German Measles Bacteriologist inspected contacts of case of Cerebro-Spinal Meningitis and took throat swabs.	
	March 25 1917		Routine	
	March 26 1917		Accommodation increased temporarily to 160 by arranging for a certain number of patients to sleep in A. block dining room. 1 Officer admitted with German Measles 1 Corporal (Berry) of this unit diagnosed German Measles 1 man of 6th Connaught Rangers diagnosed M.Y.D. ? Dysentery	

Army Form C. 2118

WAR DIARY
or
INTELLIGENCE SUMMARY
(Erase heading not required.)

Place	Date	Hour	Summary of Events and Information	Remarks and references to Appendices
METEREN	March 27/19		1 Officer admitted M.y.D. ? Measles.	
	March 28/19		Visited Tx Corps Scabies Dusting Station at CAESTRE.	
	March 29/19		Routine	
	March 30/19		Capt. W.J. Macdonald proceeded to the 177th Bde R.F.A. in temporary medical charge.	
	March 31/19		Routine. During this month all available ground in hospital compound has been planted with vegetable and flower seeds.	

Lt.J.E.Bell
Lieut. Chief Bayne
Commanding 111th Field Ambulance

WAR DIARY FOR MONTH OF APRIL, 1917.

VOLUME:- 14

UNIT:- 111th Field Ambulance R.A.M.C.

COMMITTEE FOR THE MEDICAL HISTORY OF THE WAR
Date -6 JUN. 1917

Army Form C. 2118

WAR DIARY
or
INTELLIGENCE SUMMARY
(Erase heading not required.)

Instructions regarding War Diaries and Intelligence Summaries are contained in F. S. Regs., Part II. and the Staff Manual respectively. Title Pages will be prepared in manuscript.

Place	Date	Hour	Summary of Events and Information	Remarks and references to Appendices
METEREN	April 1/1917		Routine	
	April 2/1917		Lt. Col. Bell R.A.M.C. proceeded on leave to England	
	April 3/1917		Routine	
	April 4/1917		Routine	
	April 5/1917		Routine	
	April 6/1917		Capt. J.R. McGilway R.A.M.C. rejoined the Unit from duty with 77 Bde. R.F.A.	
	April 7/1917		Routine	

1875 Wt. W593/826 1,000,000 4/15 J.B.C. & A. A.D.S.S./Forms/C. 2118.

Army Form C. 2118

WAR DIARY
or
INTELLIGENCE SUMMARY
(Erase heading not required.)

Instructions regarding War Diaries and Intelligence Summaries are contained in F.S. Regs., Part II. and the Staff Manual respectively. Title Pages will be prepared in manuscript.

Place	Date	Hour	Summary of Events and Information	Remarks and references to Appendices
NEUFEN	April 8/1917		Capt. J.R. McGilvery R.I.M.S. reported to-day having been posted to H.Q.	
	April 9/1917		Home Establishment (auth. to WO 24/m/355 (A.m.D.1) dated 2.3.3/17) Reinforcements joined the unit ##. 2 Other Ranks.	
	April 10/1917		Visit by ADMS 1st Div. Entertainment given in the evening by 11 F.A. Concert Party.	
	April 11/1917		Routine	
	April 12/1917		D.D.M.S. 2nd Army visited the unit to-day station.	
	April 13/1917		Routine	

Army Form C. 2118

WAR DIARY
or
INTELLIGENCE SUMMARY
(Erase heading not required.)

Instructions regarding War Diaries and Intelligence Summaries are contained in F.S. Regs., Part II. and the Staff Manual respectively. Title Pages will be prepared in manuscript.

Place	Date	Hour	Summary of Events and Information	Remarks and references to Appendices
METEREN	April 14 1917		Routine	
	April 15 1917		Routine	
	April 16 1917		Capt C.S. Crichton R.A.M.C. proceeded to England on termination of contract. Struck off the strength from this date.	
	April 17 1917		The following M.O.'s taken on the strength from this date: Capt E.J. Dixon R.A.M.C. T.C. Lieut J.H. Rolfe R.A.M.C. T.C.	
	April 18 1917		Routine	
	April 19 1917		Routine	
	April 20 1917		Routine. Capt J.C. Atkinson Fleming posted to & taken on the strength of this unit.	

1875 Wt. W593/826 1,000,000 4/15 J.B.C. & A. A.D.S.S./Forms/C. 2118.

Army Form C. 2118

WAR DIARY
or
INTELLIGENCE SUMMARY
(Erase heading not required.)

Instructions regarding War Diaries and Intelligence Summaries are contained in F. S. Regs., Part II. and the Staff Manual respectively. Title Pages will be prepared in manuscript.

Place	Date	Hour	Summary of Events and Information	Remarks and references to Appendices
METEREN	April 21/1917		Routine	
	April 22/1917		Routine	
	April 23/1917		Routine	
	April 24/1917		Routine	
	April 25/1917		Routine	
	April 26/1917		Routine	

Army Form C. 2118

WAR DIARY
or
INTELLIGENCE SUMMARY

(Erase heading not required.)

Place	Date	Hour	Summary of Events and Information	Remarks and references to Appendices
METEREN	26/Apr/1917 (cont)		Rejoined unit on return from leave	X.15.d. Sheet 2)
	27/Apr/1917		Weather now warm with plenty of sunshine. Garden coming on well. Mjr Bell 2nd Lieut Col Rand	
	28/Apr/1917		Routine	
	29/Apr/1917		Visited Regimental Aid Posts in line with A.D.M.S. 16th Division	

WAR DIARY
or
INTELLIGENCE SUMMARY

(Erase heading not required.)

Army Form C. 2118

Place	Date	Hour	Summary of Events and Information	Remarks and references to Appendices
METEREN	30 Apr 1917		Entertainment to patients by 141th & Amb. Concert Party.	X.15.d. Sheet 2)
			to J.J. Bell	
			Lieut. Col. Rawl	

WAR DIARY:
----------oOo----------

VOLUME:- 18

FOR MONTH OF MAY, 1917.

UNIT:- Picture, III/3rd Fd Amb ...

Army Form C. 2118

WAR DIARY
or
INTELLIGENCE SUMMARY
(Erase heading not required.)

Instructions regarding War Diaries and Intelligence Summaries are contained in F. S. Regs., Part II. and the Staff Manual respectively. Title Pages will be prepared in manuscript.

Place	Date	Hour	Summary of Events and Information	Remarks and references to Appendices
METEREN	May 1/1917		Routine	X.15-d. (Sheet 27)
	May 2/1917		Routine	
	May 3/1917		Inspection of Divisional Rest Station by Divisional Commander in which he expressed himself as very pleased with the work of the unit.	
	May 4/1917		Capt E.J. Braun Raue attached to 188th Brigade R.F.A. for temporary duty.	
	May 5/1917		Routine	

WAR DIARY
or
INTELLIGENCE SUMMARY
(Erase heading not required.)

Army Form C. 2118

Place	Date	Hour	Summary of Events and Information	Remarks and references to Appendices
METEREN	May 6/17		Capt. A.J. Hickey granted leave from 7th to 20th inst. on expiry of contract.	X.15.d. Sheet 27
	May 7/17		Capt. R.T. Grant evacuated to IInd Army Rest Station suffering from Synovitis of knee.	
	May 8/17		Capt. A.C. Atkinson-Fleming M.C. transferred to the 112th Field Ambulance on the 8th inst.	
	May 9/17		Routine	

Army Form C. 2118

WAR DIARY
or
INTELLIGENCE SUMMARY

(Erase heading not required.)

Instructions regarding War Diaries and Intelligence Summaries are contained in F.S. Regs., Part II. and the Staff Manual respectively. Title Pages will be prepared in manuscript.

Place	Date	Hour	Summary of Events and Information	Remarks and references to Appendices
METEREN	May 10/17		Horses inspected by Capt Armstrong A.V.C. New exterain fitted to gas mask and inspected by me on parade.	X. 15 of 9 thely 27
	May 11/17		Board of Survey held on 47 Horse Rugs which were ordered to be destroyed	
	May 12/17		Sick of 47th Infantry Brigade collected by this unit daily until further orders. Said Infantry Brigade is now billeted in CAESTRE area.	
	May 13/17		Dined at H.Q 47th Infantry Brigade.	

1875. Wt. W593/826 1,000,000 4/15 J.B.C. & A. A.D.S.S./Forms/C.2118.

Army Form C. 2118

WAR DIARY
or
INTELLIGENCE SUMMARY

(Erase heading not required.)

Instructions regarding War Diaries and Intelligence Summaries are contained in F. S. Regs., Part II. and the Staff Manual respectively. Title Pages will be prepared in manuscript.

Place	Date	Hour	Summary of Events and Information	Remarks and references to Appendices
METEREN	May 14 1917		Capt. E.G. Dixon rejoined unit.	X.15.a. (Photo)
	May 15 16 17 1917		Routine	
	May 18 1917		Parchment certificate from the G.O.C. 16th Division presented to gallantry and devotion to duty presented to S.M. Daniels, S.M. Harrington A.S.C. and Sgt. Nelson.	
	May 19 1917		Noon temperature 91° Fahr. 6.0 pm " 78° Fahr.	

Army Form C. 2118

WAR DIARY
or
INTELLIGENCE SUMMARY
(Erase heading not required.)

Place	Date	Hour	Summary of Events and Information	Remarks and references to Appendices
METEREN	May 20/1917		Routine	X.15.d. elect 27.
	May 21/1917		Noon temperature 74°	
	May 22/1917		Noon temperature 76°	
	May 23/1917		Noon temperature 74°	
	May 24/1917		Noon temperature 72°	

Place	Date	Hour	Summary of Events and Information	Remarks and references to Appendices
METEREN	May 26th 1917 (cont)		Visited No Corps Scabies Dressing Station CAESTRE. Arranged with O.C. of same to return 2 N.C.O's and 20 men to Head Quarters in order to act as stretcher Bearers in the forthcoming offensive. 3.0. p.m. Conference at Office of A.D.M.S. 16th Division regarding the scheme for evacuation of wounded in the forthcoming offensive. Capt. C.J. Atkinson - Hering M.C. R.A.M.C. Reinf. struck off the strength of the unit on being attached to the 8th Munster Arrdiers. Notice received that Capt. Grant Kerr has been evacuated to the Base.	X.15. d. Sheet 27

Army Form C. 2118

WAR DIARY
or
INTELLIGENCE SUMMARY
(Erase heading not required.)

Place	Date	Hour	Summary of Events and Information	Remarks and references to Appendices
METEREN	25 May 1917		Parchment Certificate for gallantry and devotion to duty awarded by the Divisional Commander to Capt. A.J. Worley and J.M.S. G. Williams both of this unit. Temp. noon 72°	X.15.01 sheet 27
	26 May 1917		Temp. noon 74°. Visit from Major Caton Revel, D.A.D.M.S. 2nd Army.	
	27 May 1917		T. noon 73°. Baths taken over by 1st Division. 10th Division still run laundry. Asked by C.R.E. to arrange improvements to soap trap. Arranged with O.C. Lowland Field Coy R.E. to build an improved form of soap trap.	

Army Form C. 2118

WAR DIARY
or
INTELLIGENCE SUMMARY
(Erase heading not required.)

Instructions regarding War Diaries and Intelligence Summaries are contained in F.S. Regs., Part II. and the Staff Manual respectively. Title Pages will be prepared in manuscript.

Place	Date	Hour	Summary of Events and Information	Remarks and references to Appendices
METEREN	28 May 1917		Temp. noon 75°. Orders received to hand over IX Corps Scabies Swamp Station to 11th Division. Visited above Station to make arrangements.	X.15.d (Sheet 27)
	29 May 1917		Whit-Monday Sports held in field at Head Quarters unit. T. noon 62° Much cooler. Handed over IX Corps Scabies Swamp Station to 34th Field Ambulance, 11th Division. Personnel returned to their various Head Quarters.	
	30 May 1917		Temp. noon 68°. Enemy shelled BAILLEUL for about an hour starting at 11.45 p.m.	

Army Form C. 2118

WAR DIARY
or
INTELLIGENCE SUMMARY
(Erase heading not required.)

Instructions regarding War Diaries and Intelligence Summaries are contained in F. S. Regs., Part II. and the Staff Manual respectively. Title Pages will be prepared in manuscript.

Place	Date	Hour	Summary of Events and Information	Remarks and references to Appendices
METEREN	31/May/1917		Temp. noon 69°. Concert given to patients by 1st Divisional Concert Troopers.	X.115.d. Sheet 27

W. J. C. Bell
Lieut. Col. R.A.M.C.

SECRET

WAR DIARY.

FOR MONTH OF JUNE, 1917.

VOLUME:- No. 19.

UNIT:- R.A.M.C. 111th Field Ambulance

B.E.F.

16th Div.
SUMMARY OF MEDICAL WAR DIARIES OF 111th F.A./8th Corps.

5th ARMY. (from 22nd June).

Western Front Operations - June - 1917.

Officer Commanding - Lt.Col. W.J.A. Bell.

SUMMARISED UNDER THE FOLLOWING HEADING :-

Phase "D" - Battle of Messines - June - 1917.

B.E.F.

16th Div.

SUMMARY OF MEDICAL WAR DIARIES OF 111th F.A. / 8th Corps.

5th ARMY.   from 22nd June.

Western Front Operations - June - 1917.

Officer Commanding - Lt.Col. W.J.A. Bell.

SUMMARISED UNDER THE FOLLOWING HEADING :-

Phase "D" - Battle of Messines - June - 1917.

B.E.F.

16th Div.
111th F.A./8th Corps. 5th ARMY.

O.C. Lt.Col. W.J.A. Bell

WESTERN FRONT.
June 1917.

PHASE "D" - Battle of Messines - June 1917.

Headquarters at PEENHOF FARM B.16.c.5.5. (27).

June 22nd.   Division arrived in 5th ARMY.

B.E.F.

16th Div.
111th F.A./8th Corps. 5th ARMY.

O.C. Lt.Col. W.J.A. Bell.

WESTERN FRONT.
June 1917.

PHASE "D" - Battle of Messines - June 1917.

Headquarters at PEENHOF FARM B.16.c.5.5. (27).

June 22nd.   Division arrived in 5th ARMY.

WAR DIARY or INTELLIGENCE SUMMARY

Army Form C. 2118

111th Field Ambulance

Place	Date	Hour	Summary of Events and Information	Remarks and references to Appendices
METHUEN	June 1 1917		Medical Arrangement for active operations received from ADMS 16th Division. Temp 74° John. Noon Q	X.15.d. Sheet 27
	June 2 1917		Capt. W.J. Macdonald RAMC and 108 other ranks (Bearers) proceeded to report to the O.C. 112th Field Ambulance at the Walking Wounded Collecting Station (M.24.d.3.8 Sheet 28). Visited Capt. Macdonald and Bearers at this Station. He and the N.C.O's are to be conducted round the Advanced Dressing Stations to-morrow. Capt. A. Massey rejoined the Unit from Leave. Temp noon 74° John. fine	See Appendix 1. D

WAR DIARY
or
INTELLIGENCE SUMMARY
(Erase heading not required.)

Army Form C. 2118

Place	Date	Hour	Summary of Events and Information	Remarks and references to Appendices
METEREN (X.15.d Sheet 27)	3 June 1917		Temp noon 72° tabn. Arie. Ry	
	4 June 1917		Capt. A.J. HICKEY Ravel and Capt. A. MASSEY Ravel detailed to report to O.C. 113th Field Ambulance at 10. a.m. for temporary duty during the operations on the 5th inst. Orders from Agnes to hold 100 stretchers in readiness to send up. Temp. noon 72° tabn. Arie. Ry	IV. 23. C. Sh. 28.
	5 June 1917		Capts A.J. HICKEY and A. MASSEY proceeded to the above duty. Temp noon 75° tabn. Arie. Ry	Appendix 1. A.

Army Form C. 2118

WAR DIARY
or
INTELLIGENCE SUMMARY
(Erase heading not required.)

Place	Date	Hour	Summary of Events and Information	Remarks and references to Appendices
METEREN X.15.d. Sh.28	6 June 1917		3 Nursing Orderlies and 10 General Duty with 100 Stretchers proceeded this morning to report to O.C. 112th Field Ambulance at Walking Wounded Collecting Station (M.24.d.3.8. Sh.28) in accordance with orders. Temp. noon. 82° Fah. Slight thunder shower in evening. 3 more motor ambulances proceeded to the 113th Field Ambulance for duty. RB	Appendix 1. C.
	7 June 1917		Attack of IX Corps began at 3.10 a.m. this morning. Visited Main Dressing Station (113th Fd Amb. LoCRE) and Walking Wounded Collecting Station (map refs above). Temp. noon. 81° Fah. Fine in morning. Violent thunder showers in the evening. RB	

Army Form C. 2118

WAR DIARY
or
INTELLIGENCE SUMMARY
(Erase heading not required.)

Instructions regarding War Diaries and Intelligence Summaries are contained in F.S. Regs, Part II. and the Staff Manual respectively. Title Pages will be prepared in manuscript.

Place	Date	Hour	Summary of Events and Information	Remarks and references to Appendices
METEREN X.15.d. Sheet 27	8 June 1917		Temp: at noon, 80° Fahr. Visited Capt. A.J. HICKEY R.A.M.C. at the LAITERIE (N.16.d.20. Sheet 28) and Capt. W.J. MACDONALD at RAMSEY'S DUGOUT and PARRAIN FARM. (N.28.b.70.95. Sheet 28)	Appendix 1. B
	9 June 1917		Capt. A. MASSEY R.A.M.C. returned from temporary duty with the 112th Field Ambulance. He has orders to proceed to CAESTRE in order to make arrangements to take over IX Corps Scabies Dressing Station from the 117th Div. Temp: noon. 75° F.	B
	10 June 1917		Capt. A.J. HICKEY, Capt. W.J. MACDONALD and Bearer Division rejoined Head Quarters. No casualties.	B

WAR DIARY
or
INTELLIGENCE SUMMARY

(Erase heading not required.)

Army Form C. 2118

Instructions regarding War Diaries and Intelligence Summaries are contained in F.S. Regs., Part II. and the Staff Manual respectively. Title Pages will be prepared in manuscript.

Place	Date	Hour	Summary of Events and Information	Remarks and references to Appendices
METEREN (X.15.d Sheet 27.)	11 June 1917		Temp. noon 86°F. 119 different units on the Sadly State of Sick and Wounded	B
	12 June 1917		Temp. noon 97°F.	B
	13 June 1917		Temp. noon 76°F. 16th Division moved to MERRIS area (F.1. Sheet 36A) This unit to received Sick from whole Division and to collect from the 49th Infantry Brigade.	B
	14 June 1917		Temp. noon 80°F. Macintosh Capes returned.	B

Army Form C. 2118

WAR DIARY
or
INTELLIGENCE SUMMARY
(Erase heading not required.)

Instructions regarding War Diaries and Intelligence Summaries are contained in F.S. Regs., Part II. and the Staff Manual respectively. Title Pages will be prepared in manuscript.

Place	Date	Hour	Summary of Events and Information	Remarks and references to Appendices
METEREN X.15.d. Sh.27	15 June 1917		Temp. noon 80°+	
	16 June 1917		Temp. noon 82°+ Detachments from Bearers of all three 16th Divisional Field Ambulances paraded here this morning and were inspected by the D.M.S. 2nd Army.	
	17 June 1917		Temp. noon 82°+ 16th Division relieved 19th Division in LOCRE area (M.28. Sheet 28) Lieut. F.H. WOLFE detached from unit for temporary duty with 8th ROYAL IRISH REGT. Temp: 10.0 pm. 80°+.	

WAR DIARY
or
INTELLIGENCE SUMMARY
(Erase heading not required.)

Army Form C. 2118

Place	Date	Hour	Summary of Events and Information	Remarks and references to Appendices
METEREN X.15.d. Sheet 27	18 June 1917		Temp. 10 a.m. 82°. Thunderstorm in evening.	
	19 June 1917		Temp. noon 70°. Violent thunderstorm during early morning. "Warning Order" received of impending movement of 16th Division to the TILQUES SOUTH Training Area (HAZEBROUCK, S.A. 1/100,000) on the 20th inst. (47th Inf. Bde Order No 138. 18th June.1917) IX Corps Scabies Bathing Station to be handed over to 59th Field Amb: 19th Division to-day. (A.D.M.S. 16th Div. No 192/10/ : 18th June 1917)	See Appendix. 2.

Army Form C. 2118

WAR DIARY
or
INTELLIGENCE SUMMARY
(Erase heading not required.)

Instructions regarding War Diaries and Intelligence Summaries are contained in F.S. Regs., Part II. and the Staff Manual respectively. Title Pages will be prepared in manuscript.

Place	Date	Hour	Summary of Events and Information	Remarks and references to Appendices
GODEWAERS-VELDE 2.0 Q.15.b.1.2 Sh. 27	20 June 1917		Capt. T.B. MARSHALL R.A.M.C. T.C. taken on the strength.	Appendix 3.
		6.40. A.M.	Unit marched to present area under orders of 47th Inf. Bde.	
			Relieved at METEREN by 35th Field Ambulance, 11th Div?	
			58 Pitch handed over.	
			Arrived in present area at 9.15 a.m.	
	21 June 1917		Collected sick of 47th Inf. Bde and evacuated to No 15 C.C.S. (HAZEBROUCK).	
PEENHOF FARM. B.16.c.5.5 Sh. 27	22 June 1917		Marched to present area. (ADMS O.O. No 20. o/- 21/6/17)	Appendix 4.
			Arrived at 12-0 noon.	

Army Form C. 2118

WAR DIARY
or
INTELLIGENCE SUMMARY
(Erase heading not required.)

Instructions regarding War Diaries and Intelligence Summaries are contained in F.S. Regs., Part II. and the Staff Manual respectively. Title Pages will be prepared in manuscript.

Place	Date	Hour	Summary of Events and Information	Remarks and references to Appendices
PEENHOF FARM. B.16.c.5.5 Sh.27	23 June 1917		Collected sick of 49th Brigade and evacuated to ST OMER. Opened Evening Station for 30 sick.	
	24 June 1917		Began scheme of Training for unit. To-day's programme as follows:- C.O's Parade 8.45 a.m. Route March 10.0 am. Parade 2-4 pm. Squad and Field Ambulance drill by Section Commanders.	
	25 June 1917		Programme similar to yesterday.	

Army Form C. 2118

WAR DIARY
or
INTELLIGENCE SUMMARY
(Erase heading not required.)

Instructions regarding War Diaries and Intelligence Summaries are contained in F.S. Regs, Part II. and the Staff Manual respectively. Title Pages will be prepared in manuscript.

Place	Date	Hour	Summary of Events and Information	Remarks and references to Appendices
PEENHOF FARM. P.16.c.5.5. Sh.27	26 June 1917		Programme similar to yesterday's. A small class is held for Officers and N.C.O.'s from 2–3.0 p.m. Section commanders take their own section from 3–4.0 p.m.	
	27 June 1917		Signaller's class started. Two men per section to undergo training. Officers are taking the section over the Medical Equipment from 3–4.0 p.m. daily	
	28 June 1917		Half holiday. Cricket match in afternoon.	

Army Form C. 2118

WAR DIARY
or
INTELLIGENCE SUMMARY
(Erase heading not required.)

Instructions regarding War Diaries and Intelligence Summaries are contained in F.S. Regs., Part II. and the Staff Manual respectively. Title Pages will be prepared in manuscript.

Place	Date	Hour	Summary of Events and Information	Remarks and references to Appendices
PEENHUF FARM. B.16.c.5.6. Sh 27	29/June/1917		Programme as before.	
	30/June/1917		Rain during entire morning. C.O's parade 9.0 am 10 – 11.0 am Field Ambulance drill 11 – 12.0 noon. Lectures on medical equipment by Section Commanders.	

W.R. Bell
Lieut Col R---
O.C. 10th Field Amb.

APPENDIX 1.

Extracts from Medical Arrangements by A.D.M.S. 16th Division, d/31.5.17

Distribution of Personnel

Unit	Officer in Charge	Personnel	Remarks
A. Main Dressing Station M.29.b.65.90	Lt.Col. W. Bennett, D.S.O., R.A.M.C.	113 Fd.Amb. {"A" Tent Sub-division, "B" Tent Sub-division} 112 Fd.Amb. {"C" Tent Sub-division}	Total Officers 9 (including Officer i/c). Supplemental men from the Division for loading and un-loading stretchers.
B. Advanced Dressing Station, FARRAIN FARM N.28.b.70.95	One M.Officer detailed by Officer Commanding 113 Fd. Ambulance.	113 Fd.Amb. {1 N.C.O and 7 men from "C" Tent Sub-division}	Total Officers 1.
C. Divisional Collecting Station for Walking Wounded. N.24.d.3.8	Lt.Col. G.J. Houghton, R.A.M.C.	112 Fd.Amb. "A" Tent Sub-division. 1 Medical Officer from 111th, Supplemented by Regt. (P). 3 nursing orderlies and 10 general duty orderlies from 111th Fd. Ambulance.	Total Officers 4 (including Officer i/c). Half personnel from above Tent Sub-division will also be required at N.14 where a Rest Post c.5.9. will be established. One Bell Tent & 2 Horse Amb. Wagons detailed by O.C. 112 Fd. Amb., and one Y.M.C.A. Hut
D. Bearers	Capt. C.H. Senger, R.A.M.C. O.C. 3 Bearer Divisions. Headquarters at Advanced Dressing Station, KEMMEL	One complete Bearer Division, minus 2 Officers, ready to move off as required under orders of O.C. Bearers. One Bearer Division, minus 2 Officers, in reserve distributed between KEMMEL, LAITERIE, and RAMSAY DUGOUT (N.23.c.3.8). The 3rd Bearer Division, minus 2 Officers in reserve at M.23.d.3.8. The O.C. Bearers to keep in touch with H.dqrs of Brigade and M.O's i/c Battalions. It is hoped that 160 men will be available as extra Regimental stretcher bearers and when distributed will come under the orders of the Regimental M.O's	Total Officers 3. (including Officer i/c.)

Appendix 2

A.D.M.S. 16th Division No 192/101 d/18.6.17.

19th Division will take over the XIXth Corps Scabies Hospital at CAESTRE from the 16th Division on the 19th inst.

The O.C. 59th Fd. Amb. is sending an advance party early in the morning and the relief will be complete in the evening.

O.C., IXth Corps Scabies Station will hand over all stores, including Red Cross Stores, and will obtain a receipt for the same.

On completion of the relief Capt Denyer, 112th Fd. Amb. will rejoin his unit at W.11.d.90.10., Sheet 27, and the personnel from 111th Fd. Ambulance will rejoin their unit at METEREN.

Appendix 3

A.D.M.S. 16th Division No. S192/103 d/19.6.17.

The 16th Division will move to the EECKE area on 20th June, 1917.

The 35th Fd. Amb, 11th Division will relieve No. 111th Fd. Amb, 16th Division at METEREN on June 20th. On the evening of the 19th inst, an advance party from No. 35 Fd. Amb. under the Quartermaster will arrive and commence the taking over of Stores, &c., including Red Cross Stores, for which a receipt must be obtained.

On the 20th inst., the No. 111th Fd. Amb. will march to the EECKE Area under orders of G.O.C, 47th Inf. Bde. O.C, No. 111 Fd. Ambulance will get in touch forthwith with the Headquarters 47th Inf Bde. and will arrange for the sending of an advance billeting party.

On the morning of the 21st inst, the O.C. No. 111 Fd. Amb. will collect sick from his own Brigade Group and evacuate them to No. 15 C.C.S, HAZEBROUCK, after being passed through the A. & D. Book.

Appendix 3.

47th Inf. Bde. Administrative Order No 4

Ref. 47th Inf. Bde. O.O. No 132 d/19/6/17.

The Brigade Group will billet tomorrow in the EECKE Area, Sheet 27 S.E. (B series) 1/20000.

Billeting Parties will meet Interpreters (who have been supplied with lists of billets as under).

1st R. Munster Fus.   GODEWAERSVELDE CHURCH 4 a.m.   Interpreter VAN de PUTTE
   Guides to meet Battalion at Godewaersvelde Church

6th R. Irish Regt.
6th Connaught Rangers } Eecke Church 4.30 a.m.   Interpreter DROZ.
   Guides to meet Battalions at Rly. Crossing in Square Q.22.c.

7th Leinster Regt.   Railway crossing in Q.23.b 4-30 a.m   Interp. CHATTE
   Guides to meet Battalion at Rly Crossing in Q.23.b.

111th Fd. Ambulance.
   This unit must arrange for its own Billeting Party and Guides.
   Area Commandant EECKE will give assistance if required.

Refilling tomorrow, 20th inst. — CHURCH SQUARE EECKE.

No tents are to be removed from present area.

Appendix H.

Extracts from O.O. N°20 issued by A.D.M.S,
16th Division, d/22/6/17.
Ref. 1/40,000 Map Sheet 27.

1. The 16th Division (less Artillery, Divisional Engineers, and Pioneer Battalion) with Divisional Supply Column will march from the EECKE area to the ERINGHEM, RUBROUCK, BROXELLE, Areas on June 22, in which area the Division will be administered by the VIIIth Corps.

2. The 111th Field Ambulance will march under the orders of the 47th Brigade. All details of billeting, rationing, &c, to be made direct with the Brigade.

3. Each Field Ambulance will arrange to collect the sick daily from its Brigade group and will provide accommodation for the detention of thirty cases suffering from minor ailments.

47th Infantry Brigade Order N° 135
(ref para. 2 above).

1. The Infantry Brigade Group (less 143 Coy. A.S.C., which will move independently) will march on June 22nd in accordance with undermentioned time-table.

2. Bde. H.Q. will open at ERINGHEM on conclusion of the march.

TIME TABLE to accompany 47 Inf. Bde. O.O. 135

UNIT	Hour of passing Starting point Road Junction IV. of STEENVOORDE, K. 31. C. 6. 2	Route to Starting-Point	Destination
111th Fd. Amb.	7.05 a.m.	Road thro' Q. 11, 10, 4, 3, 2.	PEENHOF FARM B. 16. C. 5. 5. Guides to meet Ambulance at ESQUELBEC.

Report of Arrival at B.16.C.5.5

Staff Captain,
    47th Inf. Brigade.

It is notified please, that the [unit] under my command with horse and mechanical transport complete, arrived at PEENHOF FARM at 12 noon today, the 22nd inst.

Map Reference. B. 16. C. 5. 5.   Sheet 27.

WAR DIARY.

FOR MONTH OF JULY, 1917.

VOLUME :- 20

UNIT :- 111th Field Ambulance
R.A.M.C.

COMMITTEE FOR THE
MEDICAL HISTORY OF THE WAR
Date 10 SEP. 1917

B.E.F.

16th Div.

SUMMARY OF MEDICAL WAR DIARIES OF 111th F.A./8th Corps.

5th ARMY.

19th Corps from 23rd July.

To 3rd Army on 22.8.17.

WESTERN FRONT OPERATIONS - July - August 1917.

Officer Commanding - Lt.Col. W.J.A. Bell.

SUMMARISED UNDER THE FOLLOWING HEADINGS :-

   (a) - Operations commencing 1/7/17.

   (b) - Operations commencing 1/10/17.
       Canadians attacked Passchendaele, Oct. 30th.
       Canadians took Passchendaele, Nov. 6th.

B.E.F.

16th Div.
111th F.A. / 8th Corps. 5th ARMY.   WESTERN FRONT.
                                           July-Aug. 1917.
O.C. Lt.Col. W.J.A. Bell.

19th Corps from 23rd July.

PHASE "D" 1. Passchendaele Operations, "July-Nov. 1917"

  (a) - Operations commencing 1/7/17.

Headquarters at PEENHOF FARM B.16.c.5.5.

July 16th.	Decorations. S/ A/Sgt. A.C. Hill.)
	a/L/Sgt. T. Mansell.) awarded M.M.
	Pte. R.A. Rushton.)
	Capt. A.J. Hickey awarded M.C.
23rd.	Moves and Transfer. J.15.b.5.6. (27) 19th Corps.

1.

B.E.F.

111th F.A. 19th Corps.   5th ARMY.   WESTERN FRONT.
O.C. Lt.Col. W.J.A. Bell.   July - Aug. 1917.
To 3rd Army from 22.8.17.

PHASE "D" 1. Passchendaele Operations, "July-Nov.1917".

(a)- Operations commencing 1/7/17.

Headquarters at J.15.b.5.6. (27).

July 23rd.	Moves and Transfer. To J.15.b.5.6. (27) 19th Corps.
25th.	Moves. Detachment, 2 & "B" Sec. T.S.D. to 32 C.C.S.
26th.	Moves. To Hillhoek L.20.b.7.7. (27).

B.E.F.

16th Div.
111th F.A. / 8th Corps. 5th ARMY.   WESTERN FRONT.
                                        July-Aug.1917.
O.C. Lt.Col. W.J.A. Bell.

19th Corps from 23rd July.

PHASE "D" 1. Passchendaele Operations,"July-Nov. 1917"

  (a) - Operations commencing 1/7/17.

Headquarters at PEENHOF FARM B.16.c.5.5.

July 16th.   Decorations. A/S/Sgt. A.C. Hill.   )
                                              a/L/Sgt. T. Mansell.) awarded M.M.
                                              Pte. R.A. Rushton.   )

Capt. A.J. Hickey awarded M.C.

23rd.   Moves and Transfer. J.15.b.5.6. (27) 19th Corps.

B.E.F.

111th F.A. 19th Corps.   5th ARMY.   WESTERN FRONT.
                                        July - Aug. 1917.

O.C. Lt.Col. W.J.A. Bell.

To 3rd Army from 22.8.17.

PHASE "D" 1. Passchendaele Operations, "July-Nov.1917".

(a)- Operations commencing 1/7/17.

Headquarters at J.15.b.56. (27).

July 23rd. Moves and Transfer. To J.15.b.5.6. (27) 19th Corps.
25th.   Moves. Detachment. 2 & "B" Sec. T.S.D. to 32 C.C.S.
26th.   Moves. To Hillhoek L.20.b.7.7. (27).

Army Form C. 2118

WAR DIARY
or
INTELLIGENCE SUMMARY

(Erase heading not required.)

Place	Date	Hour	Summary of Events and Information	Remarks and references to Appendices
PEENHOF FARM. B.16.C.5.5. Sh.27	1 July 1917		Sgt. Major T. DAVIES evacuated to C.C.S. with fracture of fibula	B
	2 July 1917		Training	B
	3 July 1917		Lieut F.H. WOLFE R.A.M.C. attached to 11th HANTS REGT. (Pioneers) and struck off the strength of the unit accordingly. Capt E.H. BLACK. R.A.M.C. joined the unit and taken on the strength. Capt W.G. LIDDERDALE. R.A.M.C. attached to the 180th Brigade. R.4.A. for temporary duty.	B

WAR DIARY or INTELLIGENCE SUMMARY

Army Form C. 2118

Place	Date	Hour	Summary of Events and Information	Remarks and references to Appendices
PEENHOF FARM. B.H.C.5.S. Sh.27.	4 July 1917		Experiments made with new method of carrying Pack in order to bring a counterbalancing weight in front.	B
	5 July 1917		Horse Transport inspected by Lieut: Col. COLLUM D.S.O. O.C. 16th Divisional Train. He expressed himself as favorably impressed by it.	B
	6 July 1917		Training	B
	7 July 1917		Three reinforcements arrived. All Privates from No 3 Stationary Hospital.	B

WAR DIARY or INTELLIGENCE SUMMARY

Army Form C. 2118

Place	Date	Hour	Summary of Events and Information	Remarks and references to Appendices
PEENHOF FARM. B.16.c.5.5. Sh. 27	8 July 1917		Capt. W.D. MACDONALD returned from leave and resumed duties of Transport Officer.	B
	9 July 1917		Capt. A. MASSEY R.A.M.C. detailed for daily duty with the 155th Coy R.E. He has also to attend the sick of a Chinese Labour Battalion.	B
	10 July 1917		Competition between the three Sections in Squad and Stretcher Drill won by B Section. Judges Capt. HARRISON, M.C. (Staff Capt. 47th Inf. Bde.) and Capt. DENYER. R.A.M.C.	B

Army Form C. 2118

WAR DIARY
or
INTELLIGENCE SUMMARY
(Erase heading not required.)

Instructions regarding War Diaries and Intelligence Summaries are contained in F.S. Regs., Part II. and the Staff Manual respectively. Title Pages will be prepared in manuscript.

Place	Date	Hour	Summary of Events and Information	Remarks and references to Appendices
PEENHOF FARM. B.16.c.6.6. Sh 27	11/12 July 1917		Routine	
	13 July 1917		Reinforcements: 3 Privates R.A.M.C	
	14 July 1917		Capt. W.G. LIDDERDALE R.A.M.C rejoined unit from duty with the 180th Bde R.F.A.	
	15 July 1917		Reinforcements: 2 Drivers A.S.C.	

WAR DIARY
or
INTELLIGENCE SUMMARY

Army Form C. 2118

Place	Date	Hour	Summary of Events and Information	Remarks and references to Appendices
VEENHOF FARM. B.16.c.6.5. Sh.27	16 July 1917		Following awarded the Military Medal: a/St.Sgt. A.C. HILL. a/L.Sgt. T. MANSELL. Pte. R.A. RUSHTON.	
	17 July 1917		Capt. W.G. LIDDERDALE proceeded on leave. The following Officer was awarded the Military Cross. Capt. A.J. HICKEY.	
	18 July 1917		Visit by ADMS 16th Division.	

Army Form C. 2118

WAR DIARY
or
INTELLIGENCE SUMMARY
(Erase heading not required.)

Instructions regarding War Diaries and Intelligence Summaries are contained in F.S. Regs., Part II. and the Staff Manual respectively. Title Pages will be prepared in manuscript.

Place	Date	Hour	Summary of Events and Information	Remarks and references to Appendices
PEENHOF FARM. SK.27 B.16.C.5.5	19 July 1917		Routine	R
	20 July 1917		Col. S.L. CUMMINS. C.M.G. A.M.S. took over duties of A.D.M.S. 16th Division vice Col. BRYAN-WATTS. D.S.O. A.M.S.	R
	21 July 1917		Routine	R
	22 July 1917		The following was promoted to A/Sgt. Major No 43579 A/Q.M.S. WILLIAMS D.	

Army Form C. 2118

WAR DIARY
or
INTELLIGENCE SUMMARY
(Erase heading not required.)

Instructions regarding War Diaries and Intelligence Summaries are contained in F.S. Regs., Part II. and the Staff Manual respectively. Title Pages will be prepared in manuscript.

Place	Date	Hour	Summary of Events and Information	Remarks and references to Appendices
PEENHOF FARM. Sh. 27 B.16.c.55.	22 July 1917 (cont)		The following were promoted to the rank of act/Sgt. No. 74864 Cpl Ellis. A. No. 64598 L/Cpl Buxton A. The following were awarded Divisional Parchment Certificates for gallant conduct in the field. Capt. A.J. HICKEY Capt. W.J. MACDONALD S/Sgt. A.C. HILL Pte. R.A. RUSHTON " A.E. RUSHTON Cpl. P.G. MORRIS Pte. E. CHANEY.	

WAR DIARY
or
INTELLIGENCE SUMMARY

(Erase heading not required.)

Army Form C. 2118

Place	Date	Hour	Summary of Events and Information	Remarks and references to Appendices
PEENHOF FARM. B.16.C.35. Sheet 27	22 July 1917 (cont)		Pte. C.E. GILLINGHAM. " I. D. THOMAS	
	26 July 1917		The unit marched to WINNEZEELE area. (J.15.c.5.6. Sh.27) and parked there. To collect sick of the 45th Inf Brigade for admission to the 113th Field Ambulance at WINNEZEELE (J.17.c.3.5. Sh:27) Arrived in new area at 9.45 a.m..	

Army Form C. 2118

WAR DIARY
or
INTELLIGENCE SUMMARY
(Erase heading not required.)

Instructions regarding War Diaries and Intelligence Summaries are contained in F.S. Regs., Part II. and the Staff Manual respectively. Title Pages will be prepared in manuscript.

Place	Date	Hour	Summary of Events and Information	Remarks and references to Appendices
WINNEZEELE 3.15.6.5.6 Sh 27	24 July 1917		Capt. E.H. BLACK detailed for temporary duty with 8th Corps Cyclist Battalion. B Section Tent Sub-division with Capt A.S. HICKEY. M.C. and Capt A. MASSEY to proceed to No. 32 C.C.S. at BRANDHOEK on the 25th inst. (A.D.M.S. 16th Div'n No. S192/119. 23.7.1917)	
	25 July 1917		B Section Tent Sub-division with two above named officers proceeded to No. 32 C.C.S. BRANDHOEK (G.12.b. Sheet 28) for temporary duty.	

1875. Wt. W593/826 1,000,000 4/15 J.B.C. & A. A.D.S.S./Forms/C. 2118.

Army Form C. 2118

WAR DIARY
or
INTELLIGENCE SUMMARY
(Erase heading not required.)

Instructions regarding War Diaries and Intelligence Summaries are contained in F. S. Regs., Part II. and the Staff Manual respectively. Title Pages will be prepared in manuscript.

Place	Date	Hour	Summary of Events and Information	Remarks and references to Appendices
HILHOEK (Sh 27. L.20.b.9.7)	July 26/1917		49th M. Brigade moved to WATOU No 2 area.	
	July 27/1917		Unit moved to location noted in margin and pushed out rond Advanced Dressing Stations and Collecting Stations of XIX Corps. Right Division. Adv. Dressing Stations at PRISON, YPRES (Sh. 28. I.7.6) KRUISSTRAAT (Sh. 28. I.13.c) Collecting Stations at MENIN ROAD (Sh 28. I.9.d) POTIJZE (Sh 28. I.4.a)	R
	July 28/1917		Went to HAM EN ARTOIS (near LILLERS) to collect Red Cross Stores.	B

Army Form C. 2118

WAR DIARY
or
INTELLIGENCE SUMMARY
(Erase heading not required.)

Instructions regarding War Diaries and Intelligence Summaries are contained in F.S. Regs., Part II. and the Staff Manual respectively. Title Pages will be prepared in manuscript.

Place	Date	Hour	Summary of Events and Information	Remarks and references to Appendices
HILHOEK Sh.29 L.20.b.9.7.	July 29 1917		Conference of Field Ambulance Commanders at Office of A.D.M.S. 16th Division. PLACE DE BERTHEM. POPERINGHE.	B
	July 30 1917		47th Inf. Brigade moved to BRANDHOEK Area. No 3.	B
	July 31 1917		Capt T.B. MARSHALL R.A.M.C. T.C. departed this unit for duty with 2/1st West Lancs. Field Ambulance. T	

Wylie Bell
Lieut Col R.A.M.C.
O.C. 114th 4ot Amb.

WAR DIARY.

FOR MONTH OF AUGUST, 1917.

VOLUME 2/

UNIT 111th Field Ambulance

RAMC

COMMITTEE FOR THE
MEDICAL HISTORY OF THE WAR
Date -5 NOV. 1917

Confidential.

War Diary

of

111 Field Ambulance

for period

from 1st August 1917 to 31st August 1917.

Volume XXI

B.E.F.

16th Div.

SUMMARY OF MEDICAL WAR DIARIES OF 111th F.A./ 8th Corps.

5th ARMY.

19th Corps from 23rd July.

To 3rd Army on 22.8.17.

WESTERN FRONT OPERATIONS - July - August 1917.

Officer Commanding - Lt.Col. W.J.A. Bell.

SUMMARISED UNDER THE FOLLOWING HEADINGS :-

(a) - Operations commencing 1/7/17.

(b) - Operations commencing 1/10/17.
Canadians attacked Passchendaele, Oct. 30th.
Canadians took Passchendaele, Nov.6th.

August 4th.	Moves.	Detachment. "C" T.S.D. to 113th F.A.
6th.	Moves.	To MOATED FARM H.2.d. 7.2. (28).
17th.	Military Situation.	16th Division relieved by 15th Division.
18th.	Moves.	Detachment. "C" T.S.D. rejoined unit.
20th.	Moves.	To EECKE Area.
22nd.	Moves and Transfer.)	To entraining post at Caestre on transfer to 3rd ARMY.

August 4th.	Moves.	Detachment. "C" T.S.D. to 113th F.A.
6th.	Moves.	To MOATED FARM H.2.d. 7.2. (28).
17th.	Military Situation.	16th Division relieved by 15th Division.
18th.	Moves.	Detachment. "C" T.S.D. rejoined unit.
20th.	Moves.	To ECKE Area.
22nd.	Moves and Transfer.	To entraining post at Caestre on transfer to 3rd ARMY.

Army Form C. 2118.

WAR DIARY
or
INTELLIGENCE SUMMARY.

(Erase heading not required.)

Instructions regarding War Diaries and Intelligence Summaries are contained in F.S. Regs., Part II. and the Staff Manual respectively. Title pages will be prepared in manuscript.

Place	Date	Hour	Summary of Events and Information	Remarks and references to Appendices
HILHOEK Shelters L.20.b.77.	Aug 1 1917		Capt. W.J. LIDDERDALE R.A.M.C. rejoined unit from leave. Very heavy rain all last night and to-day.	R
	Aug 2 1917		Rain.	R
	Aug 3 1917		Capt W.J. LIDDERDALE and Capt W.S. MACDONALD detailed for duty with O.C. 113 Field Ambulance at BRANDHOEK. (Ph:28. G.12.b.8.8)	R
	Aug 4 1917		Capt T.C. MARSHALL rejoined for duty. Assumed command of Bearer Divisions of Nos 111, 112 and 113 Field Ambulances operating in the forward area. 85 Bearers marched off for duty in forward area. To report to the O.C. 113 Field Ambulance at BRANDHOEK by 10.0 a.m.	R

Army Form C. 2118.

WAR DIARY
or
INTELLIGENCE SUMMARY.
(Erase heading not required.)

Instructions regarding War Diaries and Intelligence Summaries are contained in F. S. Regs., Part II. and the Staff Manual respectively. Title pages will be prepared in manuscript.

Place	Date	Hour	Summary of Events and Information	Remarks and references to Appendices
HIGHOEK Sh 27. L.2.6.27.	Aug 4/1/1917 (cont)		C. Section Tent Sub Division marched off for duty with O.C. 113 Field Ambulance reporting by 10 a.m. Capt T. B. MARSHALL R.A.M.C. assumed temporary command of the unit.	
				Sgd. E. Bell Lieut Col. Ramc
	Aug 5/1917		Three horsed ambulances units 6 neavy h. d. horses detailed for duty in forward areas t/c of O.C. 113 Field Ambulance. Personnel 1 Sgt. Pa.S.C., 6.8pm. A/S/C. 3 Wagon Orderlies R.A.M.C. Ordered to report at 5 p.m. I.O.R., Wds. 3 O.R. "Killed in Action": Details 111 Fd. Ambce. moved to moat to Moated Farm 528.H.2.d.7.2. "Wounded in Action": 1 O.R.	
Moated farm 528.H2.d.7.2	Aug 6/1917			
	Aug 7/1917		(1) Details 111th Fd. Ambce arrived H2.d.7.2., 9.30a.m. Opened as 111th F.A. F.S. for the treatment of slightly wounded t/c of O.C. 112 F.A. 16.97 Cases admitted up to midnight 72.	

Army Form C. 2118.

WAR DIARY
or
INTELLIGENCE SUMMARY.
(Erase heading not required.)

Instructions regarding War Diaries and Intelligence Summaries are contained in F. S. Regs., Part II. and the Staff Manual respectively. Title pages will be prepared in manuscript.

Place	Date	Hour	Summary of Events and Information	Remarks and references to Appendices
Moated Farm S2.c.H.2.d.?	Aug 7/1917 cont		O. taken on strength - Lt. J.A. Chandler (T.C.) 4 ors. A.S.C. O.R. " " 4 ors. A.S.C.	
	Aug 8/1917		Wounded in Action 4 O.R. Officer on 111th. F. Amb. - XIX Adv. Post Station. Shipped by H.Q. M.S. And D.D.M.S. Adm: 44 S 30 W.	
	Aug 9/1917		Wounded in Action 2. Killed 1. Hdq ors. A.S.C. transferred to Suffy. Admitted 28 S 8 W.	
	Aug 10/1917		Wounded in Action 1 O.R. Adm. 53 S 1 W.	
	Aug 11/1917 Aug 12/1917		Visit by D.D.M.S., D.D.M.S. Adm. 10 S. 0 W. Visit by H.Q. M.S.	
	Aug 13/1917		Adm. 47 S. 7 W.	
	Aug 14/1917		Visit by A.D.M.S. Adm. 59 S. 6 W. Adm. 33 S., 2 W.	

WAR DIARY
or
INTELLIGENCE SUMMARY.

(Erase heading not required.)

Army Form C. 2118.

Place	Date	Hour	Summary of Events and Information	Remarks and references to Appendices
Mondicel Farm S2F H.2.d.7.2.	Aug 15/17		Reinf. taken on strength 2 N.C.'s arrived 16/8/17. Evac by D.A.M.S. Capt. 305th	
	16/17		Arrival for duty of T/S.M.B. ENDACOTT, A. Taken on strength, Lieut Capt D.M.S. Div. of wounds 1. M. 3.	
	2/17		Relief of Div. by 15 Div.	
	4/17			
	Aug 17/1917		Relief of 16th Division	T. B. Marshall Capt. R.A.M.C. B
	Aug 18/1917		"C" Tent Sub-Division rejoined from 113th Field Ambulance & returned to day with all the Bearers except 60 (30 from this unit and 30 from the 112th Field Ambulance) who are remaining behind for another day under Capt. A.J. Vickory R.C. Reinf. Assumed command of the unit again	

WAR DIARY
or
INTELLIGENCE SUMMARY.

(Erase heading not required.)

Army Form C. 2118.

Place	Date	Hour	Summary of Events and Information	Remarks and references to Appendices
MOATED FARM Sh 28 A.2.d.7.2	Aug 18/1917 (cont)		Visit by D.D.M.S. XIXth Corps. The following N.C.Os. and men have been recommended by me to higher authorities for gallantry and devotion to duty in their work as Bearers: Lance-Corpl. IMRIE. J Pte. CHANEY. E " HAUGHAN. J.T. Dvr SEATON. F.T. Pte. CRANE. E " MOORE. F " GILLINGHAM. C.E " NELSON. W " NISBET. T " HOPKINS. F.J	

Army Form C. 2118.

WAR DIARY
or
INTELLIGENCE SUMMARY.
(Erase heading not required.)

Instructions regarding War Diaries and Intelligence Summaries are contained in F. S. Regs., Part II. and the Staff Manual respectively. Title pages will be prepared in manuscript.

Place	Date	Hour	Summary of Events and Information	Remarks and references to Appendices
MOATED FARM. Sh. 28. H.2.d.7.2.	Aug 18 1917 (cont)		Pte KELLY. F.M. " MARSHALL. J " MOSES. L. " PEACOCK. P also Capt. W.J. MACDONALD. and Lieut. F.G. CHANDLER. Bearers & Collection Point Subs Div. rejoined H.Q	B
	Aug 19 1917			
	Aug 20 1917		Unit moved to EECKE area LT. CHANDER (F.G.) reported to 16th Div. D.A.C. for temporary duty	
EECKE	Aug 21 1917		Routine	

Army Form C. 2118.

WAR DIARY
or
INTELLIGENCE SUMMARY.
(Erase heading not required.)

Place	Date	Hour	Summary of Events and Information	Remarks and references to Appendices
	Aug 22/1917		Unit marched to entraining point (Caëstre) at 2.30 a.m. horsed off 6.30 a.m. Detained at BAPAUME at 2.15 p.m. marched to GOMIECOURT arriving at 5.45 p.m. Visit by A.D.M.S. 18th Div.	
GOMIECOURT (57.c.A.2.3.d.1.1.)	Aug 23/1917		Routine & kit inspection.	
	Aug 24/1917		Routine - visit to Moy ENVILLE by O.C. to meet A.D.M.S. 18th Div. visited all posts in the line	
	Aug 25/1917		Routine. Recd. of 47 Inf. Bde. order no. 155 re relief of 21st Div. in the line by the 18th Div.	
	Aug 26/1917		Visit by A.D.M.S. to confer with M.O. of 47 Bde frondo. Capt. R.J. VERNOR R.A.M.C. T.C. 113th Field Ambulance reported for duty.	

Army Form C. 2118.

WAR DIARY
or
INTELLIGENCE SUMMARY.
(Erase heading not required.)

Instructions regarding War Diaries and Intelligence Summaries are contained in F. S. Regs., Part II. and the Staff Manual respectively. Title pages will be prepared in manuscript.

Place	Date	Hour	Summary of Events and Information	Remarks and references to Appendices
	Aug 23/1917		"C" Section completed with personnel from A & B sections & Capt. E. H. Black R.A.M.C. T.C. M.D. Sta. Amb. & accompanied by Capt. R. J. Vernon R.A.M.C. 113th Fd. Amb. moved off at 8 a.m. to take over A.D.S. 2nd Lebeer (T=7 hrs) 2nd Lieber (T=7 hrs). Phet. 51 B. from section of 64th Fd. Amb. 21st Div. 14 P.E. R.A.M.C. joined as reinforcements.	
HAMELINCOURT (51 b S 29.d.9.6)	Aug 24/1917		Unit less "C" Section "B" Sect. tent subdivision arrived HAMELIN- COURT (51 b S 29.d.9.6) to relieve H.Q. 64th Fd. Amb. 21st Div. Visited A.D.S.	
	Aug 25/1917		Visited A.D.S. with A.D.M.S. 18th Div.	
	Aug 26/1917		6 Pts. R.A.M.C. Attached for duty with 1st Divnl. Indus Coy. Visited A.D.S.	

WAR DIARY
or
INTELLIGENCE SUMMARY.

(Erase heading not required.)

Army Form C. 2118.

Place	Date	Hour	Summary of Events and Information	Remarks and references to Appendices
	Aug 30th 1917		Visited posts in line - "B" Sect. Feat. Sub-Div. returned from duty from 32nd C.C.S	
	Aug 31st 1917		Routine	

A.Y. Mitchell
Capt. R.A.M.C.
for O.C. 111 Fd Amb.

Army Form C. 2118.

WAR DIARY
or
INTELLIGENCE SUMMARY.
(Erase heading not required.)

Instructions regarding War Diaries and Intelligence Summaries are contained in F. S. Regs., Part II. and the Staff Manual respectively. Title pages will be prepared in manuscript.

Place	Date	Hour	Summary of Events and Information	Remarks and references to Appendices
	Aug 30th 1911		Visit paid in truck "B" A.S. Vet. Lab Sir returned from duty from 32 C.C.S	
	Aug 31st 1911		Routine	

A.G. Alderdon
Capt. R.A.M.C.
for O.C. Mt. Fd. Amb.

WAR DIARY.

FOR MONTH OF SEPTEMBER, 1917.

VOLUME 22

UNIT:- R.A.M.C. 11th Field Ambulance

COMMITTEE FOR THE
MEDICAL HISTORY OF THE WAR
Date -5 NOV. 1917

Confidential

War Diary

of

111 Field Ambulance

for period

from 1st September 1917 to 30th September 1917

Volume XXII

Army Form C. 2118.

WAR DIARY
or
INTELLIGENCE SUMMARY.
(Erase heading not required.)

Instructions regarding War Diaries and Intelligence Summaries are contained in F. S. Regs., Part II. and the Staff Manual respectively. Title pages will be prepared in manuscript.

Place	Date	Hour	Summary of Events and Information	Remarks and references to Appendices
#4 MELLICOOR 51.b.5.29.9.8	Sept 1st 1917		Routine	
	Sept 2nd 1917		Routine	
	Sept 3rd 1917		Routine	
	Sept 4th 1917		Visit of inspection by D.M.S III Army. DDMS II Corps. ADMS 16th D.V. A.D.S. Inspected — 3 Horses Bowels Received.	
	Sept 5th 1917		Conference of ADsMS Sanitary Officers in the Camp. Taken on Strength — 1 N.C.O (Sgt Chipperton) — Lieut Chandler returned for duty with this unit from 16th Div. D.A.C.	
	Sept 6th 1917		Capt A Fraser R.A.M.C detailed for duty with 1st R Munster Fus. Lt Chandler R.A. M.C went to A.D.S. for duty.	

WAR DIARY
or
INTELLIGENCE SUMMARY.

(Erase heading not required.)

Army Form C. 2118.

Place	Date	Hour	Summary of Events and Information	Remarks and references to Appendices
HAMELINCOURT 51°S29.d.9.6	Sept 6th 1917		10 P.B. men taken to Strength to replace 10 A.S.C. Batmen ordered to Base	
	Sept 7th 1917		10 Category "A" Batmen A.S.C. despatched to Base (Auth. L of C. Orders No. E/420/3 dated 23/8/17)	
	Sept 8th 1917		Routine	
	Sept 9th 1917		1 Officer (2Lt. H.F. Jottling 7th Leinsters) admitted gassed — died 2.30 pm	
	Sept 10th 1917		Capt. Macdonald & Capt. S.H. Black detailed for two a course of instruction in Gas at Div. Gas School. Officer buried at Boyelles T. 3.a.1.17. — Gas alert.	
	Sept 11th 1917		Capt. C.J. Vickery MC 9th Lt. F.G. Chandler detached for a course of instruction in Gas at Div. Gas School. — Relieved John of various job & reported by Sanitary Corps of 16th Div. Train	

Army Form C. 2118.

WAR DIARY
or
INTELLIGENCE SUMMARY.
(Erase heading not required.)

Place	Date	Hour	Summary of Events and Information	Remarks and references to Appendices
HAMELINCOURT 57D.SW.a.9.6	Sept 12 1916		Renhi - Visited posts in the line with D.A.D.M.S. also A.D.S.	
	Sept 13 1916		Routine.	
	Sept 14 1916		2 Nissen Bow Huts drawn.	
	Sept 15 1916		Capt. E.H. Black R.A.M.C. detailed for temporary duty with 6th Connaught - Capt. D.J. Macdonald R.A.M.C. takes over charge of A.D.S. from Capt. Black. Return of Lieut. Col. Bp. E. Bell D.S.O. from sick leave to Battalion. Nissen Bow Huts drawn.	
			Resumed command of the unit	W.G. Lithall Capt. R.A.M.C. Bp. E. Bell Lieut. Col. R.A.M.C.

Army Form C. 2118.

WAR DIARY
or
INTELLIGENCE SUMMARY.

(Erase heading not required.)

Instructions regarding War Diaries and Intelligence Summaries are contained in F. S. Regs., Part II. and the Staff Manual respectively. Title pages will be prepared in manuscript.

Place	Date	Hour	Summary of Events and Information	Remarks and references to Appendices
MARELIN COURT				
516, Sept d.g.c.	Sept 16 10/9/17		General inspection of Camp.	
	Sept 17		Visit by S.D.M.S. to Corps. (Visited Advanced Dump Station	Q
			Visit to Huts A.D. LANDERs proceeded on leave to England. Period of leave 18/9/17 to 28/9/17 (There is Plit 3)	
			Bertie	Q
	Sept 18 17/9		Inspection by A.D.M.S. 16th Div. of Advanced Dump Station and Main Dressing Station	Q
	Sept 1 7/17 7/9			Q

2353 Wt. W2544/1454 700,000 5/15 D. D. & L. A.D.S.S./Forms/C. 2118.

WAR DIARY
or
INTELLIGENCE SUMMARY.

Army Form C. 2118.

Place	Date	Hour	Summary of Events and Information	Remarks and references to Appendices
HAPLINCOURT S.4.d.9.6 Sh.51.B	Sept 20 1917		Nature	B
	Sept 21		Marched Advanced Dump Station STIEGER (T.21.t.5.2) via the beau Metzy Rd at FACTORY CROISILLE (T.24.t.2.3) Ambulance Car Stand (KNUCKLES) (T.23.d.1.5) QUARRY (T.18.b.7.2) KNUCKLE (V.19.b.6.3) and RAILWAY CUTTING (V.25.b.7.3) all on Sh.51.B QUARRY and RAILWAY POSTS are the Regimental aid Posts.	
	Sept 22		Conference (A.D. M.S. VI Corps at trem Every Station (	B
	23 1917		Routine	

Army Form C. 2118

WAR DIARY
or
INTELLIGENCE SUMMARY.
(Erase heading not required.)

Place	Date	Hour	Summary of Events and Information	Remarks and references to Appendices
HAMELINCOURT Sqd 16 Sh. 51B.	Sept 24 1917		O.T.M.S. known east of Main Dressing Station	
	Sept 25 1917		Visited A.D.S. in Shell Hole dug out. No proper shelf. 157th & 156th Coy R.E. definitely constructing	
	Sept 26 1917		1. O.K. of this unit wounded near ARTILLERY POST (B.6.9.5.) (Sh. 51B) Conv. of 3rd Army at 112. K. Evacuated in officers Tent which was installed door to door. Capt. Tice J. Sinha Officer brought his lorry here today. Attached to this unit (in rations and moves with it) No.	
	Sept 27 1917		Capt. F.G. CHANDLER R.A.M.C.T.C. posted to No. 48 C.C.S. for duty as physician and anaesthetist	

WAR DIARY
or
INTELLIGENCE SUMMARY.

Army Form C. 2118.

Place	Date	Hour	Summary of Events and Information	Remarks and references to Appendices
HAMELINCOURT St.Ld.9 & 6 R.5.(S)	Sept 26/1917 (cont)		Struck off the strength of the unit (note) Advanced Dressing Station CRUISILLE —	
	Sept 27/1917		Tool. W. Gratten at Advanced Dressing Station ST-LEGER Visited Artillery Beaver Post. Inspected Trench Tramway with a view to carrying stretcher cases from the first touch posts two stretchers fitted without any on to tramway without any superstructure except the adjustable sides. Conference of A.D's M.S. at Main Dressing Stations	
	Sept 27/1917		Worked FACTORY and KNUCKLE Posts Awaited cases under shell fire at CRUISILLE 10th a view to long term to be evacuated to Dressing Station.	

WAR DIARY or INTELLIGENCE SUMMARY

Army Form C. 2118.

Place	Date	Hour	Summary of Events and Information	Remarks and references to Appendices
HAMELINCOURT	Aug 29 1914		Three German P.O.W. have been evacuated by the Spaniards in the 15th Century. They would have excellent entrenching systems, it would apparently be difficult of the enemy shelling the vicinity of the church which they are very fine from to do.	
	Sept 20 1914		The Military Medal has been granted to the following men of this Unit: 64125 Pte (K/c) J. IMRIE R.A.M.C. 75192 " E. CHANEY R.A.M.C. 64466 " J.T. HAUGHAM R.A.M.C. The two last received the ribbon from me at the Advanced Dressing Station this evening and at the rest at the Main Dressing Station in the afternoon.	

Army Form C. 2118.

WAR DIARY
or
INTELLIGENCE SUMMARY.
(Erase heading not required.)

Instructions regarding War Diaries and Intelligence Summaries are contained in F. S. Regs., Part II. and the Staff Manual respectively. Title pages will be prepared in manuscript.

Place	Date	Hour	Summary of Events and Information	Remarks and references to Appendices
HAMELINCOURT	Sept. 16th Sh 51^B		Two officers of the U.S. M.C. reported to be attached to this unit for instruction. Captain CULLEN U.S.M.C. & " FORD " "	

Noel Bell
Lt Col Comdg

2353 Wt.W.2514/1454 700,000 5/15 D.D.& L. A.D.S.S./Forms/C. 2118.

WAR DIARY

FOR MONTH OF OCTOBER, 1917.

UNIT 111th Fd. Ambce Ram C.

VOLUME NUMBER 23

Confidential.

War Diary
of
111 Field Ambulance

for period

from 1st October 1917 to 31st October 1917

Volume XXII

WAR DIARY
or
INTELLIGENCE SUMMARY.
(Erase heading not required.)

Army Form C. 2118.

Place	Date	Hour	Summary of Events and Information	Remarks and references to Appendices
HAMELINCOURT S.29.d.9.6 (Sht 51 B)	Oct 1/17		Visited A.D.S. ST LEGER (T.27.6.) All map references on Sheet 51ᴮ except where otherwise stated.	B
	Oct 2/17		Visited A.D.S. ST LEGER in morning and went on to FACTORY RELAY POST (T.24.b.2.3) and Railway (RAILWAY CUTTING RELAY POST) at (U.25.b.6.3) met Capt BLACK R.A.M.C. and Capt CULLEN M.O. R.C. U.S.A. Practice run in evening of Light Railway from ST LEGER to QUARRY AID POST (T.18.b.7.15) of Bogie wheel trucks were fitted to carry four stretcher cases, shews was very successful and proved the value of the Light Railway for this work.	B

Army Form C. 2118.

WAR DIARY
or
INTELLIGENCE SUMMARY.
(Erase heading not required.)

Instructions regarding War Diaries and Intelligence Summaries are contained in F. S. Regs., Part II. and the Staff Manual respectively. Title pages will be prepared in manuscript.

Place	Date	Hour	Summary of Events and Information	Remarks and references to Appendices
HAMELINCOURT S.24.d.9.6.	Oct 3/17		Visited A.D.S.	B
	Oct 4/17		Routine	B
	Oct 5/17		Visited A.D.S. Inspection by A.D.M.S. 16th Division	B
	Oct 6/17		Visited AMIENS. Capt. A. MASSEY returned out from PARIS leave and assumed command of A.D.S. ST LEGER.	B
	Oct 7/17		Counter Fire began at 1.0. A.M.	B

2353 Wt. W2544/1454 700,000 5/15 D. D. & L. A.D.S.S./Forms/C. 2118.

Army Form C. 2118.

WAR DIARY
or
INTELLIGENCE SUMMARY.
(Erase heading not required.)

Instructions regarding War Diaries and Intelligence Summaries are contained in F. S. Regs., Part II. and the Staff Manual respectively. Title pages will be prepared in manuscript.

Place	Date	Hour	Summary of Events and Information	Remarks and references to Appendices
HAMELINCOURT S.29.d.9.6.	Oct 8/9/17		Routine	B
	Oct 10/1917		3 Trench Tramway Trolleys prepared for carrying stretchers to be kept at GUYNNESS DUMP SIDING — ECOUST (Sh 57c C.2) They will be for conveyance of wounded door Railway Reserve as far as Sh 51.B U.25 a.5.6	B
	Oct 11/1917		3 Sets of adjustments for Stretchers carrying on Bogie Shell wagons on Light Railway sent to A.D.S. ST LEGER	B

Army Form C. 2118.

WAR DIARY
or
INTELLIGENCE SUMMARY.
(Erase heading not required.)

Place	Date	Hour	Summary of Events and Information	Remarks and references to Appendices
HAMELIN- COURT S.29.d.9.6	Oct 12 1917		Gas projector attack by our Troops in Right Section. Few of our men were slightly gassed by cylinders which fell short.	B
	Oct 13 1917		Visited new Artillery Post dug-out to-day. The dug-out is not yet timbered. (T.30.d.5.5)	B.
	Oct 14 1917		Saw M.O. 1/c 177 Brigade R.F.A. about timbering of dug-out.	B
	Oct 15 1917		Raid by 7th Leinsters. About 80 men went over Two prisoners taken. Two officers and few men wounded. Beards from KNUCKLE POST (U.17.b.6.3) Superintended	Appx I B

2353 Wt. W2544/1454 700,000 5/15 D. D. & L. A.D.S.S./Forms/C. 2118.

Army Form C. 2118.

WAR DIARY
or
INTELLIGENCE SUMMARY.
(Erase heading not required.)

Instructions regarding War Diaries and Intelligence Summaries are contained in F. S. Regs., Part II. and the Staff Manual respectively. Title pages will be prepared in manuscript.

Place	Date	Hour	Summary of Events and Information	Remarks and references to Appendices
HAMELIN COURT (S.24.d.4.6)	Oct 16 1917		Informal visit by Brig. Genl. Perriera commanding 47th Infy. Brigade. Explained himself as being pleased with the medical arrangements in practice	B
	Oct 17 1917			B
	Oct 18 1917		Work started on new Advanced Dressing Station at CROISILLE (T.23.d.3.9)	B
	Oct 19 1917		Conference with Field Ambulance Commanders held by A.D.M.S. 16th Division	B

WAR DIARY or INTELLIGENCE SUMMARY.

Army Form C. 2118.

Place	Date	Hour	Summary of Events and Information	Remarks and references to Appendices
HAMELIN COURT (S.29.d.9.6)	Oct 20 1917		Major General HICKIE, Commanding 16th Division accompanied by the Deputy of the D.F.O.R.D inspected the Indian Burying Station.	R
	Oct 21 1917		General EDWARDS D.S.A Army inspected Indian Burying Station and delivered Burying Station.	
	Oct 22 1917		Inspected work at new A.D.S CROISILLE (T.23.d.5.9) and RAILWAY (T.24.b.2.3.) Visited FACTORY (T.24.b.2.3.) Posts.	B
			Capt F.W. SHINE, D.S.M.S. joined this unit for one weeks duty sent to A.D.S. ST LEGER.	B
	Oct 23 1917		The D.D.M.S. and D.A. & Q.M.G VII Corps (Br-Gen TULLOCH) inspected the new Indian Burying Station.	B

Army Form C. 2118.

WAR DIARY
or
INTELLIGENCE SUMMARY.
(Erase heading not required.)

Place	Date	Hour	Summary of Events and Information	Remarks and references to Appendices
HAMELIN-COURT S29.d.9.6 & 5.B.	Oct 24/17		Visited A.D.S. ST LEGER. Received three Stuart to render Bogie Well wagon on Light Railway suitable for carrying wounded.	B
	Oct 25/17		Conference of Regimental Am. O's with A.Dm.S. at Main Dressing Station.	B
	Oct 26/17		Routine	B
	Oct 27/17		Visited RAILWAY POST (U.25.c.v.3) and handed it over to 113th Field Ambulance. Visited ECOUST where 113th Fd Amb. are constructing a new Bearer Relay Post and A.S.S. New A.D.S. at CROISILLE has now got some "elephant" shelters in situ.	B

WAR DIARY or INTELLIGENCE SUMMARY

Army Form C. 2118.

Place	Date	Hour	Summary of Events and Information	Remarks and references to Appendices
HAMELIN COURT Sqd 9.6	Oct 24 1917		Hostile shelling of CRAISILLE Men FACTORY with 5.9 Howitzer	B
	Oct (ct) 1917		Stated A.D.S. ST LEGER and made arrangements for evacuation wounded in forthcoming operations by 8/9 Australians	B
	28			
	Oct 29	5.6 P.M.	Raid by 8/9 Australian trenches 9/100 yards west our. Time 5.6 P.M. Medical arrangements attached. Defenses (Relais [Pistor?] B/8 from Factory Post (T15.b.9.2) and QUARRY POST (T15.b.9.2)	AB Appen 2
	Oct 29		15 wounded & 1 lung in a German found through. Raid was successful.	B

Army Form C. 2118.

WAR DIARY
or
INTELLIGENCE SUMMARY.
(Erase heading not required.)

Instructions regarding War Diaries and Intelligence Summaries are contained in F. S. Regs., Part II. and the Staff Manual respectively. Title pages will be prepared in manuscript.

Place	Date	Hour	Summary of Events and Information	Remarks and references to Appendices
HAMELIN-COURT S.24.d.9.6.	Oct 24 1917 (cont)		Many Germans killed and wounded and dug-outs destroyed. A few prisoners.	B
			LIEUT J.B. GREGG, U.S.A. M.C. LIEUT C.G. LYONS, U.S.A. M.C. taken on strength of this unit.	
	Oct 29 1917		Hoisted new ARTILLERY POST (B.C.A.57, H.57c) Rather heavy shelling (some of the 27th May) with 5·9 howitzer (H.E. "instantaneous" fuze) and "delayed" action.	B
	Oct 31 1917		Conference of Field Ambulance commanders with Actg. A.D.M.S. (18th Divn.) Col. S.L. Cummins C.M.G. who left the Division. Major Bell Lieut Col. Branch	B

WAR DIARY

FOR MONTH OF NOVEMBER, 1917.

VOLUME :- 24

UNIT :- 111th Field Ambulance R.A.M.C.

COMMITTEE FOR THE
MEDICAL HISTORY OF THE WAR
Date 17 JAN. 1918

C O N F I D E N T I A L.

WAR DIARY

of

111th. FIELD AMBULANCE

for

Period ------------------

from 1st. November, 1917
to 30th. November, 1917.

VOLUME XXIV.

Army Form C. 2118.

WAR DIARY
or
INTELLIGENCE SUMMARY.
(Erase heading not required.)

Instructions regarding War Diaries and Intelligence Summaries are contained in F. S. Regs., Part II. and the Staff Manual respectively. Title pages will be prepared in manuscript.

Place	Date	Hour	Summary of Events and Information	Remarks and references to Appendices
HAMELIN COURT. S.29.d.9.6.	Mar 1 / 1917		All map references on Sheet 51^g except where otherwise stated. Visited CROISILLE and inspected progress in new Advanced Dressing Station. (T.23.d.8.9.) Visited KNUCKLE POST (U.19.b.6.3.) Pulley bar now been fixed to stretcher slide and it can be raised and lowered from within. Visited FACTORY POST (T.24.c.2.3) and inspected progress of dug-out. Capt S.H. BUSBY, M.O.R.C. USA' posted to Advanced Dressing Station, ST LEGER. (T.29.c.1.5.2)	B B B
	Mar 2 / 1917			
	Mar 3 / 1917			
	4 / 17		Picantine	B

WAR DIARY
or
INTELLIGENCE SUMMARY.
(Erase heading not required.)

Army Form C. 2118.

Place	Date	Hour	Summary of Events and Information	Remarks and references to Appendices
HAMELIN-COURT S.29.d.9.6.	Nov 5 1917		Capt E.H. BLACK posted to 7th Leinster Regt. for temporary duty vice Capt WATKINS. D.S.O. R.A.M.C. on leave. Capt A.J. HICKEY. O.C. Returned from leave.	Reg
	Nov 6 1917		Routine	B
	Nov 7 1917		Capt W.S. MACDONALD. proceeded on leave	B
			Capt BUSBY. M.O. R.C. U.S.A. left this unit on being posted to the 29 C.C.S.	B
	Nov 8 1917		COLONEL J. CAMPBELL. A.M.S. the new A.D.M.S. 16th Division visited the Main Dressing Station and Advanced Dressing Station.	B

Army Form C. 2118.

WAR DIARY
or
INTELLIGENCE SUMMARY.

(Erase heading not required.)

Instructions regarding War Diaries and Intelligence Summaries are contained in F. S. Regs., Part II. and the Staff Manual respectively. Title pages will be prepared in manuscript.

Place	Date	Hour	Summary of Events and Information	Remarks and references to Appendices
HAMELIN- COURT Sept 9.16.	Nov 9	1917	Routine	DG
	Nov 10	1917	Visited ST LEGER FACTORY and CROISILLE. Advanced Dressing Station at CROISILLE. Work on new will	DG
	Nov 11	1917	going on	DG
	Nov 12	1917	Visited CROISILLE.	DG
	Nov 13	1917	Visited Regimental Aid Posts and Bearer Relay Posts with the A.D.M.S.	DG

WAR DIARY
or
INTELLIGENCE SUMMARY

Place	Date	Hour	Summary of Events and Information	Remarks and references to Appendices
HAMELIN-COURT S-eg-dg-6	Mar 13 1917		Conference of Field Ambulance Commanders with A.D.M.S. Sgt. Major T. DAVIES rejoined this unit after 4½ months absence.	B.
	Mar 14 1917		Routine	B.
	Mar 15 1917		Capt. H.Q.O. WHEELER, R.A.M.C. T.C.F. joined this unit from No 48 C.C.S.	B.
	Mar 21 1917		Routine	B.

WAR DIARY
or
INTELLIGENCE SUMMARY

(Erase heading not required.)

Army Form C. 2118.

Place	Date	Hour	Summary of Events and Information	Remarks and references to Appendices
HAMELIN-lès-COURT S.21.d.9.6.	Nov 17 1917		Visited Car Stand H.S.NN (T.28.d.77) in order to inspect him the condition of the road and to acquaint my drivers with the route to be used in the forthcoming Operation. Capt. J. FERGUSON A.M.C. rejoined this unit for temporary duty.	B
	Nov 18 1917		Visited Nos 20 and No.43 C.C.S's and made arrangements to lend them our clerks for compilation of V.32.10's, A.36's and W.& S. Books during the forthcoming Operation.	B
	Nov 19 1917		Headquarters of this unit moved to the A.D.S. ST LEGER (T.29.b.) in the evening. Capt J. FERGUSON stayed in charge of Bearers 10th Head-quarters at the (Car) Stand, CROISILLE (T.23.d.2.8)	B

2353 Wt. W2544/1454 700,000 5/15 D.D.&L. A.D.S.S./Forms/C. 2118.

WAR DIARY or INTELLIGENCE SUMMARY

Place	Date	Hour	Summary of Events and Information	Remarks and references to Appendices
HAMELIN- COURT. S.21.a.9.6.	Mar 19 1917 (cont)		Capt. J. GREGG. M.O.R.C. U.S.A. noted in charge of the Advanced Dressing Station CROISILLES. Extra Bearers sent to all Relay Posts. Twenty Bearers attached to the 48th and twenty to the 49th Brigades at the Reg: Aid Post QUARRY (T.15.d.7.5) as supplementary to the Regimental Stretcher Bearers. In addition One Supplementary Bearer sent to the M.O. of 16th Bn Dub: Fusiliers. Visited the R.A.P & QUARRY in the afternoon with the D.A.D.M.S. Conferred with the M.Officers of Battalions and 9/8 Royal Irish Fusiliers re-forthcoming Operation.	B

WAR DIARY
or
INTELLIGENCE SUMMARY.

(Erase heading not required.)

Army Form C. 2118.

Place	Date	Hour	Summary of Events and Information	Remarks and references to Appendices
ST LEGER (Sq. 6)	Nov 20 1917		The 18th Division attacked at 6.20 a.m. The objectives were all taken and over one hundred prisoners captured. The evacuation of wounded worked very smoothly. I posted myself at the back Relay Post CROISILLE and remained there until the afternoon when I returned to the Advanced Dressing Station ST LEGER. Four Ambulance cars were kept going from the Posts without ceasing constantly from CROISILLE homewards, a relief being sent out to CROISILLE so that cars ran ST LEGER and to ST LEGER from HAMELINCOURT as the wounded were jumped at that place. Ten M.A.C. Cars had been sent to the Sumner and parked up at the Main Dressing Station HUMEDINCOURT	B

Army Form C. 2118.

WAR DIARY
or
INTELLIGENCE SUMMARY.
(Erase heading not required.)

Instructions regarding War Diaries and Intelligence Summaries are contained in F. S. Regs., Part II. and the Staff Manual respectively. Title pages will be prepared in manuscript.

Place	Date	Hour	Summary of Events and Information	Remarks and references to Appendices
ST LEGER (T.eq.L)	Nov 20 1917 (cont)		Work at Advanced Dressing Station ST LEGER proceeded smoothly and uneventfully. Two Dressing Tables kept going during the first rush. The majority of wounded were dealt with by 6 weeks.	B
	Nov 20 1917 (cont)		The Action will be known as the "ACTION OF CROISILLES HEIGHTS" (D.R.O 3752 28 Nov 1917)	B
	Nov 21 1917		Visited Regimental Aid Posts at QUARRY and KNUCKLE and found everything going well. Also visited FACTORY Bearer Relay Post. One man of this Unit slightly wounded near QUARRY.	B

2353 Wt. W2544/1454 700,000 5/15 D. D. & L. A.D.S.S./Forms/C. 2118.

WAR DIARY or INTELLIGENCE SUMMARY

Army Form C. 2118.

Place	Date	Hour	Summary of Events and Information	Remarks and references to Appendices
ST LEGER (T.29.b)	Nov 22		Visited Beaver Relay Post & Advanced Dressing Station at CROISILLES and found all going well. Also Reg. Aid Post at QUARRY.	
		19/17	Capt. J. FERGUSON RAMC visited Regt: Aid Post, KNUCKLE Quarry, Batt: aid posts at CROISILLES about	
		9.30 a.m.	Recalled Capt. J.F. FERGUSON from CROISILLES in the evening	
			Withdrew all extra Bearers except for extra (Field Amb.) at QUARRY	
			Sgt. Major ENDACOTT reported to A.D.M.S. 62nd Division leaving this unit	
HAMELIN COURT (S.29.d.9.6)	Nov 23 17/17		Head Quarters of this Unit returned to HAMELINCOURT	

2353 Wt. W2544/1454 700,000 5/15 D. D. & L. A.D.S.S./Forms/C. 2118.

WAR DIARY
or
INTELLIGENCE SUMMARY.
(Erase heading not required.)

Army Form C. 2118.

Place	Date	Hour	Summary of Events and Information	Remarks and references to Appendices
HAMELIN-COURT (S29.d.9.6.)	Nov 24/1917		Thirteen Reinforcements from Base. Capt. W.S. MALDONALD R. Irish Regt returned from leave. Capt. H.Q. WHEELER Rifle Brigade proceeded on leave.	
	Nov 25/17		Capt. E.H. BLACK Rifle Brigade reported unit from 7th Leinster Regt.	B
	Nov 26/17		Routine.	B
	Nov 27/17		Capt. J. FERGUSON Reserve left this Unit to join 6th Connaught Rangers as M.O.	B

Army Form C. 2118.

WAR DIARY
or
INTELLIGENCE SUMMARY.

(Erase heading not required.)

Place	Date	Hour	Summary of Events and Information	Remarks and references to Appendices
HAMELIN COURT	Nov 28 1917		Visited New Beaver Relay Post in LINCOLN SUPPORT (C.13.b.2.3.) with O/C. No. S. 16th Division. Four men posted here.	
	Nov 29 1917		Capt. A. MASSEY. R.A.M.C. proceeded on leave.	
	Nov 30 1917		New Advanced Dressing Station at CROISILLES (T.23.c.3.9) taken over. Room for twenty from stretcher cases in 5.9 proof shelter.	

W.F. Ball
Lieut Colt. R.A.M.C.
O.C. 141st Field Ambulance

S E C R E T.   Appendix I.   file
                                          P.S. 12.

Officer Commanding,
    111th. Field Ambulance.

        The 7th. Bn. Leinster Regt. will carry out a minor offensive operation in the early morning of October 16th. Casualties, if they arise, will be evacuated principally through the "Knuckle Aid Post" where the Medical Officer in charge 7th. Leinsters will be on duty. It is possible that a few casualties may also reach the Aid Post in Railway Reserve, occupied by the Medical Officer in charge 1st. Bn. R.Munster Fus.

        To evacuate the wounded from these Aid Posts, the following arrangements will be made by you:-

1. A Medical Officer from your Unit will be detailed for duty at Knuckle Aid Post to co-operate with the Medical Officer in charge 7th. Bn. Leinster Regt. and organise the evacuation to your Dressing Stations.
    The R.A.M.C. Detachment at Knuckle Aid Post will be made up to 1 N.C.O. and 6 men.
    Two wheeled stretchers will be available at Knuckle Aid Post, as well as 10 extra stretchers and 20 blankets.
    The splints, dressings and Medical Comforts at this Aid Post will be augmented by you as you may think necessary. Twelve "hot water bottles" will be available for use with cases of surgical shock.

2. The Detachment at Factory Relay Post will be increased to 1 N.C.O. and 10 men.
    Five wheeled stretchers will be concentrated at this point. A Motor Cycle Despatch Rider will be on duty there to take messages back to Advanced Dressing Station ST.LEGER. Arrangements will be made to provide hot bovril to cases arriving at this Relay Post.

3. Two Motor Ambulance Cars will be available at the "Car Stand" CROISILLES. If required and if not prevented by shelling, cars can work up to Factory Relay Post when called for.

4. A "Light Railway" Ambulance Train consisting of a covered wagon for 12 lying down cases will be sent to ST. LEGER at an hour to be arranged later, under arrangements made by me, and will come under the orders of Officer Commanding Advanced Dressing Station ST. LEGER. It will be available to go forward to "Factory" Level Crossing CROISILLES, if required, and to convey casualties from your Advanced Dressing Station direct to Casualty Clearing Station at ACHIET-LE-GRAND. You will provide 12 stretchers.

5. Administration of Anti-tetanic Serum, Registration of Casualties and attachment of Field Medical Cards and Buff Slips will be carried out at your Advanced Dressing Station, ST. LEGER.

6. The above arrangements, in so far as they are executed by you, will be completed 10 p.m. on 15.10.1917.

Headquarters,   Colonel,
16th. Division,
13.10.1917.   A.D.M.S., 16th. Division.

Copies to 16th. Division "G"
         47th. Infantry Brigade.

SECRET.

Appendix II

Officer Commanding,

  111th. Field Ambulance.

  The 49th. Infantry Brigade will carry out a small operation in the right Sub-section of the Left Section at 5 pm. on October 29th. 1917.

  The Regimental Medical Officer 7/8th. R.Inniskilling Fus. will occupy an Advanced Aid Post at U.7.d.15.20. under arrangements by 49th. Infantry Brigade, and regimental stretcher bearers will convey casualties to the "Quarry" Aid Post from this point; walking wounded being directed, under Battalion arrangements, along JANET and NELLY Trenches to the QUARRY.

  The following arrangements are to be made by you:-
1. A Medical Officer, one N.C.O. and six men of your Unit will proceed to Quarry Aid Post to supplement the party now there.

2. One N.C.O. and four men will be posted to supplement the detachment at Factory Post, CROISILLES.

3. Three Wheeled Stretchers will be placed at the Quarry and three at Factory Post.

4. Two Ambulance Cars will be at the Advanced Dressing Station, CROISILLES, and two at the Advanced Dressing Station, ST.LEGER.

5. One Officer from your Unit, with one Motor Cyclist as messenger, will be on duty at the Advanced Dressing Station, CROISILLES (car Stand).

  The above arrangements will be completed by 4 p.m. on 29.10.1917.

  All details as to preparation for wounded and evacuation through your Main Dressing Station, are left to you.

6. Officer Commanding, 112 Field Ambulance will be ordered to provide one Officer for duty at your Main Dressing Station and Officer Commanding 113 Field Ambulance an Officer for duty at your Advanced Dressing Station, ST.LEGER.

                Colonel,

Headquarters,
16th.Division,
28.10.1917.   A.D.M.S., 16th. Division.

Copies to:-

  49th. Infantry Brigade.
  "G" 16th. Division.

WAR DIARY

FOR MONTH OF DECEMBER, 1917.

VOLUME :- 25.

UNIT :- 111th Field Ambulance R.A.M.C.

CONFIDENTIAL.

WAR DIARY.

of 111th. Field Ambulance.

for

Period : December 1 to 31, 1917.

Volume XXV.

WAR DIARY
or
INTELLIGENCE SUMMARY.
(Erase heading not required.)

Army Form C. 2118.

Place	Date	Hour	Summary of Events and Information	Remarks and references to Appendices
HAMELIN COURT X.57.B. S.29.d.9.6.	Dec 1 1917		Letter from Major General W.B. HICKIE, C.B. Commanding 16th (Irish Division) received eulogising the work of this unit before, during and after the ACTION OF CROISILLES HEIGHTS (1) Answered.	Appen I
SOMIG-COURT	Dec 2 1917		This unit moved to SOMIECOURT. Sh 57c. A.23.d.0.10. handed over to 136th F. Amb. 40th Division	
BEAULEN-COURT	Dec 3 1917		Moved to BEAULENCOURT with 47th Infantry Brigade Sh 57c. N.24.d.1.8.4.	
	Dec 4 1917		One Tent Sub-division moved to RECQUIGNY to report to the 48th Infantry Brigade. Officer Capt W.J. MACDONALD R.A.M.C. and 1 Capt J. GREGG M.O. R.C. U.S.A	

Army Form C. 2118.

WAR DIARY
or
INTELLIGENCE SUMMARY.
(Erase heading not required.)

Instructions regarding War Diaries and Intelligence Summaries are contained in F. S. Regs., Part II. and the Staff Manual respectively. Title pages will be prepared in manuscript.

Place	Date	Hour	Summary of Events and Information	Remarks and references to Appendices
BEAULENCOURT Sh 57c N24d84	Dec 4 1917 (cont)		Rejoined Head-Quarters on same day.	D
	Dec 5 1917		Collected Brigade sick	D
	Dec 6 1917		Moved to TINCOURT (HAMEL) Sh 62c J18.d.2.3. Started at 10.25 a.m. and arrived at 6.25 p.m. Reinforcements - Eight other Ranks.	D
	Dec 7 1917		Routine at Dressing Station HAMEL. Advanced party of Two Officers and Nine other Ranks proceeded to take over CIVIL HOSPITAL PERONNE	D

Army Form C. 2118.

WAR DIARY
or
INTELLIGENCE SUMMARY.
(Erase heading not required.)

Place	Date	Hour	Summary of Events and Information	Remarks and references to Appendices
TINCOURT (Sh 62c. J.18.d.8.3)	Dec 7 1917 (cont)	9.9	(Sh 62c. 1.29.b.) Bearer Sub-Division consisting of Two Officers CAPT! WJ. MACDONALD R.A.M.C. and LIEUT!/ GREGG M.O.R.C. USA and thirty six Other Ranks proceeded for duty with the 1/2nd Fd Amb:	
	Dec 8 1917		This Unit less detached personnel took over the CIVIL HOSPITAL PERONNE (Sh 62c. I.29.b.) from the 2/1 W. Lancs Field Ambulance T.F. The place is very prenions Accommodation for about 120. patients A small house used for Civilians near by was taken over.	
	Dec 9 1917		General cleaning up, reporting of duties etc etc.	

WAR DIARY
or
INTELLIGENCE SUMMARY.

(Erase heading not required.)

Army Form C. 2118.

Place	Date	Hour	Summary of Events and Information	Remarks and references to Appendices
PERONNE SH. 62.C. 1.27.b	Dec 10		General cleaning up. Sanitary constructional work and Routine Hospital duties	
	11			
	12			
	13			
	14			
	15			B
	19/17		from 100 to 150 outpatients seen daily from about 60 different units stationed in vicinity. Accommodation of Hospital is roughly a hundred beds.	
	Dec 16		Capt. H.Q.u WHEELER R.A.M.C. returned from leave	B
	17 1919		Capt A. MASSEY R.A.M.C. returned from leave.	B

WAR DIARY
or
INTELLIGENCE SUMMARY.

(Erase heading not required.)

Army Form C. 2118.

Place	Date	Hour	Summary of Events and Information	Remarks and references to Appendices
PERONNE Sh.62c L.27.d	Dec 19, 20, 21 1917		Routine Hospital Duties	
	Dec 22 1917		Lieut C. G. LYONS M.O.R.C. U.S.A detailed for temporary duty with 6th/CONNAUGHT RANGERS	
	Dec 23 1917		Hostile aircraft bombing of PERONNE and vicinity abt 5.30 p.m. Two brought in dead. Eleven wounded admitted of which two died.	

Army Form C. 2118.

WAR DIARY
or
INTELLIGENCE SUMMARY.
(Erase heading not required.)

Instructions regarding War Diaries and Intelligence Summaries are contained in F. S. Regs., Part II. and the Staff Manual respectively. Title pages will be prepared in manuscript.

Place	Date	Hour	Summary of Events and Information	Remarks and references to Appendices
CIVIL HOSPITAL PERONNE S.P. 62.c 1.27.b	Dec 24 1917		1st Lieut. C.G. Lyons, M.O.R.C. U.S.A evacuated sick (Renal Calculus) and struck off the strength of this unit	B
	Dec 25 1917		Patients and Men's Christmas Dinner and Concert Church Parade in morning	B
	Dec 26 1917		Sergeant's & Christmas Dinner	B
	Dec 27 1917		1st Lieut A. Strauss, M.O.R.C. U.S.A arrived on completion of temporary duty at the 49th C.C.S. Twice off arrived i.c a.m	B

Army Form C. 2118.

WAR DIARY
or
INTELLIGENCE SUMMARY.
(Erase heading not required.)

Instructions regarding War Diaries and Intelligence Summaries are contained in F.S. Regs., Part II. and the Staff Manual respectively. Title pages will be prepared in manuscript.

Place	Date	Hour	Summary of Events and Information	Remarks and references to Appendices
CIVIL HOSP. PERONNE Sh.62.c. 1.27.b.	Dec 29 1917		Capt. A. MASSEY. R.A.M.C. (T.C.) detailed for temporary duty with 6/CONNAUGHT RANGERS vice 1st LIEUT. C.G. LYONS evacuated sick. On the 24th inst the following of this unit were granted the Military Medal: No. 64481 Pte. (A/Cpl) A.J. Lyatts No. 69566 " " W. Jackson.	R
	Dec 30 31 1917		Routine	R

Capt E. Bell
Lieut Col. R.A.M.C.
O.C. 111th Fd Ambulance

WAR DIARY of 111 Field Ambulance.   Vol. XXV.

Appendix 1.

(1).   16th.(Irish) Division,
                                                     B.E.F.
                                             Nov.28th. 1917.

O.C. 111th. Field Ambulance.

    At the close of the First phase in this Battle of CAMBRAI I wish to express to you as Commanding Officer and to the Officers, N.C.O's and Men under your command my appreciation of all the good work before, during and after the Action of Croissiles Heights. The gallantry, self-sacrifice and devotion to duty of all ranks of the 111th. Field Ambulance have been beyond praise, & I wish you to accept & to convey to your command my gratitude and thanks.

                Sgd/ W.B.HICKIE, Maj.Gen.,
                Comdg. 16th.(Irish) Division.

(2).   Dec. 4th. 1917.

G.O.C. 16th.(Irish) Division.

Sir,
    I have the honour to thank you on behalf of all ranks of this Unit for your extremely kind letter regarding our work before, during and after the "Action of Croissiles Heights".

    This Unit is very proud of your good opinion and will always endeavour to retain it.
    I have arranged to have your letter read on parade.

                I have the honour to be,
                    Sir,
                      Your obedient Servant,

                    Sd/ W.J.E.BELL, Lieut-Col.RAMC.,
            Comdg. 111th. Field Ambulance.

WAR DIARY

FOR MONTH OF JANUARY, 1918.

VOLUME :- 26.

UNIT :- 111th Fd. Amb. R.A.M.C.

Army Form C. 2118.

WAR DIARY
or
INTELLIGENCE SUMMARY.
(Erase heading not required.)

Place	Date	Hour	Summary of Events and Information	Remarks and references to Appendices
PERONNE (CIVIL HOSPITAL) 1.27.c.	Jan 1 1918		All map references except where otherwise stated are on Sheet 62.C. Grant of the Divisional Commander's Parchment Certificates to the following Officers and other ranks of this unit: CAPT. W.J. MACDONALD. R.A.M.C. LIEUT. F.G. CHANDLER — do — CAPT. A. MASSEY " 1st LIEUT. GREGG. M.O.R.C. U.S.A CORPORAL E.F. POWELL. R.A.M.C. L/CPL J. IMRIE — do — L/CPL A. WATTS " PTE UNDERWOOD " CRUMLIN " JACKSON	

Army Form C. 2118.

WAR DIARY
or
INTELLIGENCE SUMMARY.
(Erase heading not required.)

Place	Date	Hour	Summary of Events and Information	Remarks and references to Appendices
CIVIL HOSPITAL PERONNE (1.27.6.)	June 1918 (cont)		PTE HOLMES. R.A.M.C. " FLEMING. A.S.C. M.T. " MAXWELL. A.S.C. M.T. " GILLINGHAM. R.A.M.C. " NISBETT. —do— " KELLY " " L. MOSES. " " E.E. LANE. " " J.I. HAUGHAN " " W. NELSON " " F.J. HOPKINS " " J. MARSHALL " " P. PEACOCK " " E. CHANEY. " " F. MOORE. "	

Army Form C. 2118.

WAR DIARY
or
INTELLIGENCE SUMMARY.

(Erase heading not required.)

Instructions regarding War Diaries and Intelligence Summaries are contained in F. S. Regs., Part II. and the Staff Manual respectively. Title pages will be prepared in manuscript.

Place	Date	Hour	Summary of Events and Information	Remarks and references to Appendices
CIVIL HOSPITAL PERONNE. (I.27.b)	Jan 2		Routine	
	3			
	4 1918			
	Jan 5 1918		Visited 21st Divisional Rest Station, LONGAVESNE (E.25.b)	
	Jan 6 1918		E.A. bombed the town about 6.40 a.m. Some bombs fell quite close to the Dressing Station. Casualties brought in:- 1 killed, 1 died of wounds and 4 wounded	

Army Form C. 2118

WAR DIARY
or
INTELLIGENCE SUMMARY
(Erase heading not required.)

Instructions regarding War Diaries and Intelligence Summaries are contained in F.S. Regs., Part II. and the Staff Manual respectively. Title Pages will be prepared in manuscript.

Place	Date	Hour	Summary of Events and Information	Remarks and references to Appendices
CIVIL HOSPITAL PERONNE (1.27.6)	Jan 7 1918		No 48599 Q.M.S. Williams D. left this Unit to proceed to England as a candidate for a Commission in the Royal Artillery. The A.D.M.S. 16th Division inspected the Scouring Station.	B
	Jan 8/9/10 1918		Routine	B
	Jan 11 1918		The D.M.S. V#th Army visited this Dressing Station.	B

1875. Wt. W593/826 1,000,000 4/15 J.B.C. & A. A.D.S.S./Forms/C. 2118.

Army Form. C. 2118

WAR DIARY
or
INTELLIGENCE SUMMARY
(Erase heading not required.)

Place	Date	Hour	Summary of Events and Information	Remarks and references to Appendices
CIVIL HOSPITAL PERONNE (I·27·l·)	Jan 11 1918		Routine	B.
	Jan 12 1918		1st Lieut J. GREGG, M.O. R.C. U.S.A returned to this Unit from temporary duty with the 112th Field Ambulance. Routine	B.
	Jan 13 1918			B.
	Jan 14 1918		Visit from D.D.M.S. VII Corps.	B.

Army Form C. 2118

WAR DIARY
or
INTELLIGENCE SUMMARY
(Erase heading not required.)

Instructions regarding War Diaries and Intelligence Summaries are contained in F. S. Regs., Part II. and the Staff Manual respectively. Title Pages will be prepared in manuscript.

Place	Date	Hour	Summary of Events and Information	Remarks and references to Appendices
CIVIL HOSPITAL PERONNE (1.27.t)	Jan 15	18	Capt. A.J. HICKEY. M.C. went to see Sr M.S. V Army with a view to an appointment which has been offered to him	B
	Jan 16	1948	Capt E.H. BLACK returned from leave and proceeded to VII Corps School FOUCACOURT (M.29.c) to take over medical charge.	B
			Lieut A. STRAUSS. M.R.C. U.S.A. relieved Capt. A. MASSEY as M.O. i/c 6th CONNAUGHT RANGERS	B

Army Form C. 2118

WAR DIARY
or
INTELLIGENCE SUMMARY
(Erase heading not required.)

Instructions regarding War Diaries and Intelligence Summaries are contained in F.S. Regs., Part II. and the Staff Manual respectively. Title Pages will be prepared in manuscript.

Place	Date	Hour	Summary of Events and Information	Remarks and references to Appendices
CIVIL HOSPITAL PERONNE (1/27.6)	Jan 16 1918 (cont)		The latter Officer returned to this unit. Proceeded on leave to-day PARIS and SAN REMO. Handed over command of this unit to Capt A. MASSEY. R.A.M.C.	W. G. Bell Lieut Col R.A.M.C.
	Jan 17 1918		Capt. A.J. HICKEY. M.C. proceeded on duty to D.M.S. 5th Army and is struck off the strength of this Field Ambulance today.	
	Jan 18 1918		Routine.	
	Jan 19 1918		1st Lieut J. GREGG. M.O. R.C. U.S.A. proceeded on duty to BOULOGNE for one week with a view to entering American Regular Medical Service. Lieut. STEWART. R.A.M.C. reported here for duty for one week from 112th Field Ambulance to replace Lieut J. GREGG. M.O. R.C. U.S.A. while away.	

1875. Wt. W593/826 1,000,000 4/15 J.B.C. & A. A.D.S.S./Forms/C. 2118.

Army Form C. 2118

WAR DIARY
or
INTELLIGENCE SUMMARY

(Erase heading not required.)

Instructions regarding War Diaries and Intelligence Summaries are contained in F. S. Regs., Part II. and the Staff Manual respectively. Title Pages will be prepared in manuscript.

Place	Date	Hour	Summary of Events and Information	Remarks and references to Appendices
Brgl. Hospital PERONNE (1-27-r)	Jan 20/1918		Routine.	a.m.
	21/1918		Routine.	a.m.
	22/1918		1st Lieut J GREGG. M.O.R.C. U.S.A. returned here to duty from BOULOGNE.	a.m.
	Jan 23/1918		Routine.	eve
	Jan 24/1918		The A.D.M.S. 16th Division and A.D.V.S. 16th Division paid a visit here to examine and inspect transport lines of this unit on PERONNE.	a.m.
	25/1918		The D.D.M.S 4th Corps paid a visit to CIVIL HOSPITAL to inspect this place generally.	a.m.
	26/1918		Routine.	a.m.

WAR DIARY
or
INTELLIGENCE SUMMARY

(Erase heading not required.)

Army Form C. 2118

Instructions regarding War Diaries and Intelligence Summaries are contained in F.S. Regs., Part II. and the Staff Manual respectively. Title Pages will be prepared in manuscript.

Place	Date	Hour	Summary of Events and Information	Remarks and references to Appendices
CIVIL HOSPITAL PERONNE (1°21.e)	Jan 27 1918		Routine.	am
	Jan 28 1918		Routine	am
	Jan 29 1918		E.A. machine bombed town (between 9 km + 9 p.m.) on the outskirts. No damage done. No casualties.	am
	Jan 30 1918		Routine	am
	Jan 31 1918		Routine	am

R. M. McGill
Capt D.D.S
for O.C. 111 Field Ambulance

WAR DIARY.

FOR MONTH OF FEBRUARY, 1918.

VOLUME:- 27

UNIT:- 111th Field Ambulance R.A.M.C.

Confidential

War Diary

Vol. XXVII   February 1918.

111 Field Ambulance

Army Form C. 2118

WAR DIARY
or
INTELLIGENCE SUMMARY

(Erase heading not required.)

Place	Date	Hour	Summary of Events and Information	Remarks and references to Appendices
CIVIL HOSPITAL PERONNE (I·27·6) Sh 62 c	Feb 1 1916		ADMS 16th DIVISION visited this unit to-day.	QM
	Feb 2 1916		D.S.O. Lieut Colonel W.J. BELL returned from leave to-day and resumed command of the unit of the Resumed duty on return from leave to-day.	

W. J. Bell
Lieut. Col.
O.C. 111th Field Ambulance.

Army Form C. 2118.

WAR DIARY
or
INTELLIGENCE SUMMARY.

(Erase heading not required.)

Instructions regarding War Diaries and Intelligence Summaries are contained in F. S. Regs., Part II. and the Staff Manual respectively. Title pages will be prepared in manuscript.

Place	Date	Hour	Summary of Events and Information	Remarks and references to Appendices
CIVIL HOSPITAL PERONNE 1.29.b	Feb 3 1918		All map references on Sheet 62C except where otherwise stated	
	Feb 4 1918		Routine	B
			Lieut J.B. GREGG. M.O. R.C. U.S.A. admitted to hospital with ulcer of cornea — traumatic.	B
	Feb 5 1918		Routine	
	Feb 6 1918		Visited AMIENS to arrange about getting fresh vegetables for hospital.	B

Army Form C. 2118.

WAR DIARY
or
INTELLIGENCE SUMMARY.
(Erase heading not required.)

Instructions regarding War Diaries and Intelligence Summaries are contained in F. S. Regs., Part II. and the Staff Manual respectively. Title pages will be prepared in manuscript.

Place	Date	Hour	Summary of Events and Information	Remarks and references to Appendices
CIVIL HOSPITAL	Feb 7		Routine	B
PERONNE HQ.t.	Feb 8 1918			
	Feb 5		Two N.C.O's and table Privates who have been attached to the C.R.E. since the 13th January rejoined this unit to-day.	B
	Feb 9 1918		Court of Enquiry regarding absence without leave of No 24982 Pte JONES. G. 1st WORCESTER REGT attached to this unit	B
	Feb 10 11 1918		Routine	

WAR DIARY or INTELLIGENCE SUMMARY.

Army Form C. 2118.

Place	Date	Hour	Summary of Events and Information	Remarks and references to Appendices
CIVIL HOSPITAL PERONNE	Feb 12 1918	1.27 b.	Lieut. J.A. STEWART. R.A.M.C. returned to the 112th Field Ambulance. Capt. C.F. BRADY, same reported for duty. Lieut J.B. Gregg M.O. R.C., U.S.A. returned from Hospital	B B
	Feb 13/18		Raining	B
	Feb 14/18		Weather cloudy with slight mist	B
	Feb 15/18		Cloudy in morning, brightening towards mid-day. Some bombs dropped in neighbourhood from E.A. in the evening	B

WAR DIARY
or
INTELLIGENCE SUMMARY.
(Erase heading not required.)

Army Form C. 2118.

Place	Date	Hour	Summary of Events and Information	Remarks and references to Appendices
CIVIL HOSPITAL PERONNE	Feb 16/18		Cold + bright. Frost at night. Lieut J.B. GREGG M.O.R.C. U.S.A. proceeded to 113th Field Amb. for temporary duty. E.A. dropped bombs in neighbourhood in evening.	B
	Feb 17/1918		Cold, bright and frosty. Bombing from E.A. in evening in vicinity. Capt. T.C. WATKINS D.S.O. M.C. R.A.M.C. joined this Unit for duty. Lieut J.B. GREGG M.O. R.C. U.S.A. proceeded on leave and was relieved at 113th Field Amb: by Capt. A. MASSEY R.M.C.	B
	Feb 18/1918		Cold and bright. Col. A. BOWEN. D.S.O. R.A.M.C. has returned to the 16th Division as A.D.M.S.	B

Army Form C. 2118.

WAR DIARY
or
INTELLIGENCE SUMMARY.
(Erase heading not required.)

Instructions regarding War Diaries and Intelligence Summaries are contained in F. S. Regs., Part II. and the Staff Manual respectively. Title pages will be prepared in manuscript.

Place	Date	Hour	Summary of Events and Information	Remarks and references to Appendices
CIVIL HOSPITAL PERONNE (29.6.)	19/2/18		Cold & bright.	
	20/2/18		Sent by Col. A. Bowen, DSO, AQMS. Parchment certificates distributed to the following on parade. No 54157 Sgt. Smith W.A No 64264 A/Cpl. Smith J.S No 64639 Pte Mason S No 64339 Pte O'Neil G and in absentia to: Capt: E.H. Black. Dagner (now att. VII Corps School) No 64372 Pte Fairley J. (now in Hospital)	

WAR DIARY
or
INTELLIGENCE SUMMARY.

(Erase heading not required.)

Army Form C. 2118.

Place	Date	Hour	Summary of Events and Information	Remarks and references to Appendices
CIVIL HOSPITAL PERONNE. 1.27.b.	Feb 20 1918 (cont)		Cold + bright	R
	Feb 21 1918		Cloudy in morning, brightening at mid-day	R
	Feb 22 1918		Cloudy	R
	Feb 23 1918		Bright	R
	Feb 24 1918		Bright. Capt. C.H. SEVILLE. R.A.M.C. joined this Unit for duty to-day ex 36th Division	R

Army Form C. 2118.

WAR DIARY
or
INTELLIGENCE SUMMARY.

(Erase heading not required.)

Place	Date	Hour	Summary of Events and Information	Remarks and references to Appendices
CIVIL HOSPITAL PERONNE 1.27.d.	Feb 25/18		Bright	
	Feb 26/18		Capt. C.F. BRADY. R.A.M.C. joined this Unit to report to the A.D.M.S. 36th Division	B
	Feb 27/18		Cloudy	B
			Cloudy + cold	B
	Feb 28/18		Cloudy + cold	B

10/J.A.Bell
Lieut Col. R.A.M.C.
OC. 111th Field Ambulance.

140/249.

No. 111 ? a.

COMMITTEE FOR THE
MEDICAL HISTORY OF THE WAR
Date   12 MAY 1918

WAR DIARY.

Vol XXVIII.

111th Field Ambulance.

Army Form C. 2118.

WAR DIARY
or
INTELLIGENCE SUMMARY.
(Erase heading not required.)

Place	Date	Hour	Summary of Events and Information	Remarks and references to Appendices
CIVIL HOSPITAL PERONNE. 1.27.6.	March 1 1918		All map references are on Sheet 62C except where otherwise stated. Capt. C.A. SEVILLE to 6th CONNAUGHT RANGERS for temporary duty vice LIEUT STRAUSS M.O.R.C. U.S.A on leave. All officers and other ranks mentioned in this Diary belong to the R.A.M.C. except where otherwise stated. Reinforcements. Seven men arrived from Base. Weather Cold & Snow.	

Army Form C. 2118.

WAR DIARY
or
INTELLIGENCE SUMMARY.
(Erase heading not required.)

Instructions regarding War Diaries and Intelligence Summaries are contained in F.S. Regs., Part II. and the Staff Manual respectively. Title pages will be prepared in manuscript.

Place	Date	Hour	Summary of Events and Information	Remarks and references to Appendices
CIVIL HOSPITAL PERONNE. 1.29.b.	March 2/1918		Weather. Cold. Cloudy.	B.
	March 3/1918		Capt WATKINS detailed to 2/ MUNSTER FUS'rs for temporary duty. Weather, cold, cloudy	B.
	March 4/1918		Instr. by D.M.S. V# Army, and also by D.D.M.S. VII to Corps to be prepared to take 150 lightly wounded of necessary. Lieut LYONS M.C.R.C. U.S.A rejoined unit from sick leave. Weather. Rain. Mist.	B.

Army Form C. 2118.

WAR DIARY
or
INTELLIGENCE SUMMARY.
(Erase heading not required.)

Instructions regarding War Diaries and Intelligence Summaries are contained in F.S. Regs., Part II and the Staff Manual respectively. Title pages will be prepared in manuscript.

Place	Date	Hour	Summary of Events and Information	Remarks and references to Appendices
CIVIL HOSPITAL PERONNE 1.27.b.	March 5 1918		Weather. Cold, cloudy and rain clearing to fair in afternoon	R
	March 6 1918		Weather. Rain & cold.	B
	March 7 1918		Weather. Rain & cold. Ribbon of Mons Star given to following:- Lieut Col. W.S.E. BELL No T 22354 S.S. Major WARRINGTON A. A.S.C. No M 1/06975 Sgt RHODES F. A.S.C. M.T.	B

WAR DIARY
or
INTELLIGENCE SUMMARY.

(Erase heading not required.)

Army Form C. 2118.

Place	Date	Hour	Summary of Events and Information	Remarks and references to Appendices
CIVIL HOSPITAL PERONNE	March 6 1918		No 36530 Pte. BOYLE. P. R.A.M.C.	
			No 75192 Pte. CHANEY. E. R.A.M.C. (in absentia)	
			" 126 " DAWSON. J.G. R.A.M.C.	
			" 19246 Cpl. LAING. J. R.A.M.C.	
			" 125 Pte. POBOCK. J. R.A.M.C. (in absentia)	
			" 16053 " YATES. E. R.A.M.C.	
			" 57307 " NEVITT. A.C. R.A.M.C.	
			" TS/10690 Dvr. GODWIN. R.E. A.S.C.	
			" M.S./3995 Pte. DIGGINS. G. A.S.C. M.T.	
			" 6660 " WEBB. W.G. 8th DEVON REGT. att d 111th Field Ambulance	

WAR DIARY
or
INTELLIGENCE SUMMARY.

Army Form C. 2118.

Place	Date	Hour	Summary of Events and Information	Remarks and references to Appendices
CIVIL HOSPITAL PERONNE. 127.F.	March 7 1918 (cont)		Lieut. J.B. GREGG. M.O.R.C. U.S.A rejoined from leave to the United Kingdom. Weather. Cold + fair	R
	March 8 1918		Lieut. A. STRAUSS. M.O.R.C. U.S.A attached to 6th Bn. CONNAUGHT RANGERS and struck off the strength of this unit. Weather. Cold + fair.	R
	March 9 1918		Weather. Unchanged.	R

WAR DIARY or INTELLIGENCE SUMMARY

Army Form C. 2118.

Place	Date	Hour	Summary of Events and Information	Remarks and references to Appendices
CIVIL HOSPITAL PERONNE 127.6.	March 10 1918		Capt. S.D. WATKINS. D.S.O. M.C. Rejoined the Unit. Lieut C.G. LYONS. M.O. R.C. U.S.A. Proceeded to VII th Corps School for a Course of Instruction. Weather. No change.	B
	March 11 1918		Lieut J.B. GREGG. M.O. R.C. U.S.A Proceeded to 113th Field Ambulance for temporary duty. Weather. No change.	
	March 12 1918		Capt. A. MASSEY. Proceeded to the 113th Field Ambulance for temporary duty. Weather. No change.	C

Army Form C. 2118.

WAR DIARY
or
INTELLIGENCE SUMMARY.
(Erase heading not required.)

Instructions regarding War Diaries and Intelligence Summaries are contained in F. S. Regs., Part II. and the Staff Manual respectively. Title pages will be prepared in manuscript.

Place	Date	Hour	Summary of Events and Information	Remarks and references to Appendices
CIVIL HOSPITAL PERONNE 1.27.b.	March 13 1918		Weather: No change. Inspection of Horses & Horse lines by A.D.V.S. 16th Div? and by D.D.M.S. 5th Army.	B
	March 14 1918		Capt. W.S. MACDONALD with 2 Bearer Sub-divisions departed at midnight to report to O.C. 113th Field Ambulance. 50 stretchers also sent.	B
	March 15 1918		Weather: No change. Capt. W.S. MACDONALD returned leaving Bearers with the 113th Fd Amb. Capt. H.Q.O. WHEELER rejoined the Unit from VIIth Corps Reinforcement Rest Camp.	B B

Army Form C. 2118.

WAR DIARY
or
INTELLIGENCE SUMMARY.
(Erase heading not required.)

Place	Date	Hour	Summary of Events and Information	Remarks and references to Appendices
CIVIL HOSPITAL PERONNE L.27.b	March 15 1918 (cont)		Inspection of Hospital and Horse + Transport lines by G.O.C. 16th Division. Weather. Cold & fair	B
	March 16 1918		Weather. Warmer	B
	March 17 1918		St Patrick's Day. Weather. Warmer. Slightly cloudy.	B
	March 18 1918		Capt. C.H. SEVILLE rejoined unit from 6th CONNAUGHT RANGERS. Relieved by 1st Lieut. A. STRAUSS M.O.R.C. U.S.A. Weather. warm. Slightly cloudy.	B

WAR DIARY
or
INTELLIGENCE SUMMARY.

(Erase heading not required.)

Army Form C. 2118.

Place	Date	Hour	Summary of Events and Information	Remarks and references to Appendices
CIVIL HOSPITAL PERONNE 1.27.b.	March 19 1918		Rain	
	March 20 1918		1 N.C.O. Reinforcement	
	March 21 1918		Capt W.S. MACDONALD and Capt G.D. WATKINS left unit to report to 112th Field Ambulance. Enemy started bombardment during early hours of morning and attacked about 4.40.a.m. Following casualties were reported among the Bearers of this Unit attached to the 113th Field Ambulance.	

Army Form C. 2118.

WAR DIARY
or
INTELLIGENCE SUMMARY.
(Erase heading not required.)

Place	Date	Hour	Summary of Events and Information	Remarks and references to Appendices
CIVIL HOSPITAL PERONNE. 1.27.6.	March 21 1918 (cont)		Killed. 6. Died of wounds. 1. Missing. 2. Wounded. 13. 2 remaining with the Unit Gassed. 2. N.Y.D.N. 8. 4 remaining with the Unit. Sick Evac. 1. One Talbot Motor Ambulance destroyed by shell fire	B

WAR DIARY or INTELLIGENCE SUMMARY.

Army Form C. 2118.

Place	Date	Hour	Summary of Events and Information	Remarks and references to Appendices
CIVIL HOSPITAL PERONNE 1.27.b.	March 22/18		112th Field Ambulance arrived in PERONNE, having been shelled out of their station at TINCOURT, and billeted with this Unit	
	March 23		Enemy entered PERONNE in the afternoon	
HERBECOURT (AMIENS 2617) (Sh.62c. H.32.a.9.F.)	1918	10.15 a.m.	The Unit left PERONNE at 10.15 a.m. (AMIENS Sh.17)	
	March 24	1.0 p.m.	Arrived HERBECOURT 1.0 p.m.	
		5.0 p.m.	Departed " 5.0 p.m.	
Sh. 62 c. G.27.c.4.8	1918	6.20 p.m.	Arrived road side N° CAPPY 6.20 p.m.	
		12.40 a.m.	Departed " " " 12.40 a.m.	
Sh. 62 D L.23.d.4.3		1.20 a.m.	Arrived at site 1 kilometre beyond CAPPY on CAPPY - BRAY Road about 1.30 a.m.	

Army Form C. 2118.

WAR DIARY
or
INTELLIGENCE SUMMARY.

(Erase heading not required.)

Instructions regarding War Diaries and Intelligence Summaries are contained in F. S. Regs., Part II. and the Staff Manual respectively. Title pages will be prepared in manuscript.

Place	Date	Hour	Summary of Events and Information	Remarks and references to Appendices
	March 24 1918		1st Lieut C.G. Lyons. M.O.R.C. U.S.A. evacuated to No 38 C.C.S. with sore throat.	
		10.10 p.m.	Later 38 C.C.S. MANICOURT (Sh. 62.c A.16) closed. 41 Stationary Hospital CERISY - GAILLY (Sh. 62.D.O.3) receiving. Departed Site on CAPPY - BRAY Road.	
QUERRIEU (Sh. 62 D H.17)	March 25 1918	1.30 a.m.	Arrived QUERRIEU. Capt. H.G.O WHEELER joined 1st MUNSTER FUSILIERS for temporary duty	
		5.0 p.m.	Departed QUERRIEU	

Army Form C. 2118.

WAR DIARY
or
INTELLIGENCE SUMMARY.
(Erase heading not required.)

Instructions regarding War Diaries and Intelligence Summaries are contained in F.S. Regs., Part II. and the Staff Manual respectively. Title pages will be prepared in manuscript.

Place	Date	Hour	Summary of Events and Information	Remarks and references to Appendices
Sh. 62.D P.20.A.5.4.	March 25 1918	8.30 p.m.	Arrived in site near Cross Roads S.W. of BOIS DE VAIRE	
	March 26 1918		41 Stationary Hospital CERISY-GAILLY closed. Lying cases to MOREUIL (AMIENS 24, 17) Sitting " to HARGICOURT (AMIENS 24, 17) 10th M.A.C. at VILLERS BRETONNEUX (Sh. 62.D. O.35) Later. Lying Cases to AMIENS Sitting " to NAMPS (41, 55 and 61 C.C.S.) (AMIENS 24, 17) Capt A. MASSEY and 1st Lieut J. B. GREGG M.O.R.C. U.S.A attached to 112th Field Ambulance for temporary duty	

Army Form C. 2118.

WAR DIARY
or
INTELLIGENCE SUMMARY.
(Erase heading not required.)

Place	Date	Hour	Summary of Events and Information	Remarks and references to Appendices
	March 27/18	5.0 p.m.	Departed site near X roads S.W. of BOIS DE VAIRE.	B
(Sh. 62.D. N.28.c.)	March 28 1918	7.40 p.m.	Arrived site on AMIENS - ST. QUENTIN road, 5 miles east of AMIENS (Sh 62.D. N.28.C.)	
			Parked in field at road side as above with the 112th and 113th Field Ambulance.	
			Capt. A. MASSEY and Lt. Hurst J.B. GREGG M.O.R.C. U.S.A are at the Advanced Dressing Stations at HAMELET and FOVILLOY attached to 112th Field Ambulance.	B

Army Form C. 2118.

WAR DIARY
or
INTELLIGENCE SUMMARY.
(Erase heading not required.)

Place	Date	Hour	Summary of Events and Information	Remarks and references to Appendices
	March 28th 1918		Lieut E.D. KINSEY R.A.M.C. and Lt Lieut J.H. WILSON, M.O.R.C. U.S.A. joined the Unit for temporary duty, reporting from the Base	B
	March 29th 1918		Collecting local sick and wounded and evacuating all cases coming down from the Army line in rotation for twenty four hours with the 112th and 113th Field Ambulance	B
	March 30th 1918		Capt. C.H. SEVILLE R.A.M.C. proceeded to AUBIGNY to take over medical charge of a Small (vide 18th Div.) Dressing Station and Soup Kitchen (April 2 16th Div.)	B

WAR DIARY
or
INTELLIGENCE SUMMARY.

Army Form C. 2118.

Place	Date	Hour	Summary of Events and Information	Remarks and references to Appendices
	March 31 1918		Capt. G.D. Watkins. D.S.O. M.C. and 19 other ranks departed at 10:15 p.m. to open a XIXth Corps Walking Wounded Station at AMIENS. (relieving 16th Divⁿ.) W.E. Bell Lieut. Col. R.A.M.C.	

160/2983

No. 111 F.A.

April 1918

COMMITTEE
MEDICAL HIST...
Date 9 JUL 1918

111th FIELD AMBULANCE

WAR DIARY

VOLUME XXX FOR APRIL, 1918

ORIGINAL COPY

111TH FIELD AMBULANCE.
No. 4275
Date. 1.5.18

Army Form C. 2118.

WAR DIARY
or
INTELLIGENCE SUMMARY.
(Erase heading not required.)

WO29

Place	Date	Hour	Summary of Events and Information	Remarks and references to Appendices
AMIENS — ST QUENTIN Road. Sh. 62.D N.28.c.	April 1 1918		E.A. attacked camp with machine gun in early morning.	B
N.26.d.5.6.		2.30	Moved to new site stated in margin; about a mile nearer AMIENS. XIX Corps walking wounded Station at AMIENS.	
	April 2 1918		Capt A. MASSEY rejoined from 112th Field Ambulance. Lieut WILSON. N.O.R.C. U.S.A. sent to walking wounded station AMIENS for duty.	B

WAR DIARY
or
INTELLIGENCE SUMMARY.

(Erase heading not required.)

Army Form C. 2118.

Place	Date	Hour	Summary of Events and Information	Remarks and references to Appendices
Sh. 62.D. N.e.c.d.5.6.	2/3 April 1918		Enemy shelled vicinity of camp intermittently with large plumpud shells from 9.0 p.m. to 6.0 a.m. last night (2nd — 3rd) Capt. SEVILLE rejoined unit from Reserve Station AUBIGNY, relieved by Capt. A. MASSEE.	
		3.0 p.m.	Marched off	
SALEUX (AMIENS-17)		7.30 p.m.	Arrived SALEUX	

Army Form C. 2118.

WAR DIARY
or
INTELLIGENCE SUMMARY.
(Erase heading not required.)

Place	Date	Hour	Summary of Events and Information	Remarks and references to Appendices
SALEUX (AMIENS Sh. 17)	April 4/1918	9 A.M.	Transport of the Unit moved off with 47th Brigade Transport.	
		4.0 p.m.	Personnel entrained. Capt A. MASSEY, 1/Lt J. GREGG, U.S.A. and all detached personnel having rejoined.	
	April 5/1918	12.0 midnight	Arrived BLANGY (Sh DIEPPE.16) and marched off immediately on detraining.	
MORIVAL Sh. DIEPPE.16		1.30 a.m.	Arrived MORIVAL and went into BILLETS.	
		10.30 a.m.	Transport arrived	

Army Form C. 2118.

WAR DIARY
or
INTELLIGENCE SUMMARY.

(Erase heading not required.)

Place	Date	Hour	Summary of Events and Information	Remarks and references to Appendices
MORIVAL	April 5/1918 (cont)		Collecting Ord. of 47th and 48th Inf. Brigades	B
St. DIEPPE 16.	April 6/1918		Routine	
	April 7/1918		Capt W.E. GIBLINS. M.C. joined the Unit for Duty	B
	April 8/1918		Lt. Kent J.B. GREGG. M.O.R.C. U.S.A. proceeded to 1st R. Dub. Fus. for temporary duty	B
			Capt. C.H. SEVILLE proceeded to 6th CONNAUGHT RANGERS for duty	B

Army Form C. 2118.

WAR DIARY
or
INTELLIGENCE SUMMARY.
(Erase heading not required.)

Instructions regarding War Diaries and Intelligence Summaries are contained in F.S. Regs., Part II. and the Staff Manual respectively. Title pages will be prepared in manuscript.

Place	Date	Hour	Summary of Events and Information	Remarks and references to Appendices
MORIVAL. Rd. DIEPPE 16.	April 8 1918 (cont)		Lieut E.O.KINSEY proceeded to 2nd Royal Irish Regt. to duty. Capt. H.Q.O. WHEELER proceeded to 1st Royal Munster Fusiliers for duty.	B
	April 9 1918		Departed MORIVAL: 8.15 a.m. and marched to AULT, arriving at 9.45 p.m.	B
AULT St. ABBEVILLE 14.	April 10 1918	8.0 a.m.	Departed AULT at 8.0 a.m. Marched to EU (St. ABBEVILLE 14.)	B
		11.0 a.m.	entrained	
		9.0 p.m.	Arrived ARQUES. Detrained. Marched to BANDRIGHEM.	
BANDRIGHEM. (St. HAZEBROUCK 5 'A'.)			Arrived about 9.0 p.m	

Army Form C. 2118.

WAR DIARY
or
INTELLIGENCE SUMMARY.
(Erase heading not required.)

Instructions regarding War Diaries and Intelligence Summaries are contained in F. S. Regs., Part II. and the Staff Manual respectively. Title pages will be prepared in manuscript.

Place	Date	Hour	Summary of Events and Information	Remarks and references to Appendices
BANDRIGHEM Rl. HAZEBROUCK S.A.	April 11 /18	11 a.m.	Reported BANDRIGHEM. Marched to OUVE-WIRQUIN and went into billets.	B
OUVE-WIRQUIN	April 12 /18		Now in XIII Corps 1st Army. At one hour's notice to move.	B
	April 13 /18		Routine.	B
	April 14 /18		Routine.	B

Army Form C. 2118.

WAR DIARY
or
INTELLIGENCE SUMMARY.
(Erase heading not required.)

Instructions regarding War Diaries and Intelligence Summaries are contained in F. S. Regs., Part II. and the Staff Manual respectively. Title pages will be prepared in manuscript.

Place	Date	Hour	Summary of Events and Information	Remarks and references to Appendices
OUVE-WIRQUIN & HAZEBROUCK 5.A.	April 15 1918	10.0 am	Departed OUVE-WIRQUIN and marched to Standing Camp at LA LACQUE arriving at 5.30 p.m. LA LACQUE is a large Light Railway Construction Plant which has been abandoned since the 12th inst. on account of the proximity of the enemy.	
LA LACQUE (nr AIRE) & HAZEBROUCK 5.A.	April 16 1918		One Portuguese Brigade has been attached to the 16th (Irish) Division and this Unit has been detailed as its Field Ambulance. Organization of Evacuation, Sanitation etc. Have got in touch with Medical Officers of the Portuguese Brigade and informed them of our methods.	

Army Form C. 2118.

WAR DIARY
or
INTELLIGENCE SUMMARY.
(Erase heading not required.)

Place	Date	Hour	Summary of Events and Information	Remarks and references to Appendices
LA LACQUES 2. 5A	April 16 1918 (cont)		Capt. G. WATKINS. D.S.O. M.C. appointed Sanitary Officer to the Camp. 1st Portugese Brigade received orders to move to ISBERGUE	
		4.0 p.m.	Marched off	
		4.30 p.m.	Arrived at ISBERGUE and went into billets in school after a trying Station	
ISBERGUE	April 17 1918		Interviewed S.M.O. 1st Portugese Brigade – He wishes all his men to have a bath and change of clothes. route Intte to 9.30 a.m. S. 16th Battalion on the Subject	

Army Form C. 2118.

WAR DIARY
or
INTELLIGENCE SUMMARY.

(Erase heading not required.)

Place	Date	Hour	Summary of Events and Information	Remarks and references to Appendices
ISBERGUE	April 18 1918		Resting. Lieut J.H. WILSON, M.O.R.C. U.S.A. evacuated to No 39 Stationary Hospital	
	April 19 1918		Some hostile shelling in the vicinity. Capt. H.O.O. WHEELER and 2nd Lieut J.B. GREGG, M.O. R.C. U.S.A. reported the Unit. Sent hostile shelling in the vicinity. E.A. dropped several bombs in the neighbourhood during the night.	
	April 20 1918		Capt. GIBBINS posted to 1/2nd R Welch Fusiliers. Capt W.J. LAUGHREY reported to the Unit for duty.	

Army Form C. 2118.

WAR DIARY
or
INTELLIGENCE SUMMARY.

(Erase heading not required.)

Instructions regarding War Diaries and Intelligence Summaries are contained in F. S. Regs., Part II. and the Staff Manual respectively. Title pages will be prepared in manuscript.

Place	Date	Hour	Summary of Events and Information	Remarks and references to Appendices
ISBERGUE	April 21 1918		Hostile shelling of village, with some high velocity gun of large calibre	B
	April 22 1918		Hostile shelling of village with some guns of about 4.20"	B
			E.A. struck down two rounds	
	April 23 1918		Nothing to report	B
	April 24 1918		E.A. dropped bombs in vicinity last night. Scheme of Training started to-day.	Appx I

Army Form C. 2118.

WAR DIARY
or
INTELLIGENCE SUMMARY.
(Erase heading not required.)

Place	Date	Hour	Summary of Events and Information	Remarks and references to Appendices
ISBF RGHE	April 25 1918		Venture. A few shells in village in evening. Training	
Sh 36.a H30.c.2.3	April 26 1918		The Unit moved to a field about Sh 36.a H.30.c.2.3 and opened a Evacuating Station about half a mile from AIRE. Men and officers billeted in AIRE.	
	April 27 1918		Arrangements made to get all the men bathed in AIRE. Training	

Army Form C. 2118.

WAR DIARY
or
INTELLIGENCE SUMMARY.
(Erase heading not required.)

Instructions regarding War Diaries and Intelligence Summaries are contained in F. S. Regs., Part II. and the Staff Manual respectively. Title pages will be prepared in manuscript.

Place	Date	Hour	Summary of Events and Information	Remarks and references to Appendices
Sh 36 A H.30.c.2.3.	April 28 1918.		Collecting sds from Brigade Group. Training.	Q
	April 29 1918		The following N.C.O.'s and men of this Unit received the Military Medal for gallantry and devotion to duty in action. No 50454 Pte. S. HUNTER " 252995 Sgt. W.T. TAYLOR " (4296 Pte. W. DENNING " 126 " J.G. DAWSON " 74277 " T. MILLINGTON " 100719 Cpl. P.G. MORRIS (since wounded) " 64209 Pte. F.M. KELLY	B

Army Form C. 2118.

WAR DIARY
or
INTELLIGENCE SUMMARY.
(Erase heading not required.)

Instructions regarding War Diaries and Intelligence Summaries are contained in F. S. Regs., Part II. and the Staff Manual respectively. Title pages will be prepared in manuscript.

Place	Date	Hour	Summary of Events and Information	Remarks and references to Appendices
Sh. 36A H.30.c.2.3	April 29 1918 (cont)		No 70926 Pte C.A. CONDON.	B
	April 30 1918		Collecting Fd. Training	B
				Mj E Bell Lieut Col. Raine OC. 111th Fd Amb

APPENDIX I

111 Ft Amb. w/e Tuesday 30 April 1916

TRAINING PROGRAMME

TIME	WEDNESDAY	THURSDAY	FRIDAY	SATURDAY	SUNDAY	MONDAY	TUESDAY
6.30 7 AM	Squad drill	Squad drill		Squad drill		Squad drill	Squad drill
9 am to 10 am	Physical drill	Physical drill		Physical drill		Rally Round	Physical drill
10 am to 11 am	Lecture	Lecture Regimental history & discipline		Company drill		Rally Round	Lecture Organisation of Field Amb
11 am to 12 noon	Demonstration by Section Commanders	Demonstration by Section	N O V E D			Officers' mess Arrangement A.M.O.	Demonstration by Section Commanders
2 pm to 3 pm	Co's Parade Coy Drill	Co's Parade Coy Drill		Co's Parade Coy Drill		Co's Parade Coy Drill	Co's Parade Coy Drill
3 pm to 4 pm	Lectures (1) Throwing of Bombs & hand grenades (2) Army Forms W3118, W3119, W3120, AB416 (3) Shock (4) Water Cart (5) Minutes Improvised Raft (6) The United Wales Army	Lectures to Sections on				by Major Money Lt Colchester Capt Strecker Capt M Cribbin Lt Attley Lt Whyte	

30. 4. 18

H. Col Ramo
O.C. 111 Ft Amb

APPENDIX. I.

TRAINING PROGRAMME

111th Field Ambulance.   W/E Tuesday 30th April 1918

TIME	WEDNESDAY	THURSDAY	FRIDAY	SATURDAY	SUNDAY	MONDAY	TUESDAY
6.30 to 7 am	Squad drill	Squad drill		Squad drill		Squad drill	Squad drill
9. to 10 am	Physical drill	Physical drill		Physical drill		Bathing parade	Physical drill
10. to 11 am	Lecture	Lecture on reception of cases at C.C.S.		Company drill		Bathing parade	Lecture on evacuation by hay. stretcher-bearers
11.b to 12 noon	Demonstrations by Section Commanders	Demonstrations by Section Commanders		Demonstrations by Section Commanders		Officers and N.C.O.s class Squad drill	Demonstrations by Section Commanders
2. to 3 p.	C.O's parade Company drill	C.O's parade Coy. drill		C.O's parade Company drill		C.O's parade Company drill	C.O's parade Company drill
3. to 4 p.m.	Lectures & Lantern Lecture to stretcher bearers — Treatment in applications by hay. wounded. 1. Thomas splint — W3118, W3119A, W3210. A 36 staffey hay. movement. 2. Army Form 3. Attack 4. Water cart 5. (3) wounded Treatment at R.A.P.s 6. The United States Army			By Capt. D'Kerka By " Watson By " Bowley By 120 Gregg			

Lt.Col R.A.M.C.
O.C. 111 Fd Amb.

30/4/18

SECRET.

WAR DIARY.
111th Field Ambulance.

Vol. XXX.   MAY. 1918.

Army Form C. 2118.

WAR DIARY
or
INTELLIGENCE SUMMARY.
(Erase heading not required.)

Instructions regarding War Diaries and Intelligence Summaries are contained in F. S. Regs., Part II. and the Staff Manual respectively. Title pages will be prepared in manuscript.

Place	Date	Hour	Summary of Events and Information	Remarks and references to Appendices
Sh 86A. H30.c.4.5	1/May 1918		Capt. H.O.O. WHEELER and Capt. G.D WATKINS departed to report to the A.D.M.S. 4th Division. 1/Lieut. J.E GREGG, M.O.R.C.U.S.A departed to report to the A.D.M.S. 46th Division All map references unless otherwise stated are on Sheet 86A All officers unless otherwise stated belong to the R.A.M.C. Weather fair	
	2/May 1918		Locality warm & fair	

Army Form C. 2118.

WAR DIARY
or
INTELLIGENCE SUMMARY.
(Erase heading not required.)

Instructions regarding War Diaries and Intelligence Summaries are contained in F. S. Regs., Part II. and the Staff Manual respectively. Title pages will be prepared in manuscript.

Place	Date	Hour	Summary of Events and Information	Remarks and references to Appendices
Sh. 36A H.30.c.4.3.	3 May 1918		Weather warm. ISBERGUE Shelled. 1 wounded admitted	HQ
	4 May 1918		Training	
	5 May 1918		Weather cooler. Dull in morning, fair in afternoon. Training	HQ
			Weather wet. Thunder shower - warm Sunday	HQ
	6 May 1918		Training Weather + rain	HQ

Army Form C. 2118.

WAR DIARY
or
INTELLIGENCE SUMMARY.

(Erase heading not required.)

Place	Date	Hour	Summary of Events and Information	Remarks and references to Appendices
36A	7 May 1918		Weather wet.	
H.30.C.4.3.			D.D.M.S. XI Corps visited Camp at 2.10 p.m. Training	
	8 May 1918		Weather fair. E.A. dropped bombs on AIRE during night	
	9 May 1918		Fair. 2 N.C.O's and 24 men proceeded for temporary duty to No 52 Sanitary Section AIRE. 2 N.C.O's and 24 men proceeded for temporary duty to XIth Corps Rest Station LIGNEY. (G.17.9)	

Army Form C. 2118.

WAR DIARY
or
INTELLIGENCE SUMMARY.
(Erase heading not required.)

Place	Date	Hour	Summary of Events and Information	Remarks and references to Appendices
Sh 36A	10 May 1918		Weather. Cold. fair	B
H.30.c.4.3	11 May 1918		Weather fair to cloudy. 1 Officer (Major A. MASSER) and 18 O.R. R.A.M.C. with Transport of a Tent Sub-division proceeded to LES CISEAUX (I.2) to take over Dressing Station from 112th Field Ambulance.	B

Army Form C. 2118.

WAR DIARY
or
INTELLIGENCE SUMMARY.
(Erase heading not required.)

Instructions regarding War Diaries and Intelligence Summaries are contained in F. S. Regs., Part II. and the Staff Manual respectively. Title pages will be prepared in manuscript.

Place	Date	Hour	Summary of Events and Information	Remarks and references to Appendices
Sh 36cA H.30.c.4.3.	May 12 1918		Weather fair to cloudy. Cond.	
	May 13 1918		Visit by A.D.M.S. 16th Div? Weather Cold + dull to fair A.A. activity (E.A.) 12 midnight to 2.30 a.m.	
	May 14 1918		E.A. activity 10 – 12 midnight fair	
	May 15 1918		E.A. activity during night fair	

Place	Date	Hour	Summary of Events and Information	Remarks and references to Appendices
Sh. 36 A. H·30·C·4·3.	May 16 1918		Advanced party from 42nd Fd Amb, 14th Division who relieve us to-morrow.	
			E.A. bombed AIRE heavily during the night. About 75 bombs dropped. Two about 40 yards from the men's billet. Much damage done to property but few casualties.	
	May 17 1918		Handed over to 43rd Fd Ambulance and moved to billets in VPEN D'AVAL (Commune of PELETTES) (HAZEBROUCK. 5 A. Square C.5.)	

WAR DIARY
or
INTELLIGENCE SUMMARY.

Army Form C. 2118.

Place	Date	Hour	Summary of Events and Information	Remarks and references to Appendices
OPEN NAVAL Quay (St. Hare- BROUCK 5A) Spur C.5 (Cat)	17/9/18		Major A. MASSEY rejoined the Unit with detachment from LES CISEAUX	
	Aug 18/ 1918		Fain & very hot. The Unit marched to billets in WIERRE AU BOIS (Ft. CALAIS 13.)	
(Ft. CALAIS 13.)			1 N.C.O. and 6 men detached to form small Guard station at American Concentration Camp SAMER.	

Army Form C. 2118.

WAR DIARY
or
INTELLIGENCE SUMMARY.

(Erase heading not required.)

Instructions regarding War Diaries and Intelligence Summaries are contained in F. S. Regs., Part II. and the Staff Manual respectively. Title pages will be prepared in manuscript.

Place	Date	Hour	Summary of Events and Information	Remarks and references to Appendices
(Sh.CALAIS.13)				
VIERRE AU BOIS	19 May 1918		Structure in busy list. Tents at present consist of a hum Draway Station with Camp in the Chateau grounds at	
			WIERRE AU BOIS.	
			A Small Dressing Station at the Ammunition Camp near the Station SANGER with a personnel of 1 Sergt. and 6 men.	
			A Sanitary Squad of 1 Corpl and 6 men at the same place.	
			Gen Anton Ambulance collect from the 4th American Division STF ≠ in billets	

WAR DIARY
or
INTELLIGENCE SUMMARY.

Army Form C. 2118.

Place	Date	Hour	Summary of Events and Information	Remarks and references to Appendices
(CALAIS) (SL 13)	May 19 1918 (cont)		in the DESVRES, SAMER, and DOUDEAUVILLE areas	B
WIERRE AU BOIS	May 20 1918		fair & warm	B
	May 21 1918		fair + warm	B
	May 22 1918		fair + warm 24 men reported from the 52nd Sanitary Section. St. Sgt. VINCENT and Pte CLINCH renamed temporarily attached to Sanitary Section	B

Army Form C. 2118.

WAR DIARY
or
INTELLIGENCE SUMMARY.

(Erase heading not required.)

Instructions regarding War Diaries and Intelligence Summaries are contained in F. S. Regs., Part II. and the Staff Manual respectively. Title pages will be prepared in manuscript.

Place	Date	Hour	Summary of Events and Information	Remarks and references to Appendices
(CALAIS) (Sh.13.)	1 May/23		Full Orders	
	/18		Rain	
VIERRE AU BOIS	1 Jun/4		fair	
	2/4		Lecture to American Medical Officers on the	
	3/4		late "Cut" by Major A MASSEY	
	May/25			
	1/4			
	Jun/26		Fine – Sunshine	
	2/4			
	7/8			

Army Form C. 2118.

WAR DIARY
or
INTELLIGENCE SUMMARY.
(Erase heading not required.)

Place	Date	Hour	Summary of Events and Information	Remarks and references to Appendices
VIERRE AU BOIS (CALAIS) (Sh. 13)	May 29/18		Dull. Later.	
	May 30/18		Fair. Sunshine. E.A. dropped three bombs about a kilometre away. E.A. very active round area.	R2 / R
	May 31/18		Fair. Sunshine. E.A. very active round area. Hostile photographed our area by 4 planes. 16th Division took over Bell Advd. lef. Rouen	

160/3076.

7

Juneade.

SECRET.

ORIGINAL WAR DIARY.

111th FIELD AMBULANCE

VOLUME XXXI. JUNE 1918.

Army Form C. 2118.

WAR DIARY
or
INTELLIGENCE SUMMARY.
(Erase heading not required.)

WO 31

Place	Date	Hour	Summary of Events and Information	Remarks and references to Appendices
WIERRE AU BOIS	June 1		All map references on Sheet CALAIS 13 except where otherwise mentioned.	
	2			
Yh/CALAIS 13	3		All Officers in the R.A.M.C. except where otherwise mentioned.	
	15/18		Weather fair	
June D.5.				
	June 4		27 N.C.O's and men of the 112th Field Ambulance attached temporarily to the unit were sent to the R.Q.M.C. Base Depot to-day	
	15/18			
	June 5			
	6		Weather fine + dry	
	15/18			

Place	Date	Hour	Summary of Events and Information	Remarks and references to Appendices
VIERRE AU BOIS	June 6 1918		CAPT: W.J. MACDONALD of this Unit awarded the Military Cross (London Gazette)	B
CALAIS Sh. 13.	June 7 1918		Fine. Visit by Major-General A.B. RITCHIE. C.M.G. Commanding 16th (Irish) Division	B
	June 8 1918		Fine	B
	June 9 1918		Rain to fair	B

Army Form C. 2118.

WAR DIARY
or
INTELLIGENCE SUMMARY.
(Erase heading not required.)

Place	Date	Hour	Summary of Events and Information	Remarks and references to Appendices
VIERRE AU BOIS	June 10 1918		Rain to fair Visit by A.D.M.S. 16th (Irish) Division	By
CALAIS Sh.13.	June 11 1918		fair	By
	June 12 13 1918			
	June 14 1918		fair	By
	June 15 1918		fair. 20 Other ranks of this Unit are in hospital with the recent	By

WAR DIARY or INTELLIGENCE SUMMARY

Army Form C. 2118.

Place	Date	Hour	Summary of Events and Information	Remarks and references to Appendices
WIERRE AU BOIS	June 15 1918		disease known (indistinct) as "Spanish Influenza"	B
CALAIS Sh. 13.	(cont) June 16 1918		Fair. Epidemic of Spanish Influenza still continues	B
	June 17 1918		Rain to fair. 16th (Irish) Division Head Quarters moved to ENGLAND to-day. This Unit is now attached for administration to the 34th Division in which area coming in the area	B

Army Form C. 2118.

WAR DIARY
or
INTELLIGENCE SUMMARY.
(Erase heading not required.)

Instructions regarding War Diaries and Intelligence Summaries are contained in F. S. Regs., Part II. and the Staff Manual respectively. Title pages will be prepared in manuscript.

Place	Date	Hour	Summary of Events and Information	Remarks and references to Appendices
WIERRE AU BOIS	Mar 19/1/18		Showing	B
CALAIS Pl. 13	June 20/4/18		Stormy Major W J MacDonald arrived no leave	B
	June 21/4/18 22 23/7/18		Cool, fair. Since arrived.	B

(A7094) Wt. W12639/M1293 75000. 1/17. D. D. & L., Ltd. Forms/C.2118/14.

WAR DIARY

INTELLIGENCE SUMMARY

Army Form C. 2118.

Place	Date	Hour	Summary of Events and Information	Remarks and references to Appendices
WIERRE AU BOIS	June 24/7/18		Wind. Cloudy Cold	
CALAIS Sh. 13.	June 25/7/18		Fine	
			Number of cases of Three Days fever or Spanish Influenza as still coming in. Lieut LYONS, M.O. R.E. is of the opinion that its absence is increasing in severity	R2
	June 26/7/18		Fine. Cool	R2

WAR DIARY
INTELLIGENCE SUMMARY

Army Form C. 2118.

Place	Date	Hour	Summary of Events and Information	Remarks and references to Appendices
VIERRE AU BOIS	April 1/5/18		Fair	
CALAIS St 13	April 2/5/18		Reinforcements A.S.C. M.T. 2 Privates A.S.C. H.T. 1 Driver	
			better tea	
			E.A. dropped 3 bombs in vicinity between Hangard	
			11.0 P.m.	
	April 3/5/18		Fair E.A. dropped bombs in the vicinity between 11 and 12 P.m.	W.J. Bell Lieut Col Comdg

140/3131.

Army Form C. 2118.

WAR DIARY
or
INTELLIGENCE SUMMARY.

(Erase heading not required.)

111 Inf Amm SR 32

Instructions regarding War Diaries and Intelligence Summaries are contained in F. S. Regs., Part II. and the Staff Manual respectively. Title pages will be prepared in manuscript.

Place	Date	Hour	Summary of Events and Information	Remarks and references to Appendices
WIERRE AU BOIS	July 1 1918	7 am	Air raid on BOULOGNE and district last night	
ST. CALAIS B.	July 2 1918	1 pm		
	July 3 1918		Movement order received at 11.30 pm. Started loading	
	July 4 1918		Movement orders and Amm. train received from 117th Inf Bde. Transport fully loaded moved off at 12 noon	

Army Form C. 2118.

WAR DIARY
or
INTELLIGENCE SUMMARY.
(Erase heading not required.)

Instructions regarding War Diaries and Intelligence Summaries are contained in F. S. Regs., Part II. and the Staff Manual respectively. Title pages will be prepared in manuscript.

Place	Date	Hour	Summary of Events and Information	Remarks and references to Appendices
WIERRE AU BOIS	July 4 1918 (contd)		Detrained ST MICHEL area, Ma MONT EAVE and ALETTE wd m St CALAIS 13. To follow 318th Inf Regt from A.E.F.	
St CALAIS 13	July 5 /18		Transport moved from ST MICHEL area to rail L Rest	
		LENS 11	Personnel entrained at DESVRES (Phot CALAIS 13.). They the 36th Div A.E.F. to the Front, having been accompany the	
BEAUVAL	July 6		Personnel detrained at DOULLENS at 11.30 am and marched to billets in BEAUVAL, relieving the 1/2 E. Lancs. Terr 9th Aust.	
LENS 11	1918		Transport arrived at 11.30 pm	

Army Form C. 2118.

WAR DIARY
or
INTELLIGENCE SUMMARY.
(Erase heading not required.)

Instructions regarding War Diaries and Intelligence Summaries are contained in F. S. Regs., Part II. and the Staff Manual respectively. Title pages will be prepared in manuscript.

Place	Date	Hour	Summary of Events and Information	Remarks and references to Appendices
BEAUVAL.	July 7 1/18		Major W.J. MACDONALD M.C. returned from leave & 1/2 E. LANCS. TERR: F.d Amb. deputed on leave & relieved by this unit this a/noon.	
St. LENS.II	July 8 1/18		Three Motor Ambulances collecting from 3rd and 80th Fd. Amb. A.E.F. in DOULLENS, BONNEVILLE and BEAUVAL areas. Drill. Classes.	
	July 9 1/18		Arrangement made ref: return with Col. Snyper So it for A.E.F. under him.	

Army Form C. 2118.

WAR DIARY
or
INTELLIGENCE SUMMARY.
(Erase heading not required.)

Instructions regarding War Diaries and Intelligence Summaries are contained in F. S. Regs., Part II. and the Staff Manual respectively. Title pages will be prepared in manuscript.

Place	Date	Hour	Summary of Events and Information	Remarks and references to Appendices
BEAUVAL.	July 10 1918		Gen Holmet Parade. (weather bad)	
Ph. LENS.	July 11 1918		Coth. wind sunshine	B
	July 12 1918		Routine Han	B
	July 12 1918		Routine tra	B
	July 13 1918		E.A. dropped bombs in vicinity last night Major A. MASSIE went on leave. Revd 14th to 28th inst	B

Army Form C. 2118.

WAR DIARY
or
INTELLIGENCE SUMMARY.

(Erase heading not required.)

Instructions regarding War Diaries and Intelligence Summaries are contained in F. S. Regs., Part II. and the Staff Manual respectively. Title pages will be prepared in manuscript.

Place	Date	Hour	Summary of Events and Information	Remarks and references to Appendices
BEAUVAL Sh. LENS. 1	July 14 1918		E.A. active last night prior to rain	D
	July 15 1918		Warm + close	E
	July 16 1918		Violent thunderstorm last night Warm Close	B
	July 17 1918		E.A. dropped bombs on BEAUVAL about 8.0. 9. 4 civilians reported killed	B

WAR DIARY or INTELLIGENCE SUMMARY

Army Form C. 2118.

Place	Date	Hour	Summary of Events and Information	Remarks and references to Appendices
BEAUVAL	July 17 1918 (cont)		Violent hail-storm abt 8.30 p.m. Hail stones as big as walnuts. Lasted abt a quarter an hour.	
Ph. LENS 11	July 18 1918		E.A. activity in neighbourhood at night.	B.
	July 19 1918		ditto.	B.
	July 20 1918		Cloudy.	C.

Army Form C. 2118.

WAR DIARY
or
INTELLIGENCE SUMMARY.
(Erase heading not required.)

Instructions regarding War Diaries and Intelligence Summaries are contained in F. S. Regs., Part II. and the Staff Manual respectively. Title pages will be prepared in manuscript.

Place	Date	Hour	Summary of Events and Information	Remarks and references to Appendices
BEAUVAL	July 21 1918		Cloudy	B
Pt. LENS	July 22 1918		Rain. No cases remaining in Hospital to-day	B
"	July 23 1918		Dull - hot	B
"	July 24 1918		Very hot	B

Army Form C. 2118.

WAR DIARY
or
INTELLIGENCE SUMMARY.

(Erase heading not required.)

Place	Date	Hour	Summary of Events and Information	Remarks and references to Appendices
BEAUVAL	July 25 1918		Cloudy, heavy showers	
Sh LENS	July 26 1918		Hot Dull. Visit by D.D.M.S. IV Corps (Col. SIBBARD) 1/Lt LYONS, M.O. R.C. departed to U.K. on leave	
"	July 27 1918		Wet	
	July 28 1918		Wet and cloudy	
	July 29 1918		Wet. MAJOR A MASSEY R.A.M.C. returned from leave	
	July 30 1/7/18		Fine & Warm. O/C. No. 17 Sanitary Train (Canadian) paid us a visit to-day	

Aug. 1918.

WAR DIARY 9

140/3200.

VOLUME XXXIII

AUGUST 1918

111th Field Ambulance

Original Copy.

Army Form C. 2118.

WAR DIARY
or
INTELLIGENCE SUMMARY.

(Erase heading not required.)

111 3rd Army JSL 33

Place	Date	Hour	Summary of Events and Information	Remarks and references to Appendices
BEAUVAL St. LENS	1/Aug/1918		Fair & warm. Arranged Programme of Duty and Instruction for 320 Field Hospital and 320 Ambulance Company	R
	2/Aug/1918		Rain. Instruction in Field Medical Equipment to Ambulance Coys.	R
	3/Aug/1918		Capt W.G. HARKER. A.M.C. appointed Sanitary Officer. Rain. Instruction in Sectional Equipment to Ambulance	R
	4/Aug/1918		Cloudy and hot	R

(A7092). Wt. W12839/M1293. 75,000. 1/17. D. D. & L., Ltd. Forms/C.2118/14.

Army Form C. 2118.

WAR DIARY
or
INTELLIGENCE SUMMARY.
(Erase heading not required.)

Instructions regarding War Diaries and Intelligence Summaries are contained in F. S. Regs., Part II. and the Staff Manual respectively. Title pages will be prepared in manuscript.

Place	Date	Hour	Summary of Events and Information	Remarks and references to Appendices
BEAUVAL Ⅱ. LEN. Ⅱ.	Aug 5 / 1918		Very hot. Instruction to Americans in (1) Thomas's Splint (2) Sectional Equipment	
	Aug 6 / 1918		Cloudy and dull. Fine at night. Instruction to Americans in (1) Thomas Splint (2) Sectional Equipment (3) Packing of Wagons.	
	Aug 7 / 1918		Dull. Instruction to US Troops in Packing of transport 1. Thomas' Splint 2.	

Army Form C. 2118.

WAR DIARY
or
INTELLIGENCE SUMMARY.
(Erase heading not required.)

Instructions regarding War Diaries and Intelligence Summaries are contained in F. S. Regs., Part II. and the Staff Manual respectively. Title pages will be prepared in manuscript.

Place	Date	Hour	Summary of Events and Information	Remarks and references to Appendices
BEAUVAL	Aug 8/1918		Fair to Cloudy. Continued Route March in morning of U.S. and British Troops.	
St. LENS	Aug 9/1918		Fair	B
"	Aug 10/1918		Fair and warm. Considerable E.A. activity at night. Kept troops (aerial torpedo) dropped about 10 yards from one of our billets. No casualties. Same E of enemy planes was subsequently brought down by M.G. fire from our aircraft.	B

Army Form C. 2118.

WAR DIARY
or
INTELLIGENCE SUMMARY.
(Erase heading not required.)

Instructions regarding War Diaries and Intelligence Summaries are contained in F. S. Regs., Part II and the Staff Manual respectively. Title pages will be prepared in manuscript.

Place	Date	Hour	Summary of Events and Information	Remarks and references to Appendices
BEAUVAL	Aug 11/1918		E.A. activity. Several took dropped in the neighbourhood.	
St. LENS	Aug 12/9/18		Following Officers joined the Unit for Duty	
			1/Lieut D.J. HAWK M.O.R.C.U.S.A	
			1/Lieut S. HOPPER — do —	
			Fair + warm	
	Aug 13/14/918		Fair + warm	

Army Form C. 2118.

WAR DIARY
or
INTELLIGENCE SUMMARY.

(Erase heading not required.)

Instructions regarding War Diaries and Intelligence Summaries are contained in F. S. Regs., Part II. and the Staff Manual respectively. Title pages will be prepared in manuscript.

Place	Date	Hour	Summary of Events and Information	Remarks and references to Appendices
BEAUVAL Pt LENS II.	Aug 15 / 918		E.A. activity in neighbourhood at night.	B
	Aug 16 / 918		Fair	B
	Aug 17 / 918		Cloudy	B
	Aug 19 / 918		Rain	B

Army Form C. 2118.

WAR DIARY
or
INTELLIGENCE SUMMARY.
(Erase heading not required.)

Instructions regarding War Diaries and Intelligence Summaries are contained in F. S. Regs., Part II and the Staff Manual respectively. Title pages will be prepared in manuscript.

Place	Date	Hour	Summary of Events and Information	Remarks and references to Appendices
BEAUVAL	Aug 20/1918		80th Divnl A.E.F marched to BERNAVILLE entrain	B
Ph. LENS II.			Fair. Misty at night	
	Aug 21/1918		Four large and one small Motor Ambulance to report to D.D.M.S. IV Corps for use in forthcoming attack. Awaiting orders to move. Fair + warm	B
	Aug 22/1918		Fair + warm E.A activity during night	B

Army Form C. 2118.

WAR DIARY
or
INTELLIGENCE SUMMARY.
(Erase heading not required.)

Instructions regarding War Diaries and Intelligence Summaries are contained in F. S. Regs., Part II. and the Staff Manual respectively. Title pages will be prepared in manuscript.

Place	Date	Hour	Summary of Events and Information	Remarks and references to Appendices
BEAUVAL.	Aug 23 1918		Major A MASSEY, 1/Lieut L PONS M.R.C, 1/Lieut HAWK M.R.C and	
(R. LENS II.)			1/Lieut HORNER M.R.C proceeded to IV Corps Rest Station	
			MONT RENAULT FARM (R. LENS II. C.5. N°East 9° North)	B
			with 45 Other Ranks (C Section)	
	Aug 24 1918		Arrived IV Corps Rest Station.	B
MONT RENAULT FARM (R. LENS II.)	Aug 25 1918		Head Quarters of Unit moved to IV Corps Rest Station MONT RENAULT FARM.	B

Army Form C. 2118.

WAR DIARY
or
INTELLIGENCE SUMMARY.
(Erase heading not required.)

Instructions regarding War Diaries and Intelligence Summaries are contained in F. S. Regs., Part II. and the Staff Manual respectively. Title pages will be prepared in manuscript.

Place	Date	Hour	Summary of Events and Information	Remarks and references to Appendices
MONT PIGNAULT FARM. (Pt. LENS 11)	Aug 7/1918		1 Officer and 20 Other Ranks from No. 2. N.Z. Field Ambulance New Zealand Division arrived to take over.	AB
	Aug 20/1918		Orders arrived to entrain to reinen at DOULLENS. (St. LENS.11)	
	Aug 21/1918		The Field Ambulance (less Motor Transport) proceeded to DOULLENS arriving at 5.45 p.m. Motor Transport proceeded by road to BARLIN. (Sh. 44B. K.33. a.8.d.) Remainder billeted for the night in the CITADEL, DOULLENS.	AB

Army Form C. 2118.

WAR DIARY
or
INTELLIGENCE SUMMARY.
(Erase heading not required.)

Place	Date	Hour	Summary of Events and Information	Remarks and references to Appendices
DOULLENS (nr LENS II)	Aug 29 1918		Field Ambulance entrained at F.O. A.P.	
BARLIN Sh. 44B K.33.a.8.8.	Aug 30 1918		Arrived BARLIN (Sh. 44B. K.33.a.8.8.) at 6.30 p.m. 1/Lieut C.G. LYONS M.R.C. reported to 18th Scottish Rifles for Temporary Duty. 1/Lieut S. HOPPER M.R.C. reported to 6th Div. Reception Camp for Temporary Duty. 1 N.C.O. (Sgt) and 18 men reported to No. 22 C.C.S. PERNES (Sh. 44B H.10.d.10.8.) for temporary duty	

Army Form C. 2118.

WAR DIARY
or
INTELLIGENCE SUMMARY.
(Erase heading not required.)

Instructions regarding War Diaries and Intelligence Summaries are contained in F. S. Regs., Part II and the Staff Manual respectively. Title pages will be prepared in manuscript.

Place	Date	Hour	Summary of Events and Information	Remarks and references to Appendices
BARLIN Sh.44,B K.33.a.8.3	Aug 31 1918		1/Lieut D.G. HAWK. M.R.C. U.S.A. proceeded to report to A.D.M.S. 11th Div for duty together with 1 N.C.O and 4 men	

W.T. Bell
Lieut Col R.A.M.C.
O.C. 111th Fd Amb.

16

111th Field Ambulance.

WAR DIARY. VOL. XXXIV

"Original" COPY.

COMMITTEE FOR THE
MEDICAL HISTORY OF THE WAR
Date   9 NOV. 1918

Army Form C. 2118.

WAR DIARY
or
INTELLIGENCE SUMMARY.
(Erase heading not required.)

Vol 34

Place	Date	Hour	Summary of Events and Information	Remarks and references to Appendices
BARLIN. Sh. 44.B K.33.d.8.3	Sept 1 1918		All map references on Sh. 44B unless otherwise mentioned. All Officers in the H.Q.M.C. unless otherwise mentioned. E.A activity in neighbourhood during the night.	
	Sept 2 1918		1/Lt C. J. LYONS. 110465. U.S.A. posted to 1st Scottish Rifles and struck off the strength from 30/8/18. Capt J. C. REID (S.R.) and Capt. S. W. TWIGG (T.C.) posted to the Unit and taken on the strength from the 30/8/18. Battery comrades round the Hospital Hut 10th shade	B B

Army Form C. 2118.

WAR DIARY
or
INTELLIGENCE SUMMARY.
(Erase heading not required.)

Place	Date	Hour	Summary of Events and Information	Remarks and references to Appendices
BARLIN K.3.a.8.3	Sept 3 4 5 1918		Routine weather fair to intermittently cloudy. Inclined to Thunder	B
	Sept 6 1918		last night there was hostile gas shelling in HOUCHIN a village 2 kilometres from here. In consequence the Fd. Amb. is has been placed under "Ready Zone" Restrictions	B
	Sept 7 1918		Routine	B

Army Form C. 2118.

WAR DIARY
or
INTELLIGENCE SUMMARY.
(Erase heading not required.)

Place	Date	Hour	Summary of Events and Information	Remarks and references to Appendices
BARLIN R.33.a.8.3	Sept 8/18		14 Officers arrived as reinforcements	2
	Sept 9/18		Routine	2
	Sept 10/18		112th and 113th Fd Ambulances moved without BARLIN. This Unit took over duties of Main Dressing Station for Sick of the Division. Unit by A.D.M.S. 16th Division.	2
	Sept 11/18		2 Officers temporarily attached for Duty. Capt. G. WAGNER. Capt. W.S. DOUGHERTY. M.O.R.C. U.S.A.	2

Army Form C. 2118.

WAR DIARY
or
INTELLIGENCE SUMMARY.
(Erase heading not required.)

Instructions regarding War Diaries and Intelligence Summaries are contained in F. S. Regs., Part II. and the Staff Manual respectively. Title pages will be prepared in manuscript.

Place	Date	Hour	Summary of Events and Information	Remarks and references to Appendices
R 23.a 6.3	Sept 11		Bath from 112th Field Ambulance	D
	12th (out)			
	Sept 12		Cold + rain	
	13		Visit by A.D.M.S. 16th Division	B
	13th			
	Sept 14		Officers and Discharged to Convoy Station	B
	14th			
	Sept 15		Only Sick admitted	
	15th		Gassed and wounded sent to C.C.S. Passed through	
	Sept 16 18th		[illegible] No 9 Ft Amb by Gast for that [illegible] who	

Army Form C. 2118.

WAR DIARY
or
INTELLIGENCE SUMMARY.
(Erase heading not required.)

Instructions regarding War Diaries and Intelligence Summaries are contained in F. S. Regs., Part II. and the Staff Manual respectively. Title pages will be prepared in manuscript.

Place	Date	Hour	Summary of Events and Information	Remarks and references to Appendices
Rengards	Sept 15 (cont)		all returned at 6. G.S. for that purpose	
	15/18		Fair and warm. Wind South.	
	Sept 16		Fair and warm	
	16/18		E.A. activity very slight	
	Sept 17		Artillery thunder storm in early morning	
	17/18			
	Sept 18		Proceeded on short leave to PARIS. Handed over to Major A. MASSEY.	
	18/18			

Army Form C. 2118.

WAR DIARY
or
INTELLIGENCE SUMMARY.

(Erase heading not required.)

Place	Date	Hour	Summary of Events and Information	Remarks and references to Appendices
K.33.a.8.3.	Sept. 19 1918		ADMS 1/10th Division visited the hospital.	
	Sept. 19 1918		Windy & showery	
	Sept. 20 1918		Visited 2/1st Wessex Field Ambulance (53rd Division) at VAUDRICOURT (K.4. and 5.5. (Sheet 44 B.N.)). To examine site in case of taking over from them. Two N.C.O.s (1 Sergeant and one injured) & 6 men arrived as Reinforcements.	
	Sept. 21st 1918		Visited 1/1st Wessex Field Ambulance (53rd Division) at HESDIGNEUL (E.28.c.5.3. (Sheet 44 B.A.)) with a view to taking over if we went into that area.	
	Sept. 22 1918		Weather changeable with heavy showers.	
	Sept. 23 1918		10th Division moved to new area. O.O.28. - Not 4 ans.	
	Sept. 24 1918		Dull. 1 Reinforcement for A.S.C. (Dr FARR).	

Army Form C. 2118.

WAR DIARY
or
INTELLIGENCE SUMMARY.
(Erase heading not required.)

Instructions regarding War Diaries and Intelligence Summaries are contained in F. S. Regs., Part II. and the Staff Manual respectively. Title pages will be prepared in manuscript.

Place	Date	Hour	Summary of Events and Information	Remarks and references to Appendices
K.33.a.4.3.	Sept 25 1918		Dull with occasional showers.	=h
	Sept 26 1918		N.O. 36959 Q.M.S. A.C. HILL proceeded and reported to the Commandant IV Corps Reception Camp.	
			Hon. Captain & Q.M. J. LANDER R.A.M.C. proceeded on leave to U.K.	M
	Sept 27 1918		Lt. Colonel W.J.E. BELL D.S.O. R.A.M.C. returned from leave to PARIS.	
			Visit from O.C. 46th F.A. with Lt Senior who showed him round to take over from this Unit those to be completed by him soon to remove to —	
			Weather fair	
	Sept 28 1918		Weather Dull. Rain	B

Army Form C. 2118.

WAR DIARY
or
INTELLIGENCE SUMMARY.
(Erase heading not required.)

Instructions regarding War Diaries and Intelligence Summaries are contained in F. S. Regs., Part II. and the Staff Manual respectively. Title pages will be prepared in manuscript.

Place	Date	Hour	Summary of Events and Information	Remarks and references to Appendices
K.35.a.8.3	Sept 29/18		Movement order received from A.D.M.S. 16th Div.	
J.24.b.3.8	Sept 30/18		Field Ambulance moved to J.24.b.3.8 (HALLICOURT) arriving at 1120. A Small Aid Post opened adjacent to HUT for Scottish Medical evacuation to C.C.S. personal Capt. Q. WAGNER and 1/Lt W.J. DOUGHERTY M.O.R.C. U.S.A. to other hut. (116th F.A.A.B.) patients again	Major Bell Lieut Col Reynolds

WAR DIARY
or
INTELLIGENCE SUMMARY

Army Form C. 2118.

Place	Date	Hour	Summary of Events and Information	Remarks and references to Appendices
HAILLICOURT 12h 4.30	Oct 1 1918		All ranks informed as to 4th Bn 1st 90,000 Kept when otherwise stated.	
	Oct 2 1918		All Officers in the R.A.M.C. except when mentioned	
	Oct 3 1918		Capt. M.J. LOUGHREK joined the Unit for duty. Fun. Cttee. 1 Staff Sgt. joined the Unit from the Base for Duty.	
	Oct 4 1918		Routine	

WAR DIARY
or
INTELLIGENCE SUMMARY.

Army Form C. 2118.

Place	Date	Hour	Summary of Events and Information	Remarks and references to Appendices
HALLICOURT	Oct 5/1918		Visit from A.D.M.S. 16th Division who stated that he should be prepared to move to a site in LABOURSE in a few days. The enemy has retreated from LA BASSÉE and LENS followed closely by our troops. The 16th Division is now in the 1st Corps, 5th Army. Major A. MASSEY departed on a "Gas Course" to return on the 18th inst.	B

Army Form C. 2118.

WAR DIARY
or
INTELLIGENCE SUMMARY.
(Erase heading not required.)

Instructions regarding War Diaries and Intelligence Summaries are contained in F. S. Regs., Part II. and the Staff Manual respectively. Title pages will be prepared in manuscript.

Place	Date	Hour	Summary of Events and Information	Remarks and references to Appendices
CAILLICOURT T.24.b.38.	5/10/18		12 Other Ranks rejoined from No.6. C.C.S. N.C.O and 11 men proceeded to 16th Div. Salvage Officer for temporary employment (attchd note)	B
	6/10/18		Movement order received. Strength of unit N.C.O and 18 men proceeded to new site	
LA BOURSE L.2.q.6.	7/10/18		Moved to new site arriving at 11.45 a.m. Opened Hospital in school building at 6.0 p.m. Amb't by A.D.M.S.	B

Army Form C. 2118.

WAR DIARY
or
INTELLIGENCE SUMMARY.

(Erase heading not required.)

Place	Date	Hour	Summary of Events and Information	Remarks and references to Appendices
LABOURSE	Oct 10/18		Collecting Sd from Brigade in Support Line. Weather Dull	
Lie a 16	11/18		Routine. Weather colder	
	Oct 12/18		1 Reinforcement (O.R.)	
			Capt G. F. Hunter J.F. LANDER returned from leave	
	Oct 13 /18		Weather cold. Standing	
	Oct 14/18		1 Reinforcement (O.R.)	
	Oct 15/ 1918		Weather Dull	

Army Form C. 2118.

WAR DIARY
or
INTELLIGENCE SUMMARY.
(Erase heading not required.)

Instructions regarding War Diaries and Intelligence Summaries are contained in F. S. Regs., Part II. and the Staff Manual respectively. Title pages will be prepared in manuscript.

Place	Date	Hour	Summary of Events and Information	Remarks and references to Appendices
LABOURSE L.2.a.7.6.	Oct 16 1918		Routine Weather Dull	
	Oct 17 1918		Warning movement order received. Also order to evacuate and close the Dressing Station (A.D.M.S. 16th Div.)	B
	Oct 18 1918		Tent sub-Division moved to BERCLAU (Sheet 44a B.18.d.2.8.)	M
	Oct 19 1918		Personnel and transport moved to BERCLAU (Sheet 44a B.18.d.2.R.) arrived 14.00. Lt. COLONEL. W.J.E. BELL R.S.O.R.A.M.C. went on leave. MAJOR A. MASSEY R.A.M.C. taken over temporary command of the Unit.	M

Army Form C. 2118.

WAR DIARY
or
INTELLIGENCE SUMMARY.
(Erase heading not required.)

Instructions regarding War Diaries and Intelligence Summaries are contained in F. S. Regs., Part II. and the Staff Manual respectively. Title pages will be prepared in manuscript.

Place	Date	Hour	Summary of Events and Information	Remarks and references to Appendices
BERCLAU (Sheet 44a) D.21.C.2.1.	Oct. 20 1918		March from BERCLAU at 0800 o'clock to CAMPHIN. D.21.C.21 (Sheet 44a) arriving at Catophin 1120hr	JM
CAMPHIN D.21.Q.2.1.	Oct 21 1918		Left CAMPHIN at 0900hr and arrived at PONT A. MARCQ at 1230hr (Sheet 44a E.18.d.9.1.) 111 Field Ambulance front lorries receiving a great ovation from the liberated inhabitants.	JM
PONT A. MARCQ E.18.d.9.1.	Oct 22 1918		Ambulance to review at PONT A. MARCQ. The village found full of evacuated civilians from other areas. An epidemic of Influenza raging in the village. Hospital opened by unit for treating civilian cases. Also unit stores exercising civilians to CARVIN. The canteen gives rations from our stores also medical comforts.	JM
	Oct. 23 1918		A very large number of sick civilians could not receive immediate attention to their nebulous areas. Q.M.S. GREENWOOD RAMC joins the unit from this date.	JM

D. D. & L., London, E.C.
(A10260 Wt.W5300/P713 750,000 2/18 **Sch. 52** Forms/C2118/16.)

Army Form C. 2118.

WAR DIARY
or
INTELLIGENCE SUMMARY.
(Erase heading not required.)

Instructions regarding War Diaries and Intelligence Summaries are contained in F. S. Regs., Part II. and the Staff Manual respectively. Title pages will be prepared in manuscript.

Place	Date	Hour	Summary of Events and Information	Remarks and references to Appendices
PONTANAWEQ EISDDIA	Oct 24th 1918		Visit by the A.D.M.S in the morning & the afternoon. M.N. & GENERAL GERRARD. D.M.S (Mep.) visited the civilian and military hospitals of this unit.	M
			Lt. DOUGHERTY. M.O.R.C. U.S.A arrived for duty.	M
	Oct 25th 1918		D.D.M.S. 1 Corps payed a visit. The following personnel reported for duty to this unit from 13 C.C.S	
			Sister PRESTON. A.R.N.C. J.F.N.S	
			Sister GRANT. T.F.N.S	
			Nurse ALLISON. T.F.N.S	
			Sister TOHER. Q.A.I.M.N.S.R.	
	Oct 26th 1918		The A.D.M.S payed a visit in the afternoon.	M
	Oct 27th 1918		Weather fine ordinary routine	M

Army Form C. 2118.

WAR DIARY
or
INTELLIGENCE SUMMARY.
(Erase heading not required.)

Instructions regarding War Diaries and Intelligence Summaries are contained in F. S. Regs., Part II. and the Staff Manual respectively. Title pages will be prepared in manuscript.

Place	Date	Hour	Summary of Events and Information	Remarks and references to Appendices
PONT.A.MARCQ E15d.9.1.	Oct 28 1918		The P.D.M.S. 1st Corps paid a visit in the morning. Also A.D.M.S. 16th Division	J.M.
	Oct 29 1918		In the afternoon A.D.V.S. visited the unit and examined 2 H.D. Horses which were very ill. One died in the evening.	M.
	Oct 30 1918		Civilian died in hospital from Pneumonia (later) at 16.45. In. Watts from A.D.M.S. 16th Division visited hospital & inspected 6 dental cases. Weather fine. Sister MOHER. N.A.I.M.N.S. taken ill with Pneumonia (later)	M.
	Oct 31 1918		The D.D.M.S. 1st Corps visited the unit. The wasting Physician COLONEL MILLAR. R.A.M.C. 3rd Army visited Sister MOHER. Q.A.I.M.N.S.R & was satisfied with her condition.	J.M.

Allan Macey
Major R.A.M.C

16/3/01

M⁶ 7. a.

Jan 1918

Army Form C. 2118.

WAR DIARY
or
INTELLIGENCE SUMMARY.
(Erase heading not required.)

W.D. 36

Place	Date	Hour	Summary of Events and Information	Remarks and references to Appendices
PONT A MARCQ E.18.d.9.1.	Nov 1st 1918		The D.D.M.S. 1st Corps visited the unit. Also A.D.M.S. 16th Division. Weather fine.	M
	Nov 2 1918		The D.M.S. 5th Army visited the unit & called on Sister MAHER. Perfectly pleased with everything. S/Sgt. W.W. ROBERTS joined the unit on re-enforcement.	M
	Nov 3 1918		Visit from DAME M. McCARTHY (Matron-in-Chief of British Nurses in France) to see Sister MAHER. Colonel MILLAR visited Sister MAHER and was satisfied with her progress. Weather changeable. Visit from A.D.M.S. 16th Division.	M
	Nov 4 1918		Sister GRANT proceeds to 39 Stationary Hospital LILLE 1 fr duty. The A.D.M.S. 1st Div visited the unit. Lieut-Colonel W.J.E. BELL D.S.O. R.A.M.C. returned from leave.	M
	Nov 5 1918		Made inspection of Hospital. Urine line. Sanitary arrangements &c. S/Sgt-Bell A. Lt-Col. Young	

Army Form C. 2118.

WAR DIARY
or
INTELLIGENCE SUMMARY.
(Erase heading not required.)

Place	Date	Hour	Summary of Events and Information	Remarks and references to Appendices
PONT A MARCQ	Nov 6 1918		The Unit is still in the 16th Division, I Corps, V Army. Divisional Commander. Major-General A.B. RITCHIE. C.M.G. etc. Corps Commander. Lt. General Sir ARTHUR HOLLAND K.C.B. etc. Army Commander. General Sir W.R. BIRDWOOD K.C.B. etc. Education Scheme Classes started to-day. Class in French held by Pte CUSHEN 5 - 6. P.M. Copy of Syllabus attached	Appx 1

WAR DIARY or INTELLIGENCE SUMMARY.

Army Form C. 2118.

Place	Date	Hour	Summary of Events and Information	Remarks and references to Appendices
PONTÀ MARCO	Nov 7 1918		Lt Kent W.J DOUGHERTY. M.R.C. U.S.A to rejoin 112th Fd Amb for duty	B.
	Nov 8 1918		Staff Nurse TOHER and two Sistrs Q.A.I.M.N.S. returned to 29th Stationary Hospital LILLE. Staff Nurse TOHER as a patient. Asst by A.D.M.S.	B.
	Nov 9 1918		Asst by A.D.M.S. who gave us a verbal instruction that we should prepare to receive in B. Both Military and Civil trench thaafever cleared	

Army Form C. 2118.

WAR DIARY
or
INTELLIGENCE SUMMARY.
(Erase heading not required.)

Place	Date	Hour	Summary of Events and Information	Remarks and references to Appendices
RUMES (Sheet 5 TOURNAI)	Nov 10 1918		Moved from PONT à MARCQ at 21.40 a.m. in orders received from 8th Div.	
	Nov 11 1918		Arrived at RUMES at 6.15 p.m. and found Hospital to receive sick fitted with B. Armistice with Germans came into force at 11 a.m.	
	Nov 12 1918		Hospital now in working order to receive 40 sick	
	Nov 13 1918		Routine	

WAR DIARY
or
INTELLIGENCE SUMMARY.
(Erase heading not required.)

Army Form C. 2118.

Place	Date	Hour	Summary of Events and Information	Remarks and references to Appendices
ROMES Ph. S	Nov 14 /18		Rec'd warning order from A.D.M.S that we shall probably move soon and shall be [illegible]	
TOURNAI	Nov 15 /17/18		Animals [illegible] Orders came through the night to move this morning Moved off at H.30 a.m. arriving at HAUT FOR 8h 19A F.30 d and going into huts	
ARDERIE	Nov 16 /18		Moved off at 8.30 a.m arriving at LATTANT 44A K.21.a and going into Recently vacated hut. During Station [illegible] Arthur	

WAR DIARY
INTELLIGENCE SUMMARY
(Erase heading not required.)

Army Form C. 2118.

Place	Date	Hour	Summary of Events and Information	Remarks and references to Appendices
LA TAN- ANDERIE Sh 4LA K21.a	Nov 17 18 1918		Passing station taken over a Lazzarow standing our found which was freshly entrained last formed by the Germans as an officers hospital. Two enemy German RE to the No. not all and sundry had g the op 01 a bullet and driving from the no men (R) RA men + 1 other Great men and clean linen	
	Nov 17 1918		Visit by A.D.M.S.	

WAR DIARY
or
INTELLIGENCE SUMMARY.

(Erase heading not required.)

Army Form C. 2118.

Place	Date	Hour	Summary of Events and Information	Remarks and references to Appendices
LA TAN-	Nov		Visit of Major General Ritchie. G.O.C. 16th	
GO DENIS	20		Division.	
Sh 44A	1918			
Kreva	Nov			
	21		Visit by Brigadier General Clayton.	
	1918			
	Nov		Routine.	
	22			
	23			
	24			
	25			
	1918			

Army Form C. 2118.

WAR DIARY
or
INTELLIGENCE SUMMARY.
(Erase heading not required.)

Instructions regarding War Diaries and Intelligence Summaries are contained in F. S. Regs., Part II. and the Staff Manual respectively. Title pages will be prepared in manuscript.

Place	Date	Hour	Summary of Events and Information	Remarks and references to Appendices
LA TAN-	Nov			Appendix
AUDERIE	26		Classes started with revised syllabus	II
	1918			
Sh.49.A			The 7th Class having successfully passed	
			1st Army	
K.21.a	Nov			
	27			
	28		Routine	
	29			
	30			
	31			
	Dec		Asst to A.D.M.S	
	1/2		The 7th Class having now passed the 1st Army R...	
	1/12			

Appen I

Time Table of 111th Field Ambulance Classes
for November 1918

French	Mathematics	Music
Nov. 6	Nov. 8	Nov 7.
" 9	" 21	
" 11	" 23	
" 12	" 26	
" 13		
" 14		
" 18		
" 19		
" 20		
" 22		
" 25		

Classes in above subjects were held on following
dates from 5.0 pm till 6.0 pm

W Macdonald Capt
Major 111th Field Ambce
3/0 111th F.A.

Appendix II

General Arrangements of 111th Field Ambulance School

Commencing from Nov 25th 1918

Time A.M.	Monday	Tuesday	Wednesday	Thursday	Friday	Saturday	Remarks
10:30 till 11:30	Class I	Class I		Class I	Class I		Boot Dubbin + English
	II	II		II	II		
11:30 till 12:30	III	III		III	III		Shorthand Method English
	IV	IV		IV	IV		.25c — .30c
P.M.	Shorthand	French		Shorthand	French		Elementary Outline Bookkeeping
2:0 till 3:0	Agriculture *	Magnetism + Electricity *		Agriculture *	Magnetism + Electricity *		* Three Classes have not met
	Business Methods *	Bookkeeping		Business Methods *	Bookkeeping		
3:0 till 4:0	Mechanics *	Chem + Physics		Mechanics *	Chemistry + Physics		* Do

	Mathematics		Mathematics				
	Music		Music				

| Extra Subjects 5:0 till 6:0 | French | | French | | | | Class in Music Shorthand Still to be arranged |

W. J. MacDonald
Major
E.O.
111th Field Ambulance

Jas 111 Field Ambulance

WAR DIARY
or
INTELLIGENCE SUMMARY.

(Erase heading not required.)

Army Form C. 2118.

Instructions regarding War Diaries and Intelligence Summaries are contained in F. S. Regs., Part II. and the Staff Manual respectively. Title pages will be prepared in manuscript.

Place	Date	Hour	Summary of Events and Information	Remarks and references to Appendices
LA MANARDERIE Sheet 44a R.21.a.	Dec 3 1918		MAJOR A.M.MASSEY. R.A.M.C. departed on leave to U.K. MAJOR W. MACDONALD. R.A.M.C. assumed temporary command.	A.M.
	Dec 4 1918		CAPT. WHITE. R.A.M.C. 113th Field Ambulance reported for temporary duty. Visit from A/ADMS.	A.M.
	Dec 5 1918		Weather dull. Routine	A.M.
	Dec 6 1918		General Routine. Weather changeable.	A.M.
	Dec 7 1918		General Routine.	A.M.
	Dec 8 1918		General Routine.	A.M.
	Dec 9 1918		CAPT. WHITE. R.A.M.C. assumed temporary command of unit. MAJOR W. MACDONALD.D.M.C. departed on leave.	A.M.

Army Form C. 2118.

WAR DIARY
or
INTELLIGENCE SUMMARY.
(Erase heading not required.)

Instructions regarding War Diaries and Intelligence Summaries are contained in F.S. Regs., Part II. and the Staff Manual respectively. Title pages will be prepared in manuscript.

Place	Date	Hour	Summary of Events and Information	Remarks and references to Appendices
LA MANARDERIE Sheet 44 a M.21.a.	Dec 10 1918		General Routine.	a.m
	Dec 11 1918		1. W.O. and 18 men departed for I Corps Concentration camp TOURNAI.	a.m
	Dec 12 1918		General Routine.	a.m
	Dec 13 1918		Routine. 3 men departed Concentration Camp TOURNAI. MAJOR A. MR 88 EY returned from leave to Paris.	a.m
	Dec 14 1918		General Routine.	a.m
	Dec 15 1918		Routine.	a.m
	Dec 16 1918		Routine	a.m

Army Form C. 2118.

WAR DIARY
or
INTELLIGENCE SUMMARY.
(Erase heading not required.)

Instructions regarding War Diaries and Intelligence Summaries are contained in F. S. Regs., Part II. and the Staff Manual respectively. Title pages will be prepared in manuscript.

Place	Date	Hour	Summary of Events and Information	Remarks and references to Appendices
LATANARDERIE Sheet 44a K.21.a.	Dec 17 1918		Routine. Visit from A/ADMS. 10 men reported for Elborpe transportation Camp.	a.m.
	Dec 18 1918		Routine	a.m.
	Dec 19 1918		Routine. Visit from A/ADMS	a.m.
	Dec 20 1918		Routine. Wet Weather	a.m.
	Dec 21 1918		Routine. Water still bad.	a.m.
	Dec 22 1918		Routine.	a.m.
	Dec 23 1918		CAPT. WHITE departed for duty with 112th Field Ambulance	a.m.
	Dec 24 1918		Routine. Visit A ADMS.	a.m.

Army Form C. 2118.

WAR DIARY
or
INTELLIGENCE SUMMARY.
(Erase heading not required.)

Instructions regarding War Diaries and Intelligence Summaries are contained in F. S. Regs., Part II. and the Staff Manual respectively. Title pages will be prepared in manuscript.

Place	Date	Hour	Summary of Events and Information	Remarks and references to Appendices
LA TANROERIE Sheet 44a K.21.a.	Dec. 25 1918		Christmas Festivities with the units. Weather dull & wet.	a.m.
	Dec. 26 1918		Divisional staff clinical Meeting at AVELIN. MAJOR. MACDONALD'S took CHARGIE with a new	a.m.
	Dec. 27 1918		Lt. Colonel. W.J.E. BELL. returns to unit and relinquishes acting ADMS. of Division	a.m.
	Dec. 28 1918		MAJOR. W.J. MACDONALD.M.C. argued west for leave to United Kingdom	a.m.
	Dec. 29 1918		Routine	

Army Form C. 2118.

WAR DIARY
or
INTELLIGENCE SUMMARY.
(Erase heading not required.)

Place	Date	Hour	Summary of Events and Information	Remarks and references to Appendices
LA TAN – ARDERIE S.22 A.44 K.21.a	Dec 30 1918		Routine. B	
	Dec 31 1918		Routine. Work consists of collecting material from surrounding area. Hospital accommodates about 40. Lovely full. There has been holiday in the "Education" during Christmas week. A large number of German delayed mines went off to-day in the neighbourhood.	

J.E. Bell
Lieut./Col.
Laure

16 DIV
Box 1674

111th Field Ambulance

War Diary XXXVII

WAR DIARY
INTELLIGENCE SUMMARY

Army Form C. 2118

Place	Date	Hour	Summary of Events and Information	Remarks and references to Appendices
LA THAN- ARDEN St 44 R.21.a			A common place of German "booby traps" is a manure heap containing the mine or a "aim" gas. A mine of this type exploded recently near by.	
			Weather brighter to-day than it has been for some time but still cloudy.	B
			16th Division 1st Corps. 1st Army. Clear in morning, to cloudy + rain in evening, "Education" started again to-day.	

Army Form C. 2118.

WAR DIARY
or
INTELLIGENCE SUMMARY

(Erase heading not required.)

Instructions regarding War Diaries and Intelligence Summaries are contained in F. S. Regs., Part II. and the Staff Manual respectively. Title pages will be prepared in manuscript.

Place	Date	Hour	Summary of Events and Information	Remarks and references to Appendices
LA TANARDERIE SH 44^a K.21.a	Jan 3 1919		Routine. Weather cloudy & dull	R
	Jan 4 5 6 7 1919		Routine. Weather wet	B
	Jan 8 1919		Weather fair & sunny in morning. Visit by the A.D.M.S. Who inspected the Hospital.	B

Army Form C. 2118.

WAR DIARY
or
INTELLIGENCE SUMMARY.
(Erase heading not required.)

Instructions regarding War Diaries and Intelligence Summaries are contained in F. S. Regs., Part II. and the Staff Manual respectively. Title pages will be prepared in manuscript.

Place	Date	Hour	Summary of Events and Information	Remarks and references to Appendices
Lt TINTARD				
ERIE			hostive	B
R.44.a				
K.21.a				
			Proposed lecture on demobilisation	B
			Sunday	
			lecture to men on demobilisation	B
				B
			Nature	B

Army Form C. 2118.

WAR DIARY
or
INTELLIGENCE SUMMARY.
(Erase heading not required.)

Instructions regarding War Diaries and Intelligence Summaries are contained in F. S. Regs., Part II. and the Staff Manual respectively. Title pages will be prepared in manuscript.

Place	Date	Hour	Summary of Events and Information	Remarks and references to Appendices
LA TARGETTE	Jan 13/16		Six men demobilised	B
ERIE B.4.4.A	Jan 14/16		Ventures	B
K.21.c.	Jan 15/16		Major A. BASSET went on leave	B
	Jan 16/16		Major VERNON joined for temporary duty from the 113th Field Ambulance	B

Army Form C. 2118.

WAR DIARY
or
INTELLIGENCE SUMMARY.
(Erase heading not required.)

Instructions regarding War Diaries and Intelligence Summaries are contained in F.S. Regs., Part II. and the Staff Manual respectively. Title pages will be prepared in manuscript.

Place	Date	Hour	Summary of Events and Information	Remarks and references to Appendices
LA TOMBE-ENE A.44.a K.21.a	1/5/19		Routine	B
	4/5/19		Major VERNON proceeded to England on Special Leave	B
	2/5/19 3/5/19		Routine	B
	4/5/19			B
	5/5/19		17 Other Ranks demobilised	B

Army Form C. 2118.

WAR DIARY
or
INTELLIGENCE SUMMARY.
(Erase heading not required.)

Instructions regarding War Diaries and Intelligence Summaries are contained in F. S. Regs., Part II. and the Staff Manual respectively. Title pages will be prepared in manuscript.

Place	Date	Hour	Summary of Events and Information	Remarks and references to Appendices
MATMARDÈRE				
XA 44 A	2/1		C in hand	
X 21 a	3			
	4/15			
			Visit by D.D.M.S. 1st Corps.	
	1/1	24		
	1/15			
			Return. Snow + frost	
	1/5			
	2/15		Snow + frost	
	1/15		fine	
	1/5			
	1/15			
	1/1			

Army Form C. 2118.

WAR DIARY
or
INTELLIGENCE SUMMARY.
(Erase heading not required.)

Instructions regarding War Diaries and Intelligence Summaries are contained in F.S. Regs., Part II. and the Staff Manual respectively. Title pages will be prepared in manuscript.

Place	Date	Hour	Summary of Events and Information	Remarks and references to Appendices
EN TAQQA DEIRE S.6.46.A K.21.a	29 Jan 1917		C.O's Parade	B
	30 Jan 1917		Rostha	
			Weather. Snow & freezing Ice having been received by members of this unit during the month.	B
	31 Jan 1917		The following have been Mentioned in Despatches London Gazette Jan	B
			MAJOR A. MASSEY Au.74864 S/f ELBRO A	

Army Form C. 2118.

WAR DIARY
or
INTELLIGENCE SUMMARY.
(Erase heading not required.)

Instructions regarding War Diaries and Intelligence Summaries are contained in F. S. Regs., Part II. and the Staff Manual respectively. Title pages will be prepared in manuscript.

Place	Date	Hour	Summary of Events and Information	Remarks and references to Appendices
LA TOMBE ERIE Y. 44. C.19 K.21.a (C.0)	30/1		The following Divisional Parchment Certificates were received — T2/024531 Dvr CRANEY E. R.A.S.C. M.T. M1/106975 S/L ROUVIER F. R.A.S.C. M.T. Gallant conduct and devotion to duty at YPRES. Aug 1917 69690 Pte SHAW. F. R.A.M.C. Gallant conduct and devotion to duty at LEMPIRE March 1918. Presented on Parade 15 Jan 1919	B

Army Form C. 2118.

WAR DIARY
or
INTELLIGENCE SUMMARY
(Erase heading not required.)

Instructions regarding War Diaries and Intelligence Summaries are contained in F. S. Regs., Part II. and the Staff Manual respectively. Title pages will be prepared in manuscript.

Place	Date	Hour	Summary of Events and Information	Remarks and references to Appendices
LA TAMARDE ERIEN N.44 K.1.a.	1919 Jan 5th (cont.)		64602 Sgt LILLEY P. R.A.M.C. 71327 Pte CUSHEN E.E. R.A.M.C. Continuous good work from December 1915 to December 1918. Presented on Parade 15/1/'19.	
			4355 L. Sgt. Vincent. A. R.A.M.C. Gallant conduct and devotion to duty at YPRES. August 1917. Presented on Parade 23 Jan 1919.	

Army Form C. 2118.

WAR DIARY
or
INTELLIGENCE SUMMARY.
(Erase heading not required.)

Instructions regarding War Diaries and Intelligence Summaries are contained in F.S. Regs., Part II. and the Staff Manual respectively. Title pages will be prepared in manuscript.

Place	Date	Hour	Summary of Events and Information	Remarks and references to Appendices
LA THAN- ARDERIE SH.44.A K.21.a (cont)			Owing to the following not being with the Unit the Prudent Certificates were posted to their home addresses. 46565 Sjt TURNBULL J.C. R.A.M.C. 31611 L.Cpl. DOWDESWELL G.E. R.A.M.C. Continuous Service with from December 1915 to December 1918. 74930 Pte Rumbold (Rudbold) G. R.A.M.C. Gallant conduct and devotion to duty at CROISILLE HEIGHTS Nov 1917 by A. Bell O.C. 111th Field Amb. Lieut Col R.A.M.C	

Jan 4, 1919.

111 1/4 Fd Ambulance
January 1919

List of Classes for January

Subject	Unit	Instructors	Day & time	Average Attendance
European History	111 1/4 Fd Amb.	Maj Hastones R.a.m.c. C/o Downes S. Pte Cushen E.E.	Monday, Tuesday, Thursday, Friday 15:00 to 16:00 hr.	30
Trench (Beginners)	111 1/4 Fd Amb.	Pte Cushen E.E.	Tuesday, Friday 14:00 to 15:00 hr	20
Trench (Advanced)	111 1/4 Fd Amb.	Pte Cushen E.E.	Monday, Thursday 17:00 to 18:00 hr.	21
Elementary Arithmetic	111 1/4 Fd Amb.	Pte Cushen E.E.	Monday, Thursday 15:00 to 16 hr	14
Practical Mathematics	111 1/4 Fd Amb.	C/o Downes S.	Tuesday, Friday 11:00 to 15:00 hr	7
Engine Mechanics	111 1/4 Fd Amb.	Pte Stone A.S.C.M.T.	Wednesday, Thursday 11:00 to 12:00 hr	4
Shorthand	111 1/4 Fd Amb.	C/o Davis D.	Monday, Thursday 12:00 to own	4
Book-keeping	111 1/4 Fd Amb.	Pte McAuley J.	Tuesday, Friday 16:00 to 15:00 hrs	4
Elementary Physics	111 1/4 Fd Amb.	Sgt Smith W.A	Tuesday, Friday 11:00 to 12:00 hr.	5
Music	111 1/4 Fd Amb.	Sgt Lilley P.	Tuesday, Friday 14:00 to 15:00 hr.	8

111th Field Ambulance

Education   Time Table

Monday	Tuesday	Thursday	Friday	Time
Shorthand Chemistry Arithmetic	French Book-Keeping Mathematics	Shorthand Chemistry Arithmetic	French Book-Keeping Mathematics	14.00 hours " "
European History 15.00 hrs				
French	Music	French	Music	17.00 hrs

Parchment Certificates   Appendix III

T2/024531 Dvr Crane E. R.A.S.C. M.T.
M/106745 Sgt. Rhodes P. R.A.S.C. M.T.
Gallant conduct and devotion to duty
Ypres August 1917

69690 Pte Shaw R. R.A.M.C.
Gallant conduct and devotion to duty
Lempire March 1918

The above were presented on parade 15/1/19.

64603 Sgt Lilley R. R.A.M.C.
X   46565 " Turnbull J.C. R.A.M.C.
X   31661 L/Cpl Dowdeswell J.F. R.A.M.C.
74324 Pte Cushen E.L. R.A.M.C.
Continuous good work from December 1915
to December 1918
The above were presented on parade 15/1/19

43554 Sgt Vincent A. R.A.M.C.
Gallant conduct and devotion to duty
Ypres August 1917

74930 Pte Rumbold G. R.A.M.C.
X Gallant conduct and devotion to duty
Croiselle Heights November 1917

The above were presented on parade 23/1/19

X Owing to the above not being with the unit the parchment certificates were posted to their home addresses together with a letter of congratulation from the C.O.

No. 111 Field Ambulance

Army Form C. 2118.

WAR DIARY
or
INTELLIGENCE SUMMARY.
(Erase heading not required.)

Instructions regarding War Diaries and Intelligence Summaries are contained in F. S. Regs., Part II. and the Staff Manual respectively. Title pages will be prepared in manuscript.

Place	Date	Hour	Summary of Events and Information	Remarks and references to Appendices
LA TANNARD			16th Division	
ERIE			1st Corps	
K.44.a	1 1919		1st Army	
K.21.a			Weather. Snow and frost during the last week.	

Myra Bell
Lieut Col R.A.
G.C. 111th Field Artillery C.

Army Form C. 2118.

111 Field Ambulance
Vol 39

WAR DIARY
or
INTELLIGENCE SUMMARY.
(Erase heading not required.)

Instructions regarding War Diaries and Intelligence Summaries are contained in F. S. Regs., Part II. and the Staff Manual respectively. Title pages will be prepared in manuscript.

Place	Date	Hour	Summary of Events and Information	Remarks and references to Appendices
LATANAHD- ERIE Sh. 44ª Kenia	Feb 1/1919		111th Field Ambulance 16th Division 1st Corps 1st Army Two "other ranks" transferred and	R 23 23
	Feb 2/1919			
	Feb 3 4 5/1919		weather hot and even	

Army Form C. 2118.

WAR DIARY
or
INTELLIGENCE SUMMARY.
(Erase heading not required.)

Instructions regarding War Diaries and Intelligence Summaries are contained in F. S. Regs., Part II. and the Staff Manual respectively. Title pages will be prepared in manuscript.

Place	Date	Hour	Summary of Events and Information	Remarks and references to Appendices
LA TANHORDERIE Sh 44ª K 21.a.	Jan 6 1919		Routine	
	Jan 7 1919		Loud frost still present	
	Jan 8 1919		1 N.C.O and 1 man demobilised. Major A. MASSEY returned from leave	
	Jan 9 1919		Hard frost	

Army Form C. 2118.

WAR DIARY
or
INTELLIGENCE SUMMARY.
(Erase heading not required.)

Place	Date	Hour	Summary of Events and Information	Remarks and references to Appendices
LA TANAR DE NIS Sh 44 A K.21.a	Feb 10/1919		Received orders to proceed forthwith to No 1. C.C. Station - MONS for temporary duty as Officer commanding and lecture to men on Venereal Prophylaxis	
	Feb 11/1919		Handed over to A/Major A. MASSEY. R.A.M.C.	

Roy A Bell
Lieut Col. R.A.M.C.

WAR DIARY
or
INTELLIGENCE SUMMARY.

Army Form C. 2118.

Place	Date	Hour	Summary of Events and Information	Remarks and references to Appendices
LA TANNOERIE SH 44 A K.21a	Feb 12 1919		CAPT DIAMOND. R.A.M.C. arrived for temporary duty. Master for duty.	JM
	Feb 13 1919		CAPT. BRENTNALL. R.A.M.C. M.O. to 16" Durham M.G.s reported for duty. Their section	JM
	Feb 14 1919		COLONEL BOWEN D.S.O. R.A.M.C. A.D.M.S. of Division paid us a farewell visit before leaving for INDIA.	JM
	Feb 15 1919		Heavy rain the whole day. General Routine.	JM
	Feb 16 1919		Still wet. 1.O.R. Pte BALL destroyed.	JM
	Feb 17 1919		General Routine. 2.O.R. Demobilised namely Sgt Vincent and Pte MANNING.	JM
	Feb 18 1919		General Routine. Still wet.	JM

Army Form C. 2118.

WAR DIARY
or
INTELLIGENCE SUMMARY.
(Erase heading not required.)

Instructions regarding War Diaries and Intelligence Summaries are contained in F. S. Regs., Part II. and the Staff Manual respectively. Title pages will be prepared in manuscript.

Place	Date	Hour	Summary of Events and Information	Remarks and references to Appendices
LA TANARDERIE SH. 44A N.21.a	Feb 19 1919		General Routine. Weather improving	M
	Feb 20 1919		General Routine	M
	Feb 21 1919		General Routine	M
	Feb 22 1919		CAPT. DIMMOND. R.A.M.C. returned to 112 F.A. from duty 12.O.R. Unidentified 197 further received the PARKER B Trincalaigh	M
	Feb 23 1919		General Routine. Weather showery. CAPT. PRICE, R.A.M.C. reported for duty attached unit	M
	Feb 24 1919		Parchment certificates issued to the following men:— 64210 Pte. J.Y. MARTIN. R.A.M.C. 78957 Pte. F.A. DIXON R.A.M.C. 74176. 4CPL. A. CLIFFORD R.A.M.C. 2/116.3 Pte. A GREEN (R.A.S.C.M.T.) For noncombatant good work in the field	M

Army Form C. 2118.

Army Form C. 2118.

WAR DIARY
or
INTELLIGENCE SUMMARY.
(Erase heading not required.)

Instructions regarding War Diaries and Intelligence Summaries are contained in F. S. Regs, Part II. and the Staff Manual respectively. Title pages will be prepared in manuscript.

Place	Date	Hour	Summary of Events and Information	Remarks and references to Appendices
LA TANNARDERIE Sh. 14A H. 21. a.	Feb 25 1919.		CAPT Q.L. LANDER R.A.M.C. goes on leave to England.	M.
	Feb 26 1919.		CAPT. LOUGHREY R.A.M.C. returned from leave to U.K. Weather showery	M.
	Feb 27 1919.		General Routine. Weather still showery	M.
	Feb 28 1919.		General Routine; Weather Wet the whole day.	M.
			Weather improving. The 16th DIVISIONAL RACE MEETING held to-day on BERGUE AERODROME "CHARLIE" owned by the unit won the FRIEZENBURG STAKES.	M.

A Massey
Major. R.A.M.C.

Volume 39

Confidential
War Diary
(111 Field Ambulance)
March, 1919.

W.O. to D
140/3501

17 JUL 1919

Volume XXXIX

Army Form C. 2118.

WAR DIARY
or
INTELLIGENCE SUMMARY.
(Erase heading not required.)

Instructions regarding War Diaries and Intelligence Summaries are contained in F. S. Regs., Part II. and the Staff Manual respectively. Title pages will be prepared in manuscript.

Place	Date	Hour	Summary of Events and Information	Remarks and references to Appendices
Det 414 A. K.21.a.	March 1 1919		The weather here is changeable. General Routine	M
	March 2 1919		General Routine. Weather still wet.	M
	March 3 1919		General Routine. Weather improving.	M
	March 4 1919		S/SGT. TREDWELL returned from leave. A/SGT McAULEY J departed to I Army HQ.	M
	March 5 1919		Weather fine. General Routine	M
	March 6 1919		A/SGT GOLDSPINK and 8 men departed from this unit to Army of Occupation on the Rhine. Weather miserably wet.	M

Army Form C. 2118.

WAR DIARY
or
INTELLIGENCE SUMMARY.
(Erase heading not required.)

Instructions regarding War Diaries and Intelligence Summaries are contained in F. S. Regs., Part II. and the Staff Manual respectively. Title pages will be prepared in manuscript.

Place	Date	Hour	Summary of Events and Information	Remarks and references to Appendices
Shoret-Wala R.21.a.	March 7 1919		CAPT. LOUGHREY. R.A.M.C. demobilized and departed this unit. Also 3 O.R.'s which	M.
	March 8 1919		Sgt. WRIGHT, W.C. granted leave to U.K. Also 1.O.R. 2.O.R. demobilized. Weather still wet.	M.
	March 9 1919		CAPT. M. MACDONALD, D.S. Army CHARLIE won the CHAMPIONSHIP STAKES of the Division	M.
	March 10 1919		General Routine	M.
	March 11 1919		General Routine	M.
	March 11 1919		1st Lieut. S. HOPPER, MED. U.S.A. reported here for duty from 18th Scottish Rifles Vicker on the JR	M.
	March 12 1919		1 Horse Officers charger to wds (L.O.) 4 All. troops transferred to 108 Brig. R.F.A.	M.

Army Form C.2118.

War Diary
or
Intelligence Summary.

Place	Date	Hour	Summary of Events and Information	Remarks
Shc 44 a. K 21 a.	March 13 1919		One Corporal & 3 O.R.s discharged. General Routine. Weather wet.	M.
	March 14 1919.		Capt. & Q.M. LANDER, J.C. returned from leave. Weather fine	M.
	March 15 1919.		Weather fine. General Routine	M.
	March 16 1919.		Visit from Lieut Colonel. WEIR. M.C. R.A.M.C. c/ A.D.M.S. 3rd Division.	M.
	March 17 1919.		Weather wet. General Routine.	M.
	March 18 1919.		Relinquished command of the Unit its day on account of being demobilised. Capt. W.J. MACDONALD. M.O. R.A.M.C. takes command of the 111 Field Ambulance from this date. Signed:— A. Massey. Major Ra M.C. O.C. Commanding 111 Field Ambulance	M.

Army Form C.2118

War Diary
or
Intelligence Summary.

Place	Date	Hour	Summary of Events and Information	Remarks
Hut 11 A K 21 c	19-3-19		Routine	a/-
	20.3.19		Routine	a/-
	21.3.19		Routine	a/-
	22.3.19		Capt J.J. Doyle. C of E. spoke to duty troops 20.0 Divison. Army of Occupation.	a/-
	23.3.19		Routine 2/4/19	a/-
	24.3.19		Capt. Lounsgrove divine service anti 4 of A/major	a/-
	25.3.19		Div Heaq 1 & 2 R.I. Strength 2 C.R.H.A.C.H.T.D. Brigades 4 Horses transferred to 16th Div Train	a/-

Army Form C2118.

War Diary
or
Intelligence Summary.

Place	Date	Hour	Summary of Events and Information	Remarks
Sut 40 a K 21 a	26.3.19			
	27.3.19		Capt. L.K. Price leaves unit for duty with DAH at ROUEN.	
	28.3.19		Visited by Major S.	
Sut 40 a F17 c 2a TEMPLEUVE	29.3.19		Unit left THUMERIES 9.30 am arrived TEMPLEUVE 1.15 pm having lost no ponies.	
	30.3.19		1 N.C.O. & 17 private ranks TRANSFERRED to Remount Depot to await demob. 2 men left unit to catch up strength.	
	31.3.19		Held a 10 minute shoot over length of front, for temporary duty with S.O.S. info. 15 prisoners gave themselves up. A.C. 1117 4/A	

140/3550

17 JUL 1919

M. 7. a

April 1919

CONFIDENTIAL

Army Form C. 2118.

WAR DIARY
of
INTELLIGENCE SUMMARY

(Erase heading not required.)

Vol XXXX.

Instructions regarding War Diaries and Intelligence Summaries are contained in F. S. Regs., Part II. and the Staff Manual respectively. Title pages will be prepared in manuscript.

141 Field Ambulance.
From April 1st 1919
To April 30th 1919

Place	Date	Hour	Summary of Events and Information	Remarks and references to Appendices
TEMPLEUVE	1/4/19		Two O.R. transferred to 32 C.C.S. for duty	n/a
"	2/4/19		One O.R. granted leave to U.K.	n/a
"	3/4/19		One O.R. granted leave to U.K.	n/a
"	4/4/19		One O.R. granted leave to U.K. Two P.B. details transferred from 45 Worcesters to 9th K.O.R. Weather clear, fine	n/a
"	5/4/19		One O.R. granted leave to U.K.	n/a
"	6/4/19		One O.R. demobilised. Weather fine	n/a

Army Form C. 2118.

WAR DIARY
or
INTELLIGENCE SUMMARY.
(Erase heading not required.)

Instructions regarding War Diaries and Intelligence Summaries are contained in F. S. Regs., Part II. and the Staff Manual respectively. Title pages will be prepared in manuscript.

Place	Date	Hour	Summary of Events and Information	Remarks and references to Appendices
Lenfleure	7/1/19		Routine. Weather fine	up
"	8/1/19		One O.R. granted leave to U.K. weather fine	up
"	9/1/19		One O.R. proceed leave to U.K. weather dull, showery	up
"	10/1/19		Four M.A. Cars and 8 drivers have not transferred to No.1 V.R.P. weather dull.	up
"	11/1/19		Routine. Weather dull, showery	up
"	12/1/19		Routine	up
"	13/1/19		Routine	up

Army Form C. 2118.

WAR DIARY
or
INTELLIGENCE SUMMARY.
(Erase heading not required.)

Instructions regarding War Diaries and Intelligence Summaries are contained in F. S. Regs., Part II. and the Staff Manual respectively. Title pages will be prepared in manuscript.

Place	Date	Hour	Summary of Events and Information	Remarks and references to Appendices
JEMEPPE	14/2/19		Routine. Weather wet, high winds.	w/n
"	15/2/19		One O.R. granted leave to U.K. Weather wet, heavy showers, high winds.	w/n
"	16/2/19		Major W. Freeman, M.C. granted leave from 19/2/19 inclusive to 19/3/19 nine O/ricers a men's leave cancelled 19/2/19	w/n
"	17/2/19		One O.R. further leave to U.K.	w/n
"	18/2/19		T/Lt Hopkin S. M.O.R.C.U.S.A. appointed Temporary Captain from 17/2/19. Weather full dew.	w/n
"	19/2/19		One O.R. granted leave to U.K.	w/n

Army Form C. 2118.

WAR DIARY
or
INTELLIGENCE SUMMARY.
(Erase heading not required.)

Instructions regarding War Diaries and Intelligence Summaries are contained in F. S. Regs., Part II. and the Staff Manual respectively. Title pages will be prepared in manuscript.

Place	Date	Hour	Summary of Events and Information	Remarks and references to Appendices
TEMPLEUVE	20/4/19		Easter Sunday. Routine.	
"	21/4/19		One N.C.O. R. of C. H.T. demobilised	
"	22/4/19		One O.R. granted leave to U.K. Weather fine	
"	23/4/19		Routine	
"	24/4/19		Two O.R. R. of C. H.T. P.B. transferred to 1st Army H.T. Coy.	
"	25/4/19		One O.R. Started leave to U.K. Weather dull with showers. 6 O.R's demobilised.	
"	26/4/19		Routine. Weather dull and showery	

Army Form C. 2118.

WAR DIARY
or
INTELLIGENCE SUMMARY.
(Erase heading not required.)

Instructions regarding War Diaries and Intelligence Summaries are contained in F. S. Regs., Part II. and the Staff Manual respectively. Title pages will be prepared in manuscript.

Place	Date	Hour	Summary of Events and Information	Remarks and references to Appendices
TEMPLEUVE	27/1/19		2 P.B. details returned from 1st Army H.T. Coy. 1 O.R. admitted to hospital. Weather dull, showery, cold	w/n
"	28/1/19		2 O.R. East H.T. demobilised. Weather very cold, snow during morning.	w/n
"	29/1/19		2 O.R. Res. H.T. transferred to No 1 H.T. Accept. Park. Weather showery.	w/n
"	30/1/19		Routine. Weather cold, windy, with rain all day.	w/n

W. Macdonald
Major R.A.M.C.
O.C. M.G. Amb.

www.ingramcontent.com/pod-product-compliance
Lightning Source LLC
Chambersburg PA
CBHW080822010526
44111CB00015B/2594